History of NILE

A Century of Fun, Fellowship, and Philanthropy

RICHARD M. KOVAK

WESTBOW
PRESS®
A DIVISION OF THOMAS NELSON
& ZONDERVAN

WestBow Press books may be ordered through booksellers or by contacting:

WestBow Press
A Division of Thomas Nelson & Zondervan
1663 Liberty Drive
Bloomington, IN 47403
www.westbowpress.com
1 (866) 928-1240

Interior Image Credit: Courtesy of Nile Shrine Center, Mountalke Terrace, WA.

ISBN: 978-1-9736-9522-6 (sc)
ISBN: 978-1-9736-9524-0 (hc)
ISBN: 978-1-9736-9523-3 (e)

Library of Congress Control Number: 2020911741

Print information available on the last page.

WestBow Press rev. date: 07/27/2020

No great organization can fully
exist and thrive without knowledge
of its inception and genesis.

~ ANONYMOUS

Contents

Introduction

In this writer's opinion, no comprehensive nor definitive history of Nile Temple has yet been written, although laudable efforts at compiling historical accounts have been made by Frank Lazier, Past Potentate, and by Freddie Hayden, and Don Fjosland, Past Historians, and others. This book is designed to chronicle Nile's significant historical events, based on this writer's research of original documents, and series of chapters and articles form the basis for a more definitive history to be composed by a future writer.

The author wishes to thank all those who participated in the production of this book including and especially, Noble Don Moore, the longtime editor of Smile with Nile, the newspaper in which many of these articles and chapters were first published.

The book is organized chronologically by year and Potentate. National and international events are integrated into each section to give the reader the context of America's culture and society that occurred during each of Nile Temple's Potentate years.

These chapters were originally written as a series of newspaper articles published in the Nile Temple newspaper Smile with Nile from 2007 to 2012. They have been edited but each chapter still retains the charm of the original newspaper articles each one leading into the next as in a serial progression.

Any person having and wishing to provide information, documents, news articles, pictures, artifacts, souvenirs, and other items that will help develop a more comprehensive look back at Nile's glorious and fascinating history should contact this writer or the Recorder at the Nile office. The items will be photographed and/or photocopied and returned to the sender unless that person wishes to donate the items to the Nile Archives. Units and clubs are especially invited to communicate to this author the histories of their club or unit for inclusion in future installments of this history.

Nile Shrine Center Mountlake Terrace, Washington

Foreword

WHO ARE THE SHRINERS

To those readers who are not Shrine Masons and especially for those who are not Masons an explanation of certain terms, phrases and concepts used in this book may be useful. The term "Shriners" refers to members of the fraternal organization which is now known as Shriners International. All Shriners are Master Masons, but not all Masons are Shriners.

Shriners International is a Masonic society established in 1870 and is headquartered in Tampa, Florida. It was originally conceived as a respite society from pure straight line Masonic lodge ritual to encourage fun and relaxation although within the purview of general Masonic principles. Thus, a prerequisite to Shrine membership is Master Mason status. The organization takes its original cultural heritage from supposed legends about secret fraternal societies said to have existed in the casbahs and smoking dens of old Morocco and elsewhere throughout the Middle east. These legends, brought to the United States in 1870 by Billy J. Florence, a noted actor of the time, quickly became a popular novelty with a group of Masons in New York City who used to meet at the Knickerbocker Cottage, a restaurant located at 426 Sixth Avenue in that city. Florence had learned of these legends at a party given by an Arabian diplomat in Marseille, France who had staged a musical show about them and at the end of which the guests became members of an impromptu secret society. Guided by the genius of one of the members of this group, Dr. Walter M. Fleming, M.D., the Moraccan party show described by Florence became an organization of its own with a ritual, costuming (Middle East style clothing), and a fancy name: The Ancient Arabic Order of Nobles of the Mystic Shrine (A.A.O.N.M.S.). The red Moraccan fez was adopted as its distinctive head gear. The organization's initial purpose was generally to have fun away from strict lodge life, but certain charitable causes were always a part of its mission just as it is today with all Masons.

The reader should keep in mind that this period of American history (1850-1930) was rife with fraternal organizations. There were hundreds of fraternal clubs, societies and organizations by the early twentieth century and perhaps as much as 50% of all American males at the time were members of one or more of these groups. So popular was "fraternalism" in the United States that Arthur Schlessinger in the October 1944 issue of The American Historical Review called America a "nation of joiners" and many regarded this time period as the Golden Age of Fraternalism.

Fraternalism or fraternity (from the Latin frater meaning brother) is simply the organizations of people (usually males) into groups, the members of which associate together in an environment of companionship and brotherhood dedicated to their mutual intellectual, physical, financial and social benefit. Constituent groups of these organizations are variously known as lodges, chapters, castles, temples, eyries, camps, courts, groves, nests, roosts, and many other collective nouns peculiar to the type or origin of their membership.

Thus, the Shrine "temples" referred to in the text of this book are just chapters of the overall organization. In 2010, Shriners International encouraged the use of the term "Shrine center" in place of "temple" and today most of the constituent Shrine groups are known by that name.

After its founding in 1870, and a slow membership start, the Shrine organization grew rapidly with temples sprouting up all over the landscape, and occasioning in June 1876 the creation of an overall governing body which came to be known as Imperial Shrine. Annual meetings of this governing body, known as Imperial Sessions, soon became the focus points for concerted action for special charitable projects, such as relief funds for the San Francisco earthquake victims in 1906 and for European war victims in 1915.

Wanting to do more and to make their charitable impact a lasting legacy of their organization, Shriners at the 1920 Imperial Session in Portland, Oregon voted to create the Shriners Hospitals for Children system to not only financially assist children afflicted with life threatening orthopedic disorders, notably polio, but to give them medically staffed places to be treated and healed. The hospitals and their upkeep would be funded by the Shrine members and no child would be turned away because of their financial circumstance. Starting with the first hospital at Shreveport,

Louisiana in 1922, this system eventually developed into a network of 22 hospitals and clinics throughout the United States and into Canada.

Today this system of hospitals and clinics also treats pediatric burn injuries, spinal cord injuries and cleft palate problems. More than a million children have been treated over the years at no cost to the child or the parents. It is no wonder that this charitable arm of Shriners International has been called the "World's Greatest Philanthropy".

Because of its Moraccan origins, the officers of these temples or chapters took on Arabic or Middle Eastern sounding names. Collectively, the officers of a temple constituted a divan or ruling body. The President was called a Potentate. The first vice president became the Chief Rabban (after rabboni meaning teacher). The second vice president was the Assistant Rabban. Next in line came the High Priest and Prophet referring to one who had a clerical job in the group, mainly prayers before and at the end of divan meetings. The lowest member of the group was the Oriental Guide whose chief job was to guide new candidates through the initiation ceremonies. The Secretary was called a Recorder and the Treasurer was simply called the Treasurer. There were also many ancillary jobs performed by other members such as the First and Second Ceremonial Masters who prepared and conducted much of the initiation ceremonies, the Marshal who announced matters and introduced the presiding divan members, the Captain of the Guard and the Outer Guard who maintained order and oversaw the admission of members into divan meetings.

Many temples had one or more Shrine Clubs to provide venues for members of the temple in outlying areas of the temple's geographical jurisdiction to meet locally and discuss matters and concerns peculiar to their area. These Shrine clubs would usually meet on a monthly basis whereas the main temple meetings, called "stated meetings" would take place less often, being required to meet only once per calendar quarter. Temples also had within their structural system "units' which were part of the main temple and organized on the basis of particular interests or skills, such as playing in a band, marching in parades and competitions, boating, golfing, fishing, horse patrols, skiing, law enforcement, aviation and many other interests of the members. When there were enough interested members, they would petition the Potentate for a charter and, if granted, be recognized as an official "Unit" of that temple with all of its rights and privileges. Despite their diversity of interests, all of these clubs and units had as one of their primary purposes raising funds to support the main temple and the local Shriners Childrens hospitals in Spokane, Washington and Portland, Oregon.

Mention must also be made of the two main autonomous women's organizations associated with the Shriners. These are the Daughters of the Nile and the Ladies Oriental Shrine. Although independent groups, each has as one of their main missions to raise funds to support the Shriners Hospitals for Children. And this task they have done spectacularly well as will be seen in the reports on these groups in Chapter 13 of the text. They have their own rituals, costuming, ceremonies and officers. Their stated meetings are off limits to Shriners.

With all of this in mind, it is now appropriate to introduce you to Nile. Its position in the Seattle area of northwest Washington State was once considered a hindrance because of the presence in Washington State of two strong preexisting temples, Afifi Temple in Tacoma and El Katif Temple in Spokane. How Nile overcame this disadvantage and went on to become what many consider the premier Shrine center of the northwest is the story which will unfold before you in the chapters of the text of this book.

But before you indulge in the heart of this story, you may want to follow up on the history of Shriners International, a good rendition of it can be found at www.kosair.com/shrinershistory.html. More information on Shriners Hospitals for Children can be found at www.shrinersinternational. org and www.shrinershospitalsforchildren.org.

I want to thank my line and content editor, Dr. Julie Conzelmann of Superior Editing Services and all of the editors and facilitators at Westbow Press who helped make this book a reality after the raw transcript sat on my desk for the last decade. Finally, I want to dedicate this book to the Nobles and Ladies of Nile Shrine Center for their tireless work in supporting the Shriners Hospitals for Children, the World's Greatest Philanthropy, and helping to make this world a better place in which to live. As the Shrine Nobles are want to say, Es selamu aleichim - peace be with you.

Chapter One

THE RAUCOUS OUGHTS

The Raucous Nineteen Oughts

The turn of a century is always a time for optimism and opportunity. The United States (U.S.) emerged from the 1890's in an attitude of growing importance in the world due to its rapid industrialization and some would say imperialistic ambitions. In 1898, Spain's control over its new world possessions ended with America's victories in the Spanish-American war which brought U.S. dominion over Puerto Rico, Guam and the Philippines. However, the U.S. had to militarily suppress a national insurrection movement in the Philippines that had already started there against the Spanish. The rise of the iron and steel industries in the U.S. and the increased production of oil gave rise to monopolies of several sectors of business. Oil, coal, steel, and railroad barons, such as Carnegie, Rockefeller and Gould dominated U.S. industry, and financiers, such as J.P. Morgan dominated the financial world. In science, great advances were made in the discovery of radium, X-rays and quantum theory. Later, in 1903-6 Einstein would publish both his General and Special Theories of Relativity, which would open the door for modern scientific explanations of the universe.

President McKinley was reelected in 1900 but his assassination in September, 1901 brought to power the raucous Teddy Roosevelt who would march the United States into the twentieth century, found the National

Park and National Monument Systems and institute regulatory controls ("Square Deal") that would curtail railroad monopolies and control large business conglomerations. His administration also marks the start of construction of the Panama Canal begun on May 4, 1904 (Acquisition Day).

Troubles beset America and the world just as they do today. Wars included the American-Philippine War, the Second Boer War, the Russo-Japanese War, the Saudi-Rashidi War and the Kuwaiti-Rashidi War. Disasters in the United States came in the form of fires – the Great Fire of 1901 in Jacksonville, Florida, the fire at the Iroquois Theater in Chicago killing 600 people, the Great Baltimore Fire of February 7, 1904 in Baltimore, Maryland, destroying over 1500 buildings in the course of 30 hours, and the fires in San Francisco following the great San Francisco Earthquake of April 18, 1906 (a 7.8 magnitude quake which together with the ensuing fires killed 3000 people and caused an estimated $350 million in damages leaving almost 300,000 people homeless).

Great books were published: The Wonderful Wizard of Oz (L. Frank Baum), The Hound of the Baskervilles (Sir Arthur Conan Doyle), Heart of Darkness (Joseph Conrad), The Call of the Wild (Jack London), Anne of Green Gables (Lucy Maud Montgomery), and The Jungle (Upton Sinclair). American movie goers were treated to the first great success of American cinema, The Great Train Robbery. It is said that the scene in which the steam locomotive is shown coming straight on toward the audience was so realistic that many novice movie goers rushed to the back of the theaters to escape the oncoming train.

It was a decade of inventions and entrepreneurship. In 1900 came the Brownie camera (leading to the successful formation of the Eastman-Kodak company), and the debut of the diesel engine (Rudolf Diesel). George Canfield invents the first electric typewriter in 1901. Guglielmo Marconi produces the first radio receiver. Mary Whitehead invents the automobile windshield wipers. Willis Carrier invents the indoor air conditioning unit. Sir James Mackenzie of Scone, Scotland comes up with the lie detector or polygraph machine. In 1902-3, Orville and Wilbur Wright fly their powered glider at Kitty Hawk, North Carolina, the world's first fully controllable aircraft. 1906 brings the invention of the jukebox by John Gabel (Gabel Automatic Entertainer) which plays a series of gramophone records. The invention of the Photostat machine by Oscar Gregory in 1907 starts the modern era of document imaging. In 1908 Henry Ford debuts his Model T, the car which put America on wheels. And in 1909,

Leo Baekeland of Sint-Martens-Latem, Belgium invents Bakelite, an inexpensive, nonflammable plastic which replaces the previously used flammable resins.

In the Northwest part of the country a new band of entrepreneurs in the bold and bawdy town of Seattle (Gateway To Alaska) would turn Shrinedom on its ear and begin the legend of Nile Temple. As in legend as well as in actual life, an omen of greatness preceded the 1908 formation of Nile. On January 1, 1908, the tradition of dropping a ball on New Year's Eve to celebrate the New Year was inaugurated in Times Square in New York City.

FORMATION

1901-1908 The Seattle Shrine Club of Afifi Temple

The roots of Nile Temple can be traced to the Seattle Shrine Club of Afifi Temple. Nobles from the Seattle area had been commuting to Afifi Temple in Tacoma for many years by steamer, rail and horse drawn carriage. But the number of nobles being created by Afifi in the Seattle area soon made it prudent to start a Shrine Club in the growing Seattle metropolis. On January 20, 1901, an organizational meeting was called by Illustrious Sir John Arthur to form a Seattle Shrine Club. At that meeting, Arthur was elected President and H. W. Tyler was elected Secretary. A committee was formed to draw up a Constitution and bylaws. That initial Constitution and bylaws (which is set out elsewhere in this article) was submitted to Afifi and on February 3, 1901 the Constitution and bylaws were approved and the new Seattle Shrine Club was chartered to provide a home base for the many nobles in Seattle. The original Seattle Shrine Club met at the old Seattle Masonic Temple located at Second and Pike, and lasted for almost eight years until 1908 when Seattle area nobles would petition for their own temple. Of note is the fact that the Seattle Shrine Club articles (Article X) provided for the creation of a Turkish Patrol. A Marshal was appointed as Commander of the Patrol. He had the power to appoint officers and to remove them at will. The Marshal would also prescribe the style of the uniforms and the equipment to be used and fix the time and place of the Patrol's drills. The Turkish Patrol was evidently formed because later entries in the shrine club journal discuss the buying of uniforms. One of the new Shrine Club's first demonstrations of its power was to invite the Imperial Potentate to stay over an extra day in Seattle following his visit to Afifi, In April 1901 a committee of Seattle Shrine Club nobles composed of State of Washington Governor John H. McGraw, Frank Parker, W.V. Rinehart, S. Gardner Yerkes and Major J.R. Hayden was successful in persuading Imperial Sir to visit the Seattle Shrine Club where he was royally entertained. In addition, an invitation was sent to President McKinley to visit the Shrine Club when he would be visiting Seattle later that year. President McKinley would be assassinated later that year in September while he was visiting the Pan American Exposition in Buffalo, N.Y.

Leon Czolgosz, a self proclaimed anarchist, shot McKinley twice from a concealed revolver while McKinley was visiting the Temple of Music exposition on September 5, 1901, once in the shoulder and then in the stomach where the bullet lodged deep in the muscles of his back. McKinley was taken to the emergency hospital on the exposition grounds. It was decided by doctors to operate immediately rather than take him to a fully staffed hospital in Buffalo or elsewhere. The first bullet was quickly found and removed from his shoulder, but doctors could not locate the second bullet.

Unfortunately, the emergency hospital had no electric lighting even though electric lighting lit up the exteriors of the buildings on the grounds. So, light was provided by reflecting sunlight from bedpans placed around the operating table. The X ray machine, which was being demonstrated for the first time at the exposition, was not used to locate the second bullet because doctors feared what side effects it might have on the President. After doctors terminated the unsuccessful operation, McKinley appeared to recover and was sent home to Canton, Ohio to recuperate. He died several days later on September 14 from gangrene surrounding the second bullet wound.

Lack of further documentation of the Seattle Shrine Club does not permit us to examine all of its exploits over the seven years of its existence. But it is evident that Seattle area nobles were an ambitious bunch and would soon outgrow the apron strings of their mother temple and embark on far greater adventures on their own.

1908 – Organization and Dispensation

Afifi Temple in Tacoma had been in existence since it was granted dispensation by the Imperial Council in 1888 and was at the time the only Shrine Temple in the State of Washington until El Katif in Spokane was granted dispensation in 1890. Afifi nobles residing in Seattle routinely made the journey to Afifi Temple for stated meetings by dirt roads, rail, or steamer. However, Seattle's growing commercial and industrial prominence and burgeoning population growth after the turn of the century led many nobles in the Seattle area to dream of forming their own temple. One of these nobles was Ernest B. Hussey, Past Potentate of Afifi in 1903. His biography has been vividly portrayed by Historian Dennis Dorn in the December 2005 issue of SWN. Hussey and several other nobles petitioned Afifi for the opportunity to form a Seattle Temple. This request was looked upon favorably by the Afifi Divan, presumably because Shrinedom was rapidly growing and Afifi was getting a surfeit of new candidates each year. The nobility of Afifi quickly passed a motion to allow the petitioning nobles to petition Imperial for dispensation to form a new temple. On April 21, 1908, an organizational petition meeting, chaired by Noble Frank Parker of Afifi, was held at the Elks Hall in the Alaska Building in Seattle. The petition to Imperial generated at this meeting was eventually signed by 466 nobles, the largest number of signers to a petition for dispensation up to that time. That year, John C. Slater, Afifi P.P., was Afifi's Representative to Imperial. Together with Noble Frank Parker, Slater presented the petition to Imperial on July 14 at its 1908 session in St. Paul, Minnesota. On July 15, 1908, the petition was acted upon favorably and dispensation was granted to form "Nile Temple" in Seattle, Washington as the 111th temple of the Shriners of North America, Ancient Arabic Order of Nobles of the Mystic Shrine. Nile's territorial jurisdiction was established as running from south King County to the Washington/Canadian border and included all of the Alaska Territory. Other temples granted dispensation on this same date at the Imperial Session were Hillah in Ashland, Oregon and Rizpah in Madisonville, Kentucky.

The first eight members of the new Nile Temple were numerically listed on the dispensation certificate as follows: No. 1 Ernest B. Hussey, No. 2 Frank W. Parker, No. 3 Edgar C. Beede, No. 4 Elkan Morgenstern, No. 5 Henry G. Stoelting, No. 6 Frank W. Baker, No. 7 Richard Saxe Jones, and No. 8 Ralph S. Stacy. Other signers of the original petition were given alphabetical designations on the certificate.

At the first meeting after the grant of dispensation, the following officers were elected and/or appointed and installed: Ernest B. Hussey, First Potentate of Nile Temple, Ralph S. Stacey, Chief Rabban, Robert C. Hasson, Assistant Rabban, J. Bruce Gibson, High Priest and Prophet, Frank B. Lazier, Oriental Guide, Robert J. Fisher, Treasurer, Edgar C. Beede, Recorder, Daniel B. Trefethen, First Ceremonial Master, George S. McLaren, Second Ceremonial Master, Donald B. Olson, Marshal, John Rex Thompson, Captain of the Guard, Charles D. Knight, Outer Guard, and Henry G. Stoelting, Director.

Six of these members of Nile's inaugural divan went on to become Potentates of Nile (Stacey, Hasson, Lazier, Trefethen, Olson and Thompson).

Stated meetings that year were held at the Elks Hall of the Alaska Building in downtown Seattle. As news of the new temple got around Seattle, petitions to join came flooding in. A Ceremonial was planned for December, 1908. By the time the Ceremonial occurred on December 2, 1908, Nile had to rent the Moore Egyptian Theater in Seattle for the event. There were 121 new nobles initiated into the Nile that day while over 1000 nobles from far and wide attended that first Ceremonial. But more on that and the key role that the Nile Arab Patrol played at that Ceremonial in the next chapter.

Other chapters will highlight the granting of Nile's charter in 1909, Nile's pioneering efforts to hold ceremonials in Alaska and the Far East, the hosting of Imperial Sessions in 1915, 1936 and 1966, the story of how the slogan Smile with Nile came to be, Nile's growth over the years (e.g., 10,880 member nobles in 1962), its various temple homes in the greater Seattle area, its acquisition of property in the "wilderness" north of Seattle, its work for the hospitals, and how it came to be what it is today.

THE BIRTH YEARS – 1908-1909

1908 – Ernest Bertram Hussey – Nile's First Potentate

After dispensation was granted, Acting Illustrious Potentate Hussey called a meeting at the Elks Hall, Alaska Building for Wednesday September 16, 1908 to perfect the organization. On Wednesday October 28, 1908, Noble Ellis Lewis Garretson, Potentate of Afifi Temple, as the Deputy of the Imperial Potentate, instituted Nile Temple and formally installed its officers. Acting Illustrious Potentate Ernest Bertram Hussey was installed as Nile Temple's First Potentate. Nile's first regular business meeting occurred on Wednesday, November 11, 1908 when Bylaws were adopted and plans were made for the December 2, 1908 Ceremonial.

1909 – Ralph Stacy - Nile Continues to Grow

Regular stated meetings continued to be held at the Elks Hall with Potentate Hussey presiding. On May 19, 1909 Nile's second Ceremonial was to be held with Potentate Hussey presiding, but an accident at the armory, where the Ceremonial was to take place, caused the Ceremonial to be postponed. Potentate Hussey remained in office as Potentate until July 14, 1909 when a new divan was installed.

In the interim, on June 9, 1909 Nile received its charter from Imperial. That day happened to coincide with Nile's regular stated meeting at the Elks Hall where new officers were elected. On July 14, Potentate Ellis Lewis Garretson, again acting as Deputy of the Imperial Potentate, presented Nile with its charter and installed the newly elected officers. Ralph Stacey, one of the original petitioners, was installed as Potentate. The rest of the divan consisted of: Robert C. Hasson, Chief Rabban; J. Bruce Gibson, Assistant Rabban; Frank Lazier, High Priest and Prophet; Daniel Trefethen, Oriental Guide, and Edgar Beede remaining as Recorder and Robert Fisher as Treasurer.

On July 16, Nile received dispensation to travel to Nome, Alaska to conduct a Ceremonial. Several of Nile's divan members and nobles departed July 22 aboard the Steamer "Senator" to initiate new candidates almost 1500 miles away, almost unheard of in all of Shrinedom up to that time. But this was part of Nile's territory and this fledgling temple was up to the task.

Later that year, on August 25, many more candidates were made nobles on Shriners Day at the Ceremonial held at the Alaska-Yukon-Pacific Exposition Hall on the UW campus. It was estimated that almost 2,600 Shriners attended that Ceremonial which brought Nile's membership to 770 members at that point in time. Since the new Bylaws specified a December election date, the December stated meeting was election night and Robert C. Hasson was moved up from Chief Rabban to Potentate for

1910. Interestingly, Frank Lazier moved up from High Priest and Prophet to Chief Rabban. Daniel Trefethen moved up from Oriental Guide to Assistant Rabban. Henry Stoelting came up from first Ceremonial Master to High Priest and Prophet and John McLean was elected the new Oriental Guide.

At the October stated meeting it was announced that Nile would try to form a Shrine Band with Clayton B. Wilson as Musical Director. Noble Wilson had already rounded up a few players, but several key instruments were still needed. The Band uniforms were to be a costume that would "harmonize" with those currently worn by the Arab Patrol.

Nile finished 1909 with 813 members and would continue to grow through the Teens with many more adventures and startling developments. Be with us next issue when we rediscover Nile's activities and growth during America's isolationist period and later when it was drawn into the First World War.

Chapter Two

THE NINETEEN TEENS

1910-1919 America Comes of Age – The Great World War and Nile Temple's Rise to Glory

The second decade of the Twentieth Century brought America firmly into the world arena. By the end of this decade America was not only a recognized military and political force in the world, but a leader in the fight for world peace. During the 1910s, the confusing tangle of European military alliances, made as a result of the previous decades of wars, would be put to its sternest test and would ultimately disintegrate in the Great War (World War I), which was triggered by the assassination of Archduke Franz Ferdinand of Austria by a Serbian nationalist on June 28, 1914. The Great War would last until late 1918 and claim the lives of hundreds of thousands until an armistice was declared on November 11. Final peace does not come until the Treaty of Versailles signed on June 28, 1919. Obliterated by the Great War were the empires of Germany, the Ottomans and Austria-Hungary. Other major political changes which occurred during this decade were the Mexican Revolution in 1910 which led to the ouster of Mexican dictator Porfirio Diaz, the Russian Revolution in 1917 which led to the assassination of the Czar and his family and the rise of the first communist government, the Easter Rising in Ireland which eventually led to the independence of Ireland, the Jallianwala Bagh massacre which provided the impetus for the Indian Independence Movement and the Xinhai Revolution which overthrew the ruling Qing Dynasty and led to the establishment of the Republic of China.

Amidst the distractions of world wars and revolutions, during this decade Gideon Sundbeck patents the first modern zipper, Harry Brearley invents stainless steel, Charles Strite produces the first pop-up toaster, the Titanic sinks, and Nile Temple commences its Rise To Glory in full form.

1910 - Robert C. Hasson - Establishes Succession Order

At the December 1909 stated meeting, Chief Rabban Robert C. Hasson was elected Potentate and the orderly succession of divan members up the divan ladder was established. Nile had 610 members at the end of 1908 and 813 at the end of 1909. By the end of 1910 Nile's membership would jump to 927 primarily based on two successful ceremonials held at the Odd Fellows Hall, Tenth Avenue and East Pine Street on May 18 and November 3, 1910. On April 12 of that year, a special train composed solely of Shriners from many of the Northwest temples departed from the downtown railroad terminal in Seattle for the Imperial Session held that year in New Orleans.

Nile's path to glory was accelerating.

1911- Frank Lazier - Shapes the Nile Style

Remember the brother in need and remember the ladies were two of Potentate Frank Lazier's tenets during his year. Frank, who would later become Nile's longest serving Recorder, wrote to the nobles on February 4, 1911:

> Life, at best, is serious enough, and the spirit of fraternity and fellowship developed by the Shrine does much to lighten our burdens and dispel the shadows that hover over us. And that is well. But we should not play so hard that we forget there is work to be done; that misfortune is always in our midst; that many, perhaps of our own, are out of work, and in actual need. With an earnest desire to help, that I feel will be endorsed by every member, I am going to establish an Employment Bureau in connection with

Nile Temple…A brother comes to me seeking assistance. Not often for money, but for a chance to earn it. The scope of my information is limited. I can do but little. The same holds true with each individual noble. But if we can get all the Nobles working toward a given point, much should be accomplished…It is mighty hard to be out of work, and particularly if one is in a strange land. And the world is not, as a rule, overly kind to one in that condition. Perhaps we can make it feel more kindly toward him, through our solicitation. Let us make the effort.

~Frank Lazier, 1911.

Immigration at this point in America's history was impacting cities where the immigrants finally wound up. In Seattle, unemployment was becoming a growing problem and Nile, along with some of the blue lodges were to become the first social service organizations in the Northwest. (Recall that there was no Social Security, Unemployment Bureau or other such agencies until the Franklin D. Roosevelt administration programs of the 1930's.)

Lazier also instituted a Ladies Night with the nobles. It was originally supposed to occur in April, but the new Seattle Scottish Rite Temple had not yet been completed. However, the event was held with great participation and success on September 16 at the Scottish Rite Temple, located at corner of Broadway and Harvard Avenue in the City of Seattle. stated meetings continued to be held at the Elks Hall with ceremonials conducted at the Odd Fellows Hall. The May Ceremonial was attended by Imperial Potentate Fred A. Hines who was mightily impressed by the energy and ingenuity of Nile's units, the Arab Patrol, and the Nile Temple Orchestra, later to be the Band. Of the Patrol Potentate Hunes said that year:

The patrols are among the strongest attractions of the Order. They bring praise to it; they create interest; they do advertising that counts; they attract membership; cause favorable comment from outside spectators and inject life and energy into every Shrine that is fortunate enough to have one.

(For more information on the history of the formation of the Nile Patrol see the June, 2007 issue of Smile with Nile).

1912 – Daniel B. Trefethen – Nile's First Attorney Potentate Accelerates Nile's Rise to Glory

Dan Trefethen was an attorney in Seattle when he became Potentate. He was the founder of a law firm which endured for many years and from which came other Nile Potentates. He started off the year by conducting a mock Supreme Court hearing over the alleged conspiracy of former Seattle Mayor, Noble George Dilling to pass the perquisites of that office to Noble Thomas Parish, the present Mayor of Seattle. Many other Seattle city officials, who were also nobles, would be involved in this fun event, including City Comptroller candidate, Noble Harry Carroll (who later was elected to that office). Unfortunately, one of Trefethen's saddest duties early that year was to announce the passing of Ernest C. Beede, Nile's first and only Recorder at the time. Noble Beede, a 33rd Degree Mason, was given great memorial honors by the Scottish Rite Sovereign Grand Inspector General and the Inspectors General Honorary at the Scottish Rite Temple on March 10. That year on April 12, the HMS Titanic sank after striking an iceberg in the North Atlantic on its maiden voyage from England to the United States

The May Imperial Session in Los Angeles proved to be another turning point in Nile's Rise To Glory in Shrinedom. Al Malaikah Temple in Los Angeles would host Imperial. They had heard of Nile's growth (Nile's membership would pass the 1,000-mark that year) and the strength of the other temples in the Northwest and expected a sizable contingent from up north. Nile combined with Afifi, Gizah and Al Kader temples to fill a whole train for the pilgrimage to Los Angeles. Commanding a Pullman car themselves was the Nile Arab Patrol, primed to compete for the prizes to be awarded at Imperial. According to the Post Intelligencer news report of May 10 of that year, Nile was accorded thunderous applause from the 20,000 spectators. Fifty Patrols participated at Imperial Session in Los Angeles and all were given loving cups by Imperial Potentate William R. Cunningham.

The Nome and Fairbanks Shrine Clubs were formed that year and Chief Rabban John McLean who was named the "Acting Potentate of Alaska," conducted a pilgrimage to the Land of the Midnight Sun. He and his caravan left Seattle on July 7 aboard the steamer State of California and arrived back in Seattle on the steamer Victoria on August 23. The Nile Temple Band was finally established at Nile Temple. Frank Lazier was elected Recorder to fill the post of the departed Ernest C. Beede. Nile dues were $3 per year. A Fall Ceremonial was held on November 30 of that year and Nile wound up 1912 with a total membership of 1,024.

1913 – John L. McLean - Nile opts For the Orient

Potentate John L. McLean advanced Nile's Rise To Glory by negotiating a special dispensation from Imperial for Nile to visit Manila, Philippine Islands to conduct a Ceremonial for almost 150 candidates. It was at the time the greatest pilgrimage by any temple in Shrinedom (surpassing Nile's own pilgrimages to Alaska in 1909 and 1912) – a voyage of 14,000 miles aboard the largest vessel flying the American flag at the time, the SS Minnesota, home ported in Seattle. It greatly helped that Imperial Second Ceremonial Master Ellis Lewis Garretson (Past Potentate of Afifi Temple and a strong Nile supporter) helped grease the skids with Imperial Council and Imperial Potentate Billy Irwin, and that Nile Noble Claude Meldrum was the Assistant. General Passenger Agent of the Great Northern Steamship Co., owner of the Minnesota. Finally, it was Noble Jerry Henderson, the jovial Purser of the Minnesota that alerted Nile to the demand for Shrine membership in the Orient. Dubbed the "Shrine Ship," the Minnesota, sailed on December 30, 1913 with 200 Shriners and their ladies on board. Unfortunately, McLean could not make the trip, so Potentate-elect John Rex Thompson went in his place.

Nevertheless, McLean had a good year. Ceremonials on June 7 and December 12 (attended by Imperial Potentate W.W. "Billy" Irwin) brought in another load of new nobles allowing Nile to finish 1913 with over 1400 members. A Grand Ball was held at the armory and the 1915 Shrine Committee was established to generate support and funds to lure the 1915 Imperial Council Session to Seattle.

1914 –John Rex Thompson - The "Thriller in Manila"

Potentate John Rex Thompson started out the new year sailing aboard the SS Minnesota to Manila. And what a tremendous boost that gave to Nile. The Ceremonial was staged in Manila on January 31 at the Bamboo Oasis Shrine Club and garnered 142 new Shriners. At Nile, Chief Rabban Donald

B. Olson was Acting Potentate. He helped rally Nile's forces for the "Assault at Atlanta," the code name for Nile's bid to secure the 1915 Imperial Session for Seattle.

The 1914 Imperial Session was an important stepping stone for Nile temple because it was at this session that Seattle made its bid to become the first Northwest temple to host Imperial. A competition had developed between San Francisco (Islam Temple) and Seattle for the right to host the 1915 Session. San Francisco was backed by most of the California temples whereas Seattle had the backing of the Oregon, Washington, Montana, Idaho, and western Canadian temples. Nile Past Potentate J.L. McLean brought 255 Nile members to Atlanta on a 3000-mile train trip each way. The fight was on to convince the Imperial Council to award the next session to Seattle. Of course, it helped that Ellis Lewis Garretson, Past Potentate of Afifi, was Imperial Second Ceremonial Master and was actively lobbying for Seattle. Still, it was no sure thing.

(For more information on this item see the July/August 2007 issue of Smile with Nile).

1914 ended with a visit by Imperial Potentate Dr. Frederick R. Smith to Nile Temple and another successful year-end Ceremonial which brought Nile's membership total to 1,731. Unfortunately, the Great World War broke out that year casting a dealt pall over Europe that would eventually cover the United States and Nile Temple a few years later.

1915– Joseph A. Swalwell –
The Imperial Session in Seattle

Much has been written about the 1915 41st Imperial Council Session held July 13-15 in Seattle (See the account of this historic event in Chapter 13 of this series published in the July/August 2007 issue of Smile with Nile). But in addition to this great event, other indications of the growth of Nile Temple occurred. An Auxiliary Patrol was formed of 32 nobles and three officers. They were outfitted with the same Zouave uniforms and acted as an escort at Imperial with the regular Patrol. Vacancies in the ranks of the regular Patrol would be filled from the Auxiliary Patrol by draft. A Ceremonial was held at the Seattle Hippodrome on June 14 bringing in one the largest classes of new nobles to date. Another pilgrimage was made to Alaska. This time to Juneau, only an 1800-mile round trip, for a

$50 travel cost. Again, several new nobles were initiated. The new Seattle Masonic Temple was being built at Harvard and East Pine Streets. Eighteen Masonic bodies contributed to the cost of building this $250,000 edifice with Nile being one of the major contributors and stockholders in the Seattle Masonic Temple Corporation. And it was during this year, that the famous Smile with Nile slogan was coined.

Nile Chairman of the Imperial Session Planning Committee, J. E. Chilberg, started a contest to determine what catchy phrase might be used to publicize the Session. Among the entries was one submitted by Noble Herbert L. Schoenfeld: "Smile with Nile." This slogan proved to be a popular choice and the Planning Committee adopted it and featured it in all of its publicity literature. It caught on with Shriners from other temples and the spectacular success of the 1915 Session in Seattle caused it to become a household slogan across America. Its enduring popularity is evident to this day for when Shriners from other temples hear of a Shriner hailing from Nile Temple, they usually say: Oh yes, Smile with Nile!

1916 - Donald B. Olson– The New Seattle Masonic Temple

Nile's net membership total at the end of 1915 was 1,951 and membership would cross the 2000 mark this year. Because of this huge increase in membership the Recorder's salary was bumped by unanimous resolution from $60 per month to $150 per month. During this year, Nile invested heavily in the Seattle Masonic Temple Corporation, buying bonds, and lending other help where needed. At the balls and dances held that year, it was the Nile Patrol and the Nile Band that provided the entertainment. The Patrol drilled every Wednesday night at the armory under the command of Captain George Drever with W.D. Freeman and R.E. Sullivan as First and Second Lieutenants respectively. The Band, under the direction of Noble Harvey J. Woods, practiced every week at 1318 Second Ave in Seattle. Another pilgrimage to Manila occurred on April 8th of that year pursuant to the privilege accorded by Imperial Potentate J. Putnam Stevens and 81 new Nile members (nobles)were created. A special visitation to Nile's mother temple, Afifi, occurred on April 26 when 250 nobles traveled by a five-car train to Tacoma. A pilgrimage on October 20 by 115 nobles to Bellingham was another success. Again, the Patrol and Band outdid themselves in providing marvelous entertainment. But they were almost outdone by Mrs. Lou Singerman's dramatic reading of "The Wild Zingarella," the wild applause for which necessitated two encores.

Stated meetings continued to be held at either the Odd Fellows Hall (Tenth Ave. and East Pine) or the old Scottish Rite Temple (Broadway and Harvard). Soon meetings would be held at the New Seattle Masonic Temple (corner Harvard and Pine). The new building had three lodge rooms dubbed Doric, Ionic and Corinthian, a Shrine auditorium seating 1800 and a dining room that seated 800. After dedication of the Seattle Scottish Rite Temple on November 12 (see July/August 2007 SWN article), Nile held its first stated meeting and its first Ceremonial in that location that same month. The Masonic Tribune under Noble Sidney Smith and Brother John H. Reid would start up publication in October. And Nile finished that year with a net membership of 2,074.

1917– George R. Drever – A Short Reign - A Call to Service

Potentate George R. Drever, former Captain of the Patrol and a Major in the State of Washington National Guard never finished his term of office. After presiding over the June Ceremonial, he was called up to active service in July and would eventually serve in France as part of the American Expeditionary Force sent to assist the Allies in the Great War. President Wilson had declared our country to be in a state of war with Germany on April 2, 1917 and Congress declared war four days later. Wrote Potentate Drever when this news came out:

> Nobles of Nile, I am sure that not one of you will fail your country in this hour of her greatest need, but that you will be found in the front rank of doing all in your power to help her emerge triumphant from the conflict in the cause of freedom in which she is now engaged. And love and honor your flag. It is worthy of both, for, from its birth 140 years ago, it has never engaged in any war that has not been for liberty.

And in true Nile spirit, he continued to write:

While we perform our duty, yet should we remember that though the shadows of war hover o'er us, we are not to willfully hide from the sunshine, or try to shut happiness out of our lives, and so, we are going to have another LADIES NIGHT Wednesday, May 9th in the SHRINE AUDITORIUM.

~ George Drever, April, 1917.

An interesting side note here is that the United States did not enter the war as part of the Allied Powers, but as a self-styled "Associated Power." The United States had a very small army at this time and had to call on state National Guard units to serve, but after passing the Selective Service Act, it drafted well over 2,000,000 men and by summer 1918 was sending American soldiers to France at the rate of 10,000 a day.

A trip to the Imperial Council Session was scuttled. One of the main reasons for going was to help Al Kader Temple win the 1919 Imperial Session for Portland in return for Al Kader's great support in assisting Nile to land the 1915 Imperial Session in Seattle. However, Imperial Potentate Niedringhouse canceled all social functions at Imperial due to the war crisis and only Imperial Officers and authorized temple Representatives would attend. Chief Rabban Ivar Hyland took over as Acting Potentate and, partly due to the war call up, Nile finished the year with only a small increase to 2, 097 members.

1918– Ivan L. Hyland – The Great War Ends

This was a war year and many Nile nobles answered the call to serve in the United States military forces. Potentate Hyland presided over a very cautious Nile Temple since it was unknown how many more nobles would be called up or volunteering to take part in the American Expeditionary Force. Typical of the atmosphere at Nile was the entertainment at stated meetings. At the regular stated meeting in March the entertainment arranged by Past Potentate Dan Trefethen consisted of talks by Sergeants L.O. Bonnet and Paul Mirat. The former was an expert grenadier who fought in the Battles of Verdun, Neuport and Somme, and was awarded the Croix de Guerre for gallantry in service. The latter was one of most expert riflemen in the world and who fought at the Battles of Marne, Verdun, Somme, and Aisne, also awarded the Croix de Guerre. Frank Moulton, popular baritone of the day sang patriotic songs. Extracts from Nile nobles' letters from France were heartwarming, but in particular this one from Noble Sergeant W. H. Dobb was very instructive:

> Have helped to found a Masonic Lodge here, to be known as Liberty Lodge No. 8. Am rather proud of it, as I feel I am the only member of Lawson Consistory, of Seattle, which is one of the founders of the first (American) lodge in France.

> ~ W. H. Dobb, 1918.

How about this one from Noble Captain H. Eugene Allen:

> Thank you very much for your kind letter and dues card for 1918…I feel that I am only following the teachings of Masonry and upholding the honor of my profession by sacrificing my personal interests to serve my country in its hour of need.

> ~ H. Eugene Allen, 1918.

And from Noble Captain Thomas R. Beeman:

> My heart is warm from reading your good letter of Dec. 5th, enclosing Shrine card for 1918…Tell the Nobles that I am well and working under a full head of steam, as are all the officers and men who have been favored with an opportunity to do their bit for the great cause.

> ~ Thomas Beeman, 1918.

On March 7th, Recorder Frank Lazier sent General John J. Pershing, who was a Noble, a service flag containing a copy of the Nile Honor Roll of Nile nobles serving in the Great War. On April 12, General Pershing wrote back thanking Nile for their splendid display of patriotism.

Hyland did lead a pilgrimage to Alaska, to the cities of Anchorage,

Seward, and Cordova where several new nobles were created. On September 24, pursuant to a dispensation from Imperial Potentate Elias J. Jacoby, Nile membership (nobility) was conferred on several officers at Camp Lewis. Shortly afterward, many of these nobles were transferred to the front in Europe. A War Tax of 10% was imposed on new candidates so that in addition to the $75 initiation fee another $7.50 was collected, all War Tax monies going to support the troops overseas. Finally, on November 11th the Armistice was declared in Europe. In celebration, Nile held a Victory Ceremonial on December 7th, which brought in 85 new nobles bringing Niles total membership to 2,329. And 218 nobles serving overseas had their dues remitted for 1918 and 1919.

Not to be overlooked was The Great Pandemic of 1918 which ravished America and the world. It began early in 1918 and peaked in October of that year. Second and third waves of it lasted throughout 1919. It has been estimated that 550,00to 650,000 people in the United States died from this virus and anywhere from 17 million to 50 million people worldwide. For reasons known only to the Almighty Creator the initial first wave essentially died out in November of that year shortly after the Armistice came into existence. A remarkable coincidence for which all were thankful. Only a few of Nile's extended family were stricken with the virus and it is unknown if any Nobles died from it versus from injuries suffered in the Great War.

Note: The Great Pandemic was also known as the Spanish Flu. This was a misnomer because the flu never originated in Spain. The flu was prevalent during the war in the United States, United Kingdom, France, and Germany but because of wartime censorship there was little or no news disseminated about the devastating effects of the flu available to reporters. Spain was not under this news censorship restriction and when word got out that King Alphonse of Spain contracted the virus, eager reporters promptly dubbed the malady "The Spanish Flu."

1919 - John C. Watrous – Peace in the World

Potentate Watrous took office as the Great War was coming to a formal end (Treaty of Versailles was not signed until June 28, 1919) and President Wilson's plan for the League of Nations was underway. The highlight of the February stated meeting was an address by Past Potentate Major George R.

Drever, who had just returned direct from France on January 27, about his experiences on the French battlefront. Several nobles were commemorated via the Black Camel list, including Noble Captain Matthew L. English,. killed in action of October 4, 1918. After rallying his troops and while leading his company of tanks, on foot ahead of the first wave of infantry, Noble English was cut down by machine gun bullets. After reading the Nile News of this account, Captain E. H. Ristine wrote:

> I had a cross made with the Nile insignia on it and put it on his grave which I found a little way northeast of Exemont (France). He was a very close friend of mine…He used his tanks to help my brother's regiment in the Varennes, Cheppy Charpentry, and Baulney district, Sept. 26th to Oct. 2nd.

A Past Potentate's Ceremonial was held on May 14 with all 11 Nile Past Potentates taking the offices of the Ceremonial divan. The 50 member Nile Patrol under the command of Capt. Richard Huntoon and the 50 member Nile Band under Director Harvey Woods performed admirably at this historic Ceremonial.

Another great pilgrimage to Manila took place with a Ceremonial held at the Grand Opera House in Manila on Saturday, July 5 netted 125 new nobles. And Nile went to Imperial Council Session in Indianapolis with its Patrol and Band to help Al Kader win the 1920 Imperial Session for Portland. Win it they did with the help from Nile and the other Northwest temples. It would turn out to be an epoch-making Session because at that session Imperial Potentate W. Freeland Kendrick would finally gain the vote needed to establish the Shriners Hospitals for Children system.

In November of that year Imperial Sir Kendrick would visit Seattle for Nile's Fall Ceremonial. While in Seattle, he and his lady christened the launch of the Liberty ship SS Nile (changed from the Crittenden by the United States Shipping Board at the behest of influential Nile nobles). Mrs. Kendrick acted as sponsor of the ship which was built at the Skinner and Eddy Shipyard in Seattle. The Band and the Patrol escorted Mrs. Kendrick during the launch while all launch arrangements were overseen by the Anchor and Ark Association, a group made up of all the Masons who worked at the Skinner and Eddy Shipyard. See the article on the Ark and Anchor Association in Chapter 13, Special Groups and Activities.

Through four ceremonials, two in Seattle, one in Bellingham and one in Manila, 470 new nobles were created that year, the largest in the history of Nile to that point in time, allowing Nile to finish 1919 with a total membership of 2,758.

Nile would continue its Rise To Glory in the 1920's with many more pilgrimages to the Orient and to Alaska. Membership would grow and new adventures and antics would occur. Join us next issue as we revisit the 1920's with more year by year detail as to how Nile grew and prospered.

Chapter Three

THE ROARING TWENTIES

(Recently discovered materials in the Nile basement have allowed the author to revise and rewrite that part of the History of Nile dealing with the 1920's. Here for your enjoyment is an enhanced version of the story of America and Nile temple in the 1920's).

The Jazz Age or Roaring Twenties was for the most part a period of sustained economic growth following an event of enormous trauma (Great War or World War I). Wikipedia has compared this decade to those of the 1950's and 1990's when similar periods of sustained growth followed an event of national significance (World War II for the 1950's and the end of the Cold War in the late 1980's for the 1990's). However, both the United States and Nile had major problems with which to contend. Prohibition (the 18th Amendment and the Volstead Act passed and signed into law on January 16, 1919) took effect on January 17, 1920, giving rise to the unanticipated outcome of organized crime, booze running, bootlegging and gangland murders. The United States Senate voted against joining the League of Nations, dashing the hopes for a true international peace organization. The rise of Bolshevism/Communism in Russia (Lenin/Stalin) and the rise of Fascism in Italy (Mussolini) together with the depressed economy of the Weimar Republic in Germany (prelude to Hitler and Nazism) made for international tensions that would later accelerate throughout the 1930's and explode into world war in the 1940's. But for the most part life was good and getting better. Women gained the right to vote in the United States in 1920, the successful culmination of the suffragette movement. Flapper fashions, the Charleston dance, bobbed hair, talking motion pictures, and F. Scott Fitzgerald novels entertained and delighted all. Manias and fads marked the 1920's. Marathons (running, dance and whatever else that could be sustained for long periods of time) were boffo. Slang language (broads, dames and dolls, cat's meow and cat's whiskers, Joe College, jazzbo, pos-a-loot-ly and the real McCoy) became the street speech, the equivalent of texting acronyms today. Fads, such as pole sitting, crossword puzzles and Mahjong, were on everyone's must do list.

The stock market embarked on an unprecedented growth cycle that lasted all the way through the decade until October 24, 1929 (Black Thursday). Technologically, John Brodie Baird demonstrated the first working mechanical television system in 1925, Charles Lindbergh flew the Atlantic solo in the Spirit of St. Louis in 1927. The first talking picture (via soundtrack), Don Juan, appeared in 1926 followed by the first part-talkie, The Jazz Singer in 1927 and the first all-talkie, Lights of New York, in 1928. And in the same year that Howard Carter discovered the Tomb of Tutankhamun in Egypt (1922), Nile went to China and brought back Nile the camel.

1920 –Archie F. Hamill – Babe Ruth to New York

The year 1920 opened with a shocker. On January 1, Babe Ruth was traded by the Boston Red Sox to the New York Yankees for $125,000, the highest price ever paid to obtain a ball player up to that time. Potentate Hamill opened 1920 with a Ceremonial on January 29, the very day that the 18th Amendment (Prohibition) took effect. The Ceremonial netted 150 new nobles.

The Imperial Council Session to be held in Portland that year was the prime goal of Nile's units and nobles. Al Kader would be hosting Imperial Council and they expected a large delegation from their growing sister temple at Seattle. The Band and the Patrol were busy practicing and drilling for Portland. And the newly chartered Nile Chanters were preparing their songs under the able leadership of Noble David F. Davies. However, Potentate Hamill wanted another Ceremonial on June 11 to further boost Nile's ranks before the Portland Imperial Session, which would be attended by General John J. Pershing, a noble at Sesostros Temple in Lincoln, Nebraska. The June Ceremonial boosted Nile by another 618 new members. Over 10,000 Shriners eventually passed through Seattle in June of that year on their way to Portland and Nile gathered almost 1000 automobiles to squire them around Seattle and show them the Puget Sound area.

On June 21, the 60-member Band, 43-member Patrol, 20 member Chanters and other Nile members left Seattle in two special trains of the Great Northern Railroad for Portland. Several hundred other nobles headed down by automobile or on other trains so that Nile's total representation at Portland was closer to 2,000 nobles. At Portland, several thousand silk "Smile with Nile" badges were distributed along with thousands of Nile's "Seattle – Seaport of Success" booklet. The Snohomish County Shrine Club brought down a band of jazz artists that were the hit of the convention. Nile lodged at the Multnomah Hotel where Imperial stayed and held an "open house" for three days. It was at the Multnomah that Noble Forrest Adair from Yaarab Temple in Atlanta, Georgia was kept awake one night by a baritone horn player playing "I'm Forever Blowing Bubbles" over and over. He would use the text of that song the next day at Imperial Session to make the impassioned speech ("Bubbles Speech") that would convince the nobility to vote to create the Shriners Children's Hospital system. (See full account of this event in the July 2007 issue of SWN).

The hospital creation resolution that was sponsored by Imperial Potentate W. Freeland Kendrick and unanimously passed by the assembled nobility read: "That resolution be adopted, authorizing the establishment of a hospital for crippled children, to be supported by the Nobles of the Mystic Shrine, on an annual per capita basis, and to be known as the Shriners Hospital for Crippled Children." And so, began the Shriners Children's Hospital system as a result of a vote in Portland. Another Ceremonial on November 27 earned Nile another 84 members, finishing 1920 with a net membership of 3,635

1921- Charles D. Lewis – The Snohomish Suez Temple

After a fast start to the year by participating in the Pacific Coast Ceremonial in Tacoma on January 8 (23 temples participating), and a fabulous installation at the Seattle Masonic Temple auditorium on January 13, Potentate Lewis and Nile soon found themselves faced with a threat of monumental proportions. The Snohomish County Shrine Club petitioned Nile for permission to petition Imperial to start a temple in Everett to be called Suez Temple. The territory of Suez would encompass Snohomish, Skagit, Whatcom, Island and San Juan counties, leaving Nile with King, Kitsap, Clallam, and Jefferson counties and the Alaska Territory. Snohomish was to present a resolution at the April 13 Nile stated meeting requesting Nile's permission to petition Imperial for dispensation.

Potentate Lewis immediately directed a letter to all Nile nobles reminding them that a temple in Everett would make for three temples within a 60 mile stretch, that excellent modes of transportation made trips to Nile from the outlying counties easy, that there was a dearth of population in Kitsap, Clallam and Jefferson counties, and that Nile's reputation and ability to survive as a temple of destiny would be irrevocable damaged. As you can well imagine, after this impassioned plea by the potentate, the resolution was voted down by a large majority of Nile nobles. Shortly afterward, a very successful Spring Ceremonial was held on April 30. But the threat to Nile was not over. Snohomish County Shrine Club took their petition to Imperial Council Session sitting in Des Moines, Iowa on June 14-16 of that year. But it was a bad year to try to gain dispensation for a new temple. The Imperial Session had passed a resolution requiring a minimum of 600 members to petition for dispensation and, if establishment of the new temple would leave the old temple with 1,500 members or less, dispensation would not be granted.

Under these unfavorable conditions the petition to create Suez Temple failed and the threat to Nile passed. Also, at this Imperial Session, the Hospital per capita levy of $2 was passed by which no dues card could be issued without the levy being paid in addition to regular dues, thus ensuring funding of the fledging hospital system. Another pilgrimage to Alaska took place and another Ceremonial was held that fall both of which brought in many new members. And Nile hosted its first circus via the John Moore Co. of New York. Three cars were raffled off at the circus: a new Cadillac, a new Chalmers, and a new Studebaker. As luck would have it, none of the winners were Shriners or even Masons.

A young ladies and babies popularity contest was also held with the four most popular ladies and the three most popular babies receiving diamond rings. The circus ran from October 29 to November 9 in the

Arena. Nationally, Imperial contracted to build the first Shriners Hospital in St. Louis, Missouri, next to Washington University Hospital, whose eminent chief orthopedic surgeon, Dr. Nat Allison, would provide his services free to the new hospital. However, St Louis was not destined to host the very first Shriners Hospital for Children. That honor would go to Shreveport Louisiana in 1922. Nile ended 1921 with a net membership of 3,986.

1922 –Hugh Caldwell – Camels and Comedy

When Mayor of Seattle, Hugh Caldwell, assumed the office of Potentate at Nile he did so in a hurry. Because he would lead Nile's Fourth Pilgrimage to the Orient in early January, he obtained a dispensation from Imperial to be installed on December 30, 1921 instead of the usual first stated meeting in January. The pilgrimage became legendary, not only because of its great success in obtaining new members and the length and quality of the receptions in the various cities of Manila, Shanghai and Hong Kong, but because Potentate Hugh brought back a dromedary camel named Nile Camel from China, a sedan throne chair from Manila, and a rickshaw from Hong Kong. Miss Nile, as the female camel was known, was introduced to the nobility at the April 12 stated meeting. Hugh soon discovered that Nile needed a roommate at the Woodland Park Zoo, where Nile would be quartered between appearances at Nile events.

He obtained Potentate, a male camel, and had him shipped to Seattle in May. Nile spent almost $6000 that year to purchase sets, costumes, and props for its First Section, the Nile unit which typically set up and operated the ceremonials. At the January 11 Ceremonial and again at the June 3 Ceremonial the new scenic effects were presented by the First Section without having to rely upon Al Kader or Afifi for scenery and sets. Also, debuting at the June Ceremonial was the newly formed Dancing Girls unit. This unit consisted of six Oriental Dancing Girls and six Egyptian Dancing Girls (all nobles from other units). At the beginning of the year, in addition to the regular appointed divan, Caldwell appointed 25 aides with such titles as: Admiral of the Arabian Navy (Henry Seaborn), Toymaker for the Harem (Albert Berry), Guardian of the Mummies (Clarence Parker), Designer of Eunichs' Clothes (Ed Oliver) and my personal favorite, the Oompah of Swat (Edgar Webster).

In obvious delight over this fun-loving Potentate, the nobility passed a resolution at the June Ceremonial to submit Hugh's name in 1923 as a candidate for Imperial Outer Guard. Hugh took Miss Nile, the rickshaw, the sedan chair and 120 marching unit members (almost evenly split among Patrol, Band and Chanters) to Imperial Session in San Francisco that year and Nile's units became a big hit in the parade. The Second Annual Shrine Circus was held from September 30 to October 14 at the Arena and two year-end ceremonials, one at Bellingham and one at Seattle were held with much success. Nile funded and had its name put on two hospital beds at Seattle Children's Orthopedic Hospital as well as contributing by both donations and per capita levy to the Shriners Hospitals for Children. That year the first Shriner's hospital opened in September in a converted mansion in Shreveport, Louisiana. The St. Louis hospital would have to await the resolution of land acquisition issues at that site. At the end of 1922 Nile's net membership stood at 4,261 and Nile's Rise To Glory was accelerating.

1923 – "Richard W. Huntoon "Five thousand in 1923"

Potentate Huntoon's rallying theme this year was "Five Thousand in '23." Such a membership number would put Nile in rare company nationally. Only a few other temples had more than that in membership. Huntoon was the longtime Captain of the Patrol and he had the support of his unit men to make this happen. The big event that year was the Imperial Session in Washington, D.C. June 5-7. Prior to that trip, a big Ceremonial was held on May 19 at the Shrine Auditorium which brought in 200 new nobles. The pilgrimage to Washington, D.C. was very successful with a full complement of Nile's units (Patrol, Band and Chanters) in participation. On a sad note, President and Noble Warren G. Harding died in office.

That year, Nile's Second Section was formally organized as the Section Gang with a set of Bylaws, uniforms, and George T. McGillivery as Superintendent. In those days, the Presidents of Shrine Clubs were known as Sheiks. Since the first Shrine Club (Snohomish) was formed in 1911, the number of clubs had grown to 28 by 1923 (15 in Washington: Everett/Snohomish, Bellingham, Bremerton, Kent, Auburn, Concrete, Blaine, Port Townsend, Port Angeles, Anacortes, Mount Vernon, Sedro Woolley, Snoqualmie, Sumas, Vashon; 10 in Alaska: Ketchikan, Juneau, Skagway, Cordova, Valdez, Seward, Anchorage, Nenana, Fairbanks, and three in Asia: Manila, Shanghai, Yokohama). Of interesting note is the Skagit Shrine Club that year purchased 47 acres of land for $4,500 for the benefit of the Camp Fire Girls with the only stipulation that it be used as a camp for that organization. The President of the Skagit Shrine Club was Sheik W. M. Kirby and the camp came to be known as Camp Kirby.

Nile's ninth pilgrimage to Alaska netted several more nobles and the year-end Ceremonial on December 6 was a Joint Ceremonial with Gizeh Temple, attended by Imperial Potentate Conrad V. Dykeman. Afifi and Al Kader Temples also attended and Nile returned the favor by attending Afifi's and Al Kader's Imperial Potentate Ceremonials on December 8 and 9 respectively. Nile finished 1923 with a net membership of 4.951.

1924 – E.S. Goodwin – Nile Buys the Country Club Property

Potentate Goodwin, who never used his full first name anywhere but whose full name, after diligent research, was found to be Ervin Shirley Goodwin, presided over one of the most fortuitous years in Nile history. Two years earlier, Potentate Hugh Caldwell, in his outgoing address at the end of his year, expressed a desire for Nile to acquire some country property to be used as a picnic area for Nile nobles and their families and possibly as a golf course. The new Oriental Guide, Bill Eastman, was heavily involved in land acquisitions as part of his business. He located some land north of Seattle, near a heavily wooded wilderness lake, which he suggested Nile might like to use as recreational property.

After considerable inspection, study, and discussion, on March 24, 1924, the nobility approved the purchase of 92 acres on Lake Ballinger from the Ballinger Estate for the princely sum of $25,000. An additional 43 acres adjoining the Lake Ballinger property was added in April. Potentate Goodwin, Chief Rabban Walter F. Meier and the rest of the divan made plans for a picnic to celebrate this momentous purchase. And, on August 9, the First Annual Nile Temple Picnic was held on the new grounds by the shores of Lake Ballinger. 3,500 nobles, ladies and children attended that first ever Nile Picnic.

Potentate Goodwin's other major contribution to Nile was starting a series of Sunday Concerts, given by the Band, for the benefit of Nile nobles and their ladies. Ceremonials were held on March 22, May 24 and December 13 bringing in many new nobles. Imperial Session was held in Kansas City, Missouri that year but the best Patrol in the country did not attend. Instead, according to Patrol Historian Harris Bremer, Nile's Patrol voted not to attend and to donate the money reserved for the trip toward the building of a clubhouse and ballroom at the new country property. But the highlight of the year occurred at Al Kader Temple. For several years, Al Kader had been coming north for Nile's ceremonials and putting on a beautiful First Section for Nile. This year Nile's Second Section went to Al Kader for its November 29 Ceremonial and its Section Gang put on one of the best Second Sections ever witnessed at Al Kader. But the star event of the evening was the talk by 10-year-old Max Dalton of Kelso, WA. Max had his foot badly mangled in a mowing machine accident when he was much younger. The newly established Portland Shriners Hospital had started operating in 1924 and Max was one of the first patients admitted. Chief Orthopedic Surgeon Dr. Dillahunt operated on Max's foot and Max could now walk and play like any child now. Max had indicated that he would like to thank the nobles in person for his treatment. Al Kader Past Potentate Frank S. Grant brought Max down from Kelso and introduced him to the nobility. His entry into the armory was stunning. Escorted by the combined bands, Drum Corps and Patrols, Max immediately drew spontaneous applause from the 3,500 in the audience. After Frank described Max's case and treatment, Max thanked the nobles for what they had done for him, told how he had not walked for years, but now could walk and play like his classmates, how he hoped that the nobles would be as good to all the other children at the hospital as they had been to him and that he hoped someday to be a Shriner himself. Well, the ensuing applause from the audience nearly blew the roof off the Portland Armory. That same year Shriners Hospitals were also opened in St. Louis, Spokane, and Minneapolis, with Honolulu and San Francisco having opened the year before. And Nile finished 1924 with a net membership of 5,183.

1925 – Walter F. Meier – Triennial
Conclave of Knights Templar

During Potentate Meier's year several significant events occurred. Shrine Hospitals were opened in Montreal, Springfield, Massachusetts., and Salt Lake City, Utah; the first East-West Shrine College All Star Game was played in San Francisco, hosted by Islam Temple; and the Knights Templar held their Grand Encampment at their 36th Triennial Conclave in Seattle.

Since all Shriners had to be either 32nd Degree Scottish Rite Masons or York Rite Knights Templar (and most were both) the Triennial Conclave held special interest for Nile nobles. The Executive Committee in charge of arrangements for the approximately 150,000 visitors was composed almost solely of Nile nobles, including Past Potentates, Joe Swalwell, Richard Huntoon, Major Drever, and John Rex Thompson.

An illustrated pamphlet heralding Seattle's scenic, industrial, and cultural strengths was produced. The conclave attracted York Rite Masons, who were also Shriners, from all over the country and Nile's reputation as a temple of national repute continued to grow. Potentate Meier would later become Grand Master of Washington in 1927-28. Imperial Session was held in Los Angeles that year, June 2-4, and Nile's Uniformed Units chose to go by ocean going steamer, the "SS Dorothy Alexander." What a pleasant and fun trip it was when a boatload of 300 Nile Shriners traveled by sea. Nile's units put on a great show and were well received by the other temples, greatly enhancing Nile's national reputation among the temples. The highlight of Imperial was the Electrical Pageant staged by all the major movie studios of the time: Lasky, Paramount, MGM, Universal, Fox, Warner Bros. and United. Electrically lighted floats displaying highlights of the motion picture industry formed a chain of special effects never before attempted anywhere else. A Warner Bros. film of this great event was produced and shown in temples throughout Shrinedom and was shown at the Blue Mouse Theater in Seattle on December 10.

Earlier that summer on August 15, the Band, Patrol and Chanters held a joint picnic at the new Nile Country Club grounds at Lake Ballinger. But this was preceded by an even larger Nile Basket Picnic on the Nile grounds for Nile families and friends on July 11 with three thousand seven hundred 44 in attendance. A pilgrimage to Southeast Alaska and a December Ceremonial rounded out Potentate Meier's year with both events bringing in new nobles and ending 1925 with a net membership total of 5,248.

1926 – Thomas M. Askren – Nile Marches On

Nile's growing importance as a Shrine Temple made it a must stop destination on every Imperial Potentate's list. Two Imperial Potentates visited Nile in 1926. On January 7, Imperial Sir James C. Burger arrived at Nile to welcome new candidates who had just been voted upon at Nile. And on August 14, Imperial Sir David W. Crossland became the first Imperial Potentate to be received at Nile's Country Club grounds. Also attending on August 14 were Potentates George Hoag of El Katif and William D. Askren (Potentate Askrens brother) of Afifi. This is the only time on record that brothers have been Potentates of Nile and Afifi in the same year. The annual picnic was held on July 17 with over 7,000 nobles and their families in attendance. Free lemonade, peanuts, popcorn, and ice cream were provided, but families had to bring their own picnic baskets.

Of note was Noble J. M. Yeaman of Yeaman Brothers Contractors made Nile a present of a 6,000-gallon water tank, which they installed free of charge, to replace Nile's undersized 3000 gallon water tank, thus assuring Nile of plenty of water for its growing picnic outings. A cartoon lithograph of the picnic by Farwest Lithograph is included for your amusement. Other significant events included Nile's 13th pilgrimage to Alaska in August (Ketchikan, Sitka, Juneau, Skagway, and Wrangell) where several more Nile nobles were created and a Joint Ceremonial with Gizeh Temple held in Victoria, B.C. on October 30. This latter event cemented a growing sister temple relationship with Gizeh which has remained the strongest of any temple relationship that Nile has with other temples. The combined bands, Patrols and Chanters of Nile and Gizeh put on a marvelous display of parades, concerts, and events for the Vancouver Island residents.

Also, that year, $5,000 was borrowed from the Dexter Horton Bank to pay off a portion of the country club land purchase and to commission a preliminary survey and design for the building of a country clubhouse by the design team of Olmstead Brothers, designers of the Woodland Park grounds in Seattle and Central Park in New York City. An additional 20 acres was acquired to bring Nile's Country Club acreage to a total of 155 acres at a total cost of $33,200. On a sad note, two Nile Past Potentates passed away within five weeks of each other, John Rex Thompson (1914) and John C. Watrous (1919). These two were the first of Nile's past potentates to journey to that Celestial Temple above. Nevertheless, Nile's fun activities attracted many new nobles to join Nile and by year end, net membership stood at 5,229.

1927 – Fred R. Harrison – The Black Camel Calls Too Soon

Potentate Harrison's year started out well. A resolution was passed at the January stated meeting authorizing Nile to borrow $10,000 to develop the

Country Club property with buildings and other improvements. A total of $50,000 was eventually approved that year to cover construction of a clubhouse, access roads and ground improvements. And that spring a beautiful clubhouse, consisting of a large ballroom with wood dance floor, a kitchen area, restrooms and additional space for meetings and dining (now the Caravan Room and Gold Room) were built.

Noble C. J. Parker of Parker & Hill Engineers also laid out plans for tennis courts, a baseball field, croquet field, outdoor dance area and bandstand and, amazingly, a layout for an 18-hole golf course. Nile re-indorsed Past Potentate Hugh Caldwell's bid for Imperial Oriental Guide (Hugh ran second in a field of five in 1926). But in March, Potentate Harrison had a full-fledged attack of shingles and had to go south to recuperate. Nonetheless, a successful ceremonial was held on June 4 and Fred attended Imperial Session in Atlantic City from June 14-16 where Hugh Caldwell was finally elected to the post of Imperial Outer Guard.

Fred was supposed to have dedicated the newly built clubhouse on the date of the 4th Annual Nile Picnic – Saturday, July 23, when tragedy struck! On Friday, July 22 at 2 PM, Fred died. The annual picnic was canceled and Nile went into mourning for its Potentate. Fred's passing in 1927 would become an eerie precedent for what would happen almost exactly 60 years later in 1987 when Potentate Fred Sethmann would die in office on July 18 of that year. Chief Rabban William Eastman very ably took over as Potentate and hosted an Imperial Potentate's Ceremonial on November 10 with Imperial Potentate Clarence M. Dunbar in attendance.

In November, though, Past Potentate Robert Hasson (1910) passed away, marking the loss of a fourth Potentate of Nile. And Nile Noble Frank Parker (Past Potentate of Afifi 1896-7) also passed away. Frank was the lead man and largely responsible for organizing the petition to Imperial Council for a dispensation to form Nile in 1908. He and Noble John C. Slater (Past Potentate Afifi) had presented Nile's petition to Imperial Council at the St. Paul session on July 14, 1908. The next day, Nile's dispensation was granted. Because of his efforts he was affectionately known as the "Daddy of Nile." A delightful Potentate's Ball was held on December 8 and Potentate Eastman started a Kiddie's Christmas party that year on December 23. That year, Nile's net membership increased only slightly to 5,267.

1928 – William A. Eastman – Nile Rolls on To Glory

During Potentate Eastman's year in office, the Country Club property was further developed with plantings of flowers and shrubs. Dances were held on the all wood floor of the clubhouse ballroom and social meetings were held in the Dining Room and Club Room. Imperial Council Session was held in Miami, Florida that year and Nile's representatives traveled by train via the Grand Canyon, Albuquerque, Houston, and New Orleans.

At Imperial, Nile Recorder Frank Lazier was elected President of the Shrine Recorders' Association (even though he could not attend due to a bout of pneumonia) and Nile's Hugh Caldwell moved up the Imperial line one notch to Imperial Captain of the Guard. Ceremonials were held on June 9 and December 1 and again bought in many new nobles. The December Ceremonial was especially large and colorful because four other temples (Gizeh, Al Kader, Afifi and El Katif) joined in with their respective bands, Patrols and Chanters and Drum Corps. Another Imperial Potentate, Frank C. Jones, was received and entertained at the Country Club grounds and a pilgrimage to Alaska took place August 14 (Nile's 14th) and a few new nobles were created. On the humorous side of things, the Nile Thursday Luncheon Club at their October 24 get together held a mock political debate between impersonators of the two United States presidential candidates, Herbert Hoover, and Al Smith. Luncheon Club President Judge William. Steinert read telegrams that the candidates were on their way to attend the luncheon. "Al Smith" wired that he was coming by airplane and that it didn't bother him because he was used to being "up in the air." "Hoover," ably represented by Noble Bill Butt, was the first to arrive and said that the Democratic Party was responsible for all the rain in Seattle because Seattle was "all wet." "Smith" arrived in the person of Hugh Caldwell and, in comparison to Noble Butt's formal frock coat and dignified bearing, wore a derby hat cocked to the back of his head, sack coat, white vest, and striped trousers so loud they could be heard in Tacoma. "Smith" prefaced his remarks by saying in remarkably accurate New Yorker accent "This is the foist toime I have had Thoisday luncheon wit youse." When asked about his read of the Republican platform, "Smith" responded "What did the Republican platform say in 1920? What did it say in 1924? I don't know what this one says either." Hoover went on to win the election that year, but Smith was funnier by far. Near the year's end on December 22, Nile put on another children's holiday event, dubbed the Annual Christmas Tree Party at the Shrine Auditorium in the Seattle Masonic Temple that was a great success. Nile finished the year with a net membership of 5,750.

1929 – Douglas Ball – the Great Crash

Although Potentate Ball had a good year in 1929, he had the dubious distinction of presiding over Nile (as President Hoover did over the country) during the start of the Great Crash of the New York stock market which continued into the 30's and essentially stunted the growth of Nile, as well as the United States economy, for several years.

Potentate Ball led a group of Nile nobles 200 strong to the Imperial Council Session held in Los Angeles at Al Malaikah Temple on June 4-6. Nile units again distinguished themselves and reasserted their claim to being some of the top units in Shrinedom. The highlight of the trip was another fantastic parade of electrically lighted floats put together by the Hollywood movie colony. Later, on June 29 back in Seattle, Nile held its ceremonial which was attended by new Imperial Potentate Leo Youngsworth. The Second Section was held on the Country Club grounds, hosted by the Section Gang. Unfortunately, we do not have a record of what nefarious stunts were executed out in the woods, although we know that the Recorder, Frank Lazier, and Second Section Director George Drever traveled to the Shrine Directors' Association Convention in Grand Rapids, Michigan earlier that year and came back with some new stunts.

The ceremonial was again very successful. A Veteran Patrol was formed with Past Potentate Bill Eastman elected as president. This new unit promptly took over the staging of Nile's fifth Annual Picnic which occurred on July 13 at the Country Club grounds. Besides the games and goodies for the children, the adults had a ball with two dances, one inside the clubhouse and one on the huge outdoor dance platform and two three inning baseball games on the ball field, one between the Chanters and the Band and the other between the Patrol and the Veteran Patrol. Dance music was provided by the Band and a song concert by given by the Chanters.

A 15th pilgrimage to Southeast Alaska and Fairbanks took place on August 4-27. Many new nobles were created, including Noble A.L. McCord, who was at work prospecting for gold over 500 miles from Fairbanks shortly before the ceremonial was to take place. When word reached him about the upcoming ceremonial, he left his dig and walked 90 miles to the Tenana River where he built a raft. He floated 50 miles downstream through dangerous rapids and swirling currents. He then arranged with a trapper to borrow a small boat and floated another 275 miles downstream to a point where a road existed. He obtained a ride in an automobile to travel the last 100 miles to Fairbanks and arrived there in time for the ceremonial.

Nile reached out to the greater Seattle community that year in two significant ways. The Seattle Chamber of Commerce sponsored a "Charmed Land" public relations campaign that year. At the heart of it was the selling of colorful woolen blankets from Jacobs Oregon City Woolens. Participating private entities would receive a portion of the proceeds for their efforts in marketing these woolen blankets which, it was hoped, would gain a fair amount of national publicity for Seattle. Nile took part and sold many blankets throughout the Seattle area via its Publicity and Entertainment Fund Committee and earned a considerable amount of money for its efforts. And the Nile Band gave an awesome concert on KOMO radio on April 4 in connection with the Charmed Land Song Contest.

On December 7, Nile held a 21st Birthday Ceremonial, commemorating its formation in 1908. Recorder Frank Lazier wrote the first historical account of Nile's history for that ceremonial's program. Although Black Thursday occurred on October 24, the market did a slight rebound before falling again on Black Tuesday October 29. The full effects of the crash would not be felt until the following years. Nile held its Third Annual Christmas Party for the children and ended 1929 with a net membership total of just under 6,000.

Nile would endure the 30's and the Great Depression which was sparked by the Great Crash. We will examine the causes and concerns of that historic event in the next article – The Turbulent Thirties.

Chapter Four

THE TURBULENT THIRTIES

The 1930'a were a turbulent time in United States history. Rocked by the New York stock market crash in October, 1929, the world's economies struggled to adjust to a severely modified economic climate. In the United States, the actual crash was preceded by a five-year run up of stock prices. Many people put their whole life's savings into stocks and many more borrowed money to invest in stocks. The Dow Jones Industrial Average peaked at 381.17 in early September, 1929 just before stocks started to dive. From September to mid-October, the market lost 17% of its value. After a small recovery the market took a big dive culminating in "Black Thursday" on October 24, 1929 when almost 13 million shares were traded. Leading financiers attempted to stem the tide of decline by buying huge amounts of blue-chip stocks. But the panic continued. News spread across the country. On Monday October 28, more selling occurred, another 12 million shares traded, and on "Black Tuesday" October 29, amid news that President Hoover would not veto the pending Hawley-Smoot Tariff Act (in effect doubling taxes on imported goods), 16.4 million shares were traded, a number not exceeded until 1969. The market had altogether lost close to half its value (48%) in less than a week. Temporary respites occurred and the market even climbed back to 294 in April 1930. But it thereafter continued to decline to a low of 41.22 on July 8, 1932.

Many commentators have speculated on the actual causes of the Great Crash. Chief among the theories was the "get rich quick" mentality which gripped many small investors prior to the crash. An incredible number of stocks were bought and sold at many times their price to earnings ratio. As the stock market and the prices of stocks continued to steadily rise through the 1920's, many investors used up their savings and then borrowed both from banks and their brokers to buy more and more stocks. As in the 1990's, it seemed like the boom would continue forever. Once the supply of new money dwindled to the point of not being able to fuel the binge stock buying and selling started to occur with its concomitant effect on lowering stock prices, the steam went out from the boom market. Banks and brokers started calling in their loans and many investors borrowers could not respond. Bad loans made by the banks with little security to back them up except for the speculative stocks of their borrowers came back to haunt them and soon they could not keep up with normal financial business transactions. As word of the banks' inability to transact financial business got around, other people rushed to pull their savings from these banks. Recall that at this time most banks were very small local banks or at most modest regional banks and there was no Federal Deposit Insurance Corporation (FDIC) to insure bank deposits. Once banks started to go under, the whole financial atmosphere of the country changed and stocks continued to dip. Selling of massive amounts of stocks occurred and the events of October 1929 ensued. Caveat: there are other theories about the Great Crash, including the Keynesian, Marxist, and Austrian theories, but this author considers the above theory very logical and explanatory of what happened.

The Great Depression which followed the stock market crash emanated from people's fears of doing any more borrowing. Add to that many banks had failed due to runs on the banks from panicky depositors. Now there were many fewer small banks to loan money. Without borrowed money, businesses languished, fewer goods were produced and even fewer durable goods were purchased. The Smoot-Hawley Tariff Act raised the prices of many imported goods and other countries soon retaliated by putting high tariffs on American goods sold abroad. Nature also conspired against the country. The Dust Bowl of the summer of 1930 and for much of the 1930's bankrupted many small farmers and ranchers. As in John Steinbeck's novel, Grapes of Wrath, many families left their homes and properties and fled to California and elsewhere. The average income of the American family fell 40% from 1929 to 1932, from $2,300 to $1,500. In the latter part of the 1930's the economy recovered quite a bit. American ingenuity, resourcefulness, and pluck, with a little help from President Franklin D. Roosevelt's social welfare programs, allowed the United States to stabilize its economy and not suffer the fate of other countries which succumbed to political dictatorships (Germany, Italy, Spain) as a solution to the worldwide Great Depression. Interestingly, the Union of Soviet Socialist Republics (USSR) was largely unaffected by the Great Depression because it had shifted from a capitalist economy to a totally socialist economy and was pretty much self-sufficient during this time frame.

Nevertheless, it was the advent of the Second World War with its huge buildup of manufactured military goods and its employment of a large number of people that finally pulled the world's economies out of the doldrums of the Great Depression.

But Americans were as resilient as ever during these years as was Nile Temple. Consider that in 1931 the world's tallest building at the time, the Empire State Building, was completed and opened. The Chrysler Building and Rockefeller Center were also completed in the early 1930's, monuments to progress. The Golden Age of radio kept homebound Americans amused and inspired. Jack Benny, Fred Allen, George Burns and Gracie Allen, and Fibber McGee and Molly all left Americans laughing during these down days. And the Lone Ranger, the Shadow, Green Hornet and Jack Armstrong took us to worlds where the worries of today were left behind. Radio stirred the imagination and saved our sanities during these years. By 1939, over 80% of all Americans owned a radio or had one in their homes. (Younger readers must recall that in the 1930's there were no TVs, no computers, no iPods, no electronic gaming devices and no cell phones). Imaginations were tweaked to their maximum by Orson Welles' broadcast of the H.G. Wells Martian invasion thriller, War of the Worlds, on October 30, 1938.

As the United States economy started to improve during the 1930's, music tastes shifted from the sweet jazz sound of the early 1930's to the lively swing music of the middle and late 1930's. Dance music by Duke Ellington, Glenn Miller and Tommy Dorsey filled the radio waves and the dance halls. Broadway composers wrote songs for musicals that made people sit up and feel good. Such hits as Strike Up the Band and Girl Crazy (George and Ira Gershwin), Anything Goes and Red, Hot and Blue (Cole Porter) are still played today. "Talkies" (talking pictures), having been introduced in the late 1920's, were taken to a new level in the 1930's as

Hollywood churned out such movies as the Wizard of Oz, the Good Ship Lollipop, the Busby Berkeley extravaganzas, the horror films of Dracula, Frankenstein and King Kong, and the immortal Gone With the Wind. And the first full length animated film, Snow White and the Seven Dwarfs by Disney premiered in 1937.

And at Nile, the nobles and their ladies and families soldiered on despite the Great Depression, the threats of war and the changing political environments. Nile lost over 700 memberships between 1932 and 1940. But ceremonials and installations were still held, parties thrown, pilgrimages taken, and fun meetings and social events continued. Shriners and their families could escape the dreariness of the depression years by picnicking at Nile's Lake Ballinger picnic grounds. The clubhouse had been completed in 1928 and, by the early 1930's, the grounds had been developed into formal picnic areas, and a wading pool and playfield for the children. Horseshoe courts, Dutch ovens for cooking dinners, a baseball field, and a large outdoor dance platform delighted the adults. Indoors, the clubhouse offered a large dance floor in the Pyramid Ballroom, a dining room, a kitchen, and another smaller meeting room. And as we shall see below, the potentates, divans, units, and clubs during those years offered a myriad of diversions and events for the membership's pleasure.

1930 – Paul Watt - Traveling Pote

Potentate Watt claimed to have traveled to and visited every Shrine club and unit in his realm. Not only that, but on several of these trips he took the Chanters, Band, and Divan to liven up the visits. Nile had lost a net of 209 members in 1929 (from 5115 to 4906) and Watt wanted to make this loss up in a hurry. Several ceremonials were held, but the one that really gratified him was the one in Port Angeles on May 17. In March, Nile had hosted a dinner for the Shriners of Clallam and Jefferson counties at the Masonic Temple in Port Angeles. The Olympic Peninsula Shrine Club had been pretty quiet for several years prior and Nile wanted to wake them up. A few live wires got together and elected Noble Tom Owen (Port Angeles City Engineer) as president. He and the other new officers wanted a ceremonial in Port Angeles to help drive membership. Potentate Watt told them that if they could get 20 candidates, Nile would put on a full ceremonial for them in PA. They got 18 and the ceremonial that was put on was a huge success.

A Spring Ceremonial on May 31 at Nile netted 90 more new nobles. The Family Picnic on July 12 was highlighted by a Prohibition Debate between Imperial First Ceremonial Master Hugh Caldwell and Potentate Watt. No information presently exists as to which personage took which side of the debate, but it is rumored that both participants celebrated thereafter with special refreshments.

1930 marked the formation of a Golf Course Committee to build an 18-hole golf course at the clubhouse grounds. A Nile Golf Club would be formed, consisting of 400 members paying $330 a piece to fund the construction of the course. Although the golf course would have to wait, tennis courts were added and the horseshoe courts improved and expanded. The Winter Ceremonial on December 13 brought in another 20 nobles and Nile finished the year with a net membership of 5,009.

1931 – Van S. McKenny – The Depression Deepens but Nile Sails On

Potentate McKenny's year started off with a trans-Pacific pilgrimage to Asia aboard the SS President Grant from January 25 to March 18, Nile's fifth Orient pilgrimage). Ceremonials were conducted in Yokohama, Kobe, Shanghai, Hong Kong, and Manila – 18,000 miles of Smile with Nile. Numerous new nobles were created. This pilgrimage was followed with a trip to Ketchikan, Cordova and Fairbanks, Nile's sixteenth pilgrimage to Alaska from August 4-27 where another 35 nobles were created. In between these trips, the Nile Family Picnic on July 25 drew a turnout of 5500 Nile nobles, ladies, and kids, one of the largest picnics ever held at Nile. The highlight of the picnic was the competition between the First and Second Platoons of Nile's Patrol for the Hugh M. Caldwell Cup, donated by Past Potentate Hugh Caldwell. And the Dance Committee arranged for two separate dance bands to perform, one for the outdoor dance platform and one for the clubhouse ballroom.

At the Pacific Northwest Shrine Association (PNSA) meeting in Spokane, May 16 that year, Nile also had the largest delegation in attendance. The year concluded with a Winter Ceremonial on December 5 which brought in another 31 new nobles. However, 271 nobles had to be suspended for non-payment of dues and Nile finished 1931 with a net membership of 4,896.

1932 – Don H. Evans – The New Deal Era Starts

Potentate Evans' year got off to a generous start when Nile nobles voted at the January stated meeting to create Life Memberships. All nobles who paid 15 years' worth of dues ($12 in 1932) would become Life Members. However, they would still be responsible to pay the per capita to Imperial and the Hospital levy (.50 and $2.00 respectively in those days). 1932 was not kind to America, with the depression deepening and the Dust Bowl continuing. President Hoover's days were numbered.

In all honesty Hoover did try to pull the country out of the depression with his emphasis on voluntary cooperation between business and government to restart the economy. But Franklin D. Roosevelt would be elected President in November 1932 and from 1933 on the country would move in a whole different direction. But at Nile, the nobles and ladies kept their faith in their country and in one another. Nile Temple took over the Shrine Luncheon Club to give it more stature and support. This Club was immensely popular and became more so with its emphasis on high quality programs, entertainment, and speakers. An Ice Carnival was held at the Ice Arena in November featuring the Shipstad and Johnson Ice Follies. A Valentine's Dance, Potentates Ball and a Spring Party were held. At the Fifty-Eighth Annual Imperial Session in San Francisco during July 26-28, a huge Electrical Lights Parade was again staged by Hollywood studios with Harold Lloyd as Grand Marshal and Imperial Potentate Thomas J. Houston as Special Guest. Of course, Nile units attended in force, but there are no written reports of competitions or awards.

Ceremonials were held on June 4 and December 14 with both events bringing in some new nobles, but the latter ceremonial was without its traditional dinner due to lack of funds. And in 1932 Past Potentate Bill Eastman started the tradition of putting trees along the Country Club property driveway with the names of Past Potentates on them. This project, which consisted of planting pin oak and tulip trees along the Country Club grounds drive way was carried out by the Country Club Committee. Potentate Evans was very pleased to dedicate this amazing feat at the Nile Family Picnic on July 16. As the year closed, the United States and the world would be looking to see what the new president would do. Nile membership sank to under 4,500.

1933 – Howard M. Findlay – Nile's Silver Anniversary

Potentate Findlay could not have come into office at a more auspicious time. President Roosevelt was about to turn the country on its head with his New Deal programs and Potentate Findlay chose to inspire Nile nobles with a super celebration of Nile's Silver (25th) Anniversary of its formation. As he stated in his opening message to Nile:

> There has never been a time, certainly not within the memory of any of us, when there has existed a greater need for the spreading of sunshine and brotherly love – the very essence of the inspiration which prompted and brought into being the organization of the Ancient Arabic Order of Nobles of the Mystic Shrine.
>
> Let us make this year – the twenty-fifth anniversary of Nile Temple – a real jubilee. To this end, many activities have been arranged for your pleasure, and it is the sincere hope and wish of your Potentate that you will participate in them, and that your visits to the Oasis of your Temple will be frequent, pleasant, and happy ones.

And indeed, Potentate Findlay made it happen. In addition to the dances, balls and party events, a special Silver Anniversary Ceremonial was held on May 13 at the Shrine Auditorium of the Seattle Masonic Temple with Imperial Potentate Earl C. Mills in attendance. Many new nobles were created. Dinner was once again served and the man whom the country had come to call O. M. D. (Old Man Depression) was on the run. Another successful picnic was held at the Country Club grounds. A baseball game between the Patrol and Band/Chanters team provide a lot of laughs and musical entertainment. No money to build a golf course, but the nobles enjoyed a tournament of Barnyard Golf. A 15-day pilgrimage to southeastern Alaska aboard the SS Yukon brought in a few more nobles. Parties at Halloween, Thanksgiving and Christmas, together with a Winter Ceremonial on December 16 rounded out the year. The only sad note was the passing of renowned Band Director Harvey J. Woods on August 29. His musical march compositions were well known throughout the country and were respected as works of serious merit. Nile finished 1933 with a net membership of 3,216.

1934 – John A. Bennett – "Smile with Nile" Begins

In 1934, one of Potentate Bennett's most cherished dreams came into being –Volume 1, Number 1 of Smile with Nile (SWN) debuted in February of that year. It contained in one publication the Potentate's message, news from units and clubs, announcements, the audit and treasurer's reports, sickness and distress, and advertisements. Previously, a variety of postcards, brochures, foldouts, and booklets, some with the name Smile with Nile on them and some with just Nile Temple adorning their mastheads were sent out to nobles to apprise them of happenings, events, stated meetings, ceremonials, and travel opportunities. The first before and after pictures of children from the Portland Shrine Hospital appeared in the April issue. The unit columns in this first volume of SWN consisted of: Toots From The Band, Tunes From The Chanters, and Tracks From The Patrol. Recall that these were the only Uniformed Units in existence back then. One newsworthy item was that Past Potentate Walter F. Meier dropped into Nile to say hello. He was now the Grand Exalted Ruler of the Grand Lodge of Elks and had been dubbed the Flying Exalted Ruler because of his trips to 345 Elks Clubs around the country.

News from other organizations began pouring in. The Shrine Clubs, notably the Northwest Shrine Club, and other organizations started reporting to the membership at large on their activities with one of the most frequent columns coming from the Daughters of the Nile. In civic news, Noble Charles L. Smith a member of the Patrol was elected mayor of Seattle. On May 1, Imperial Potentate John N. Sebrell visited to pay his respects to Nile Temple. Looking up at a Smile with Nile electrical sign he said: "Nobles, you have the greatest slogan that was ever known, for it contains a word that, in action, has brought more happiness into the world than anything else–the word Smile." At the Sixtieth Imperial Council Session in Minneapolis on June 19-21, the way was cleared for Seattle to host the 1936 Imperial Session where Hugh Caldwell would be installed as Imperial Potentate. Successful ceremonials were held on June 2 and December 15 and Nile's Fourth Annual Ice Carnival took place at the Ice Arena on December 8. The Chanters once again sponsored, hosted, and performed at the Kiddies Christmas Party on December 21. And the current political joke going around was: "The danger in (Congress)passing so many relief measures is that we will never know which one saved us." The 1934 membership tally increased to 3,521.

The Turbulent Thirties will be continued in the next issue of Smile with Nile. We will explore what Franklin D. Roosevelt did or tried to for the country, how Seattle made out hosting the 1936 Imperial Council Session and how the events of the late thirties finally started to bring the country out of the Great Depression.

THE TURBULENT THIRTIES –
THE NEW DEAL ERA

During Nile's Silver Anniversary Year of 1933, Franklin Delano Roosevelt came into office and began a frenetic 100 Days of reform and relief to spur the nation's economy out of the Great Depression. The first New Deal effort was a short-term recovery program aimed chiefly at banking reform laws and emergency relief programs. Later, a second New Deal program from 1935-1936 aimed to ensure long term protection for union workers, tenant farmers and migrant workers. Created during these time periods were the so-called "alphabet soup" agencies: Social Security Administration (SSA), the Federal Deposit Insurance Corporation (FDIC), the National Recovery Administration (NRA), the Federal Housing Administration (FHA) the Tennessee Valley Authority (TVA) and the Securities and Exchange Commission (SEC). A lot of bureaucracy, yes, but mandated by the times. Recall that by March 4, 1933, almost every bank in the country had been closed by the governors of the various states. By Executive Order, the President kept them closed until new legislation could be passed. The Emergency Banking Act, passed and signed into law on March 9, allowed the reopening of most banks under Treasury Department supervision. Money flowed back into the reopened banks, but over 4,000 local banks had to be merged into larger banks.

Depositors of these merged banks received 85 cents on the dollar. The establishment of the FDIC in June, 1933, insuring deposits up to $5000, helped to end the run on banks which had exacerbated the economic downturn of 1929-1933. The farm crisis was met with the Agricultural Adjustment Administration which called for crop reductions and domestic allotments of various farm products together with subsidies for farmers who idled some of their land. The idea was to provide price supports for crops and other farm products by allowing less to be produced to keep prices up.

Richard M. Kovak

And farmers did benefit for the first three years, but consumers who were forced to pay high prices for farm commodities were furious. In 1936, the United States Supreme Court declared the Agricultural Adjustment Act unconstitutional and it had to be replaced with a system of direct subsidies to farmers that exists to this very day. But most people were put back to work through the various government programs enacted to create large public projects which would employ tens of thousands of those out of work. Thus, the Tennessee Valley Administration dam project not only put a lot of people to work but also curbed flooding, helped generate electricity and caused the modernization of many farms in the area. The Works Progress Administration, the Civilian Conservation Corps, the United States Forest Service, and the National Youth Administration provided continuing work for thousands of men, women, and youths across the country. In 1937, during President Roosevelt's second term of office, the economy dipped again with unemployment rising to 19% from 14.3%.

Facing mounting criticism that he had only made the Great Depression last longer by not allowing big business the freedom to resolve the economic woes of the country, he rejected advice to cut spending and balance the budget. Instead, he embarked on a $5 billion spending program in 1938 to jump start the economy again. The economy did respond and improved slowly up through 1940. But it was the massive government spending on the war effort, the employment of almost 12 million men and women in the military, and the wage and price controls associated with that era that finally brought the United States out of the Depression. Consider that in 1929 government spending was only 3% of the Gross National Product. Through the 1930's, government spending tripled, but still was only about 10% of the GNP. As we shall see in a later article on the 1940's, government spending during the war years reached a high of 40% of GNP in 1944.

A bigger form of relief for many was the repeal of Prohibition. Congress, in response to years of pleading by citizens, adopted a resolution to add the 21st Amendment to the United States Constitution which in effect repealed the Volstead Act of 1919. Ratification by the necessary number of states, 36, took place on December 5, 1933 when Utah ratified and the Volstead Act and the 18th Amendment was confined to history as the nation's bars and liquor establishments were back in business. It should also be noted that the repeal of Prohibition was part of Roosevelt's campaign platform in 1932 on the ground that repeal would provide a multitude of jobs and economy stimulation for a nation bearing the burden of the Great Depression. Once he was elected in November 1932, Prohibition had little chance of survival.

The 1930's saw the production of many public art projects. Murals were painted on many government buildings and funds from the Works Progress Administration (WPA) gave Gutzon Borglum the financial ability to complete the great Mount Rushmore sculptures (1934 – Washington; 1936 – Jefferson; 1937 – Lincoln and 1939 – Theodore Roosevelt). And civil engineering feats, such as Hoover Dam, completed in 1935, and the great lodges in the National Park System benefited from government spending during this era. With little money to travel, most people stayed home and listened to the radio or played board games. Ironically, one of the most popular board games was Monopoly, introduced by Parker Brothers in 1935. It was said that 20,000 games were sold in one week when it first appeared.

At Nile, the nobles and their ladies still had their social events, meetings, parades, and their beloved Country Club grounds. And in 1936, one of their own, Hugh Caldwell, was slated to become Imperial Potentate.

1935 – Orvis B. Joseph - Country Club Mortgage Burned

O. B. Joseph came into office at a public installation at the Civic Auditorium, Nile's first public installation since 1931. In February, a Blue Ribbon from Imperial for most reinstatements (419) during 1934 was presented to Nile. A ceremonial on May 11 brought in 32 new nobles and the ceremonial in Tacoma on May 18 brought in a few more. A big event occurred at the 61st Imperial Session in Washington, D. C., June 11-13 when Nile was awarded host temple status of the 62nd Imperial Session because Hugh Caldwell, P.P. of Nile was to be installed in Seattle as Imperial Potentate. But a bigger event in some people's minds occurred at the Annual Family Picnic on July 27 when, in the presence of Imperial Potentate Leonard P. Steuart, Nile divan officers burned the mortgage of the Country Club property (152 acres at the time). In the heart of the Great Depression, Nile was able to pay off the mortgage and now owned the Country Club Grounds free and clear.

On August 3, Potentate O. B. left Seattle for Nile's 18th pilgrimage to Alaska. Visits and ceremonials occurring at Ketchikan, Wrangell, Juneau, Anchorage and Fairbanks netted several new nobles and many happy memories. Of note was a visit to Petersburg where the Nile group was taken to another ship, the North King, where the men were initiated into the ultra-exclusive Fraternal Order of The Frozen Gobblers of the Golden North. Apparently, this turned out to be a hilarious gag decree well delivered by the Captain of that ship and his Chief Engineer. At Fairbanks, the Nile Ceremonial at the Moose Hall was attended by none other than Noble Will Rogers who was quite amused by the proceedings.

After their return to Seattle, Potentate O.B. and his Divan spent most of the rest of the year helping Joe Swalwell, Chairman of the 1936 Executive Committee, in preparing for next year's Imperial Session. But there was still time for a Winter Ceremonial on November 30 at the Shrine Auditorium, the Fifth Ice Carnival at the Ice Arena on December 7, and the Kiddies Christmas Party on December 23. And the Nile Band gave a radio concert on radio station KOL on December 16. Nile finished the year with a net membership of 3,623.

1936 – Tom Holman – Imperial Session in Seattle

In 1936, Hugh Caldwell was Deputy Imperial Potentate. In those days the Imperial Council Session was held in the home jurisdiction of the incoming Imperial Potentate. So, Nile was privileged to host the Sixty-Second Imperial Session in Seattle on July 13-16 because its own man would be installed as Imperial Potentate during this session. Tom Holman was Nile Potentate that year and he selected Noble Joseph A. Swalwell as president and Chairman of the Executive Committee to make the arrangements for the Imperial Session. And what a job he and his committees performed! Over 55,000 Shriners attended this event despite the economic effects of the Depression.

The Old Times Building (former home of the Seattle Times newspaper) in downtown Seattle was transformed into Shrine Headquarters. The fifth floor was made into an Egyptian temple for meetings and social events. The fourth floor was the domain of the Chanters who featured a picturesque Klondike Dance Hall. The third floor held offices, a pressroom, a switchboard, and a completely equipped first aid hospital. The second floor was Band headquarters and the first floor housed executive offices, registration desks and other administrative activities. On most of the floors were spacious lounges for female guests. A beautiful program book was published. The book extolled the virtues and advantages of not only Seattle, but also Tacoma and the rest of the Northwest. Hotels were booked to capacity and even private homes could not accommodate all the visiting Shriners. So, a Fez City was created, consisting of hundreds of Pullman cars parked near the King Street and Union Pacific Railway stations just south of the business district. Fez City would eventually hold 10,000 Shriners. Street lights were installed in the lanes between the tracks. And the railway companies put in sanitary facilities, power lines, phone connections, running water and shower baths, and porter service. All the cars were air-conditioned. It was only a short walk from Fez City to the Seattle downtown area, but what a relief for Shrine and city planners to have housing of this magnitude so close to heart of the city.

The Grand Parade held on Tuesday July 14, 1936 presented 126 units with over 5,000 marching Shriners. The parade lasted almost three hours. 50,000 other Shriners were among the 300,000 people who watched the parade from the sidelines. It was the greatest number of people ever assembled for a single event in the history of the Northwest said Chief William Cole of the Washington State Patrol whose officers were called on to assist Seattle Police to manage the huge throng. An anecdote of note is in order here. A bit of Shrine courtesy by the Al Malaikah band from Los Angeles drove the crowds into a frenzy. They repeatedly played "Bow Down To Washington" as they marched. And, even though they would occasionally play other schools' fight songs, whenever they returned to "Bow Down," which they did frequently, the crowds went wild.

Many events were held on the University of Washington campus including the massed bands concert witnessed by 20,000 spectators at Husky Stadium. This band, composed of 2,500 band members from 40 different temples consisted of 300 trombones, 166 sousaphones, 800 clarinets, 400 trumpets, 100 saxophones, 500 horns, 30 bassoons, 50 piccolos and many other instruments. They played a rousing concert program ending with the Smile with Nile March composed and directed by Noble William G. Marshall, Director of the Nile Band

Hollywood movie stars of the day arrived: Allan Jones, Sally O'Neil, William Farnum, Patsy Ruth Miller. Ironically, silent film star Monte Blue served as a very talkative Master of Ceremonies for several events. Great fun was had when Ms. Miller and Ms. O' Neil were met at the airport by Past Potentate. Van S. McKenney, who was accompanied by a detachment from the Nile Patrol and Potentate the camel from the Woodland Park Zoo.

Upon being introduced to the two starlets, Potentate immediately stretched out his neck, chomped down on and ate the bouquet of roses and ferns that Ms. Miller was carrying and then beckoned Ms. O'Neil to jump on for a ride which she promptly did in her white culotte pants. Policemen assigned to control the crowds obtained the autographs of the stars on blank traffic tickets. Clark Gable was to have been there, but had to cancel because of studio business down in Los Angeles. However, the two female stars so captivated the crowds that Clark was not missed for very long.

The business of the Imperial Session was short and ended on a melancholy note. Nile's Hugh Caldwell was unanimously elected Imperial Potentate, but immediately resigned the office because of failing health and the press of his business. Instead, he nominated next in line Clyde I. Webster to fill the post and Noble Webster was unanimously elected. Nevertheless, the 1936 Imperial Session will go down in history as one of the best ever because of the planning, organization, ingenuity, and hospitality of Nile Shriners. Hugh was elected as an ad vitam member of the Imperial Council meaning that he could hold the title of Imperial Sir for life. A comprehensive account of this event has been compiled by Nile Past Potentate and Recorder Frank B. Lazier and is part of the Nile Archives and History of Nile Project. See a fuller account of this event in Chapter 13.

The other major event that occurred in 1936 was the formation of Nile's Legion of Honor unit. Talked about for years, this unit came into being largely through the efforts of Noble Colonel Robert M. Watkins. The spur to formation was the coincidence at the 1936 Imperial Session of the National Association of Legions of Honor annual meeting. Aware of Nile's intentions, National Commander Henry H. Green (Yaarab Temple, Atlanta, Georgia.) brought three Legion of Honor drill teams to Seattle, which performed with the utmost military precision. Sensing the opportunity, Watkins approached Nile Potentate Tom Holman for permission to form a Nile LOH unit that year. Potentate Holman gave his permission to Watkins and his committee to investigate the feasibility of such a unit.

The committee's report was presented at the December 10, 1936 stated meeting, officially accepted, and the new unit was sanctioned to come into being. On the following day, the first Nile LOH meeting occurred with Colonel Chester Chastek elected as Commander, Watkins as Senior Vice Commander and Kenneth Hodges as Junior Vice Commander. 41 members were signed up including members of the Nile Drum and Bugle Corps. Petition was immediately made to the National Association of Legions of Honor (NALOH) for a charter and on

December 21, 1936 the national organization elected Nile Legion of Honors its 10th member unit. Colonel Watkins was elected Commander for 1937. The Legion served Nile long and gloriously and much more will be said about its activities in future articles, including hosting the national conventions in 1954 and 1985.

Other events did happen at Nile during 1936 including the Potentate's Ceremonial on April 25 (71 new nobles), the Imperial Ceremonial on June27 (129 new nobles), the coast to coast broadcast of the Nile Band and Chanters on CBS radio on April 18, the sixth pilgrimage to the Orient (Manila, Hong Kong, Shanghai and Yokohama), a Thanksgiving Ceremonial on November 28 (11 new nobles) and the Sixth Ice Carnival on December 11-12. Most remarkable of these was the trip to the Orient. For on that trip in Manila at the Ceremonial conducted at the Bamboo Oasis Shrine Club, a young military officer by the name of Douglas MacArthur was made a Nile Shriner. In January of 1936 the Grand Master of the Grand Lodge of the Philippines made MacArthur a Mason on sight. Because many United States military officers were members of Bamboo Oasis Shrine Club, word of Nile's impeding pilgrimage from July 18 to August 16 came to MacArthur and he petitioned for membership. Since that date he became one of Nile's most famous and storied members. And sadly, Potentate the camel died later that year survived by his lady, Miss Nile, and son, Outer Guard. Membership finished at 3825.

1937 – Carl E. Croson – A Quieter Year at Nile

It was hard to follow such a spectacular year as 1936. But Potentate Croson kept up the events that had by now become a pattern at Nile. Dance and bridge parties were held monthly at the Country Club, A Potentate's Ball on February 6, a Summer Ceremonial on May 22, the Annual Picnic on July 24, a Fall Ceremonial on November 27, and the Seventh Annual Ice carnival on December 10-11 all kept up a rhythm and flow of normalcy for Nile's nobles and their ladies. In 1937, the Great Depression deepened and the economy took a severe downturn.

In the world at large, the harbingers of world war were starting to occur. Japan invaded China which received defensive support from Russia. Hitler's Nazi Party was gathering strength in Germany and Mussolini flexed the muscles of his Fascist Party in Italy. Yet Nile valiantly soldiered on. Nile's

Units attended the Pacific Northwest Shrine conference in Victoria, B.C., and the Nile units acquitted themselves well. However, a more impressive showing by Nile's Uniformed Units was made in Detroit at the Imperial Session on June22-24. 127 Uniformed unit men showed up in Detroit along with scores of other Nile nobles and their ladies. In the Imperial Parade and in restaurants, bars and hotels, Nile's Band and Chanters units both played and sang "Bow Down To Washington" with great enthusiasm in part due to the University of Washington's recent national regatta rowing successes at Poughkeepsie, New York (UW swept the Varsity, Jayvee and Freshman rowing races at the national collegiate regatta for the second consecutive year). The year ended with a great Kiddies' Christmas Party on December 23 staged by the Chanters who put on a circus show for the kids and the adults that was worthy of Ringling Brothers and Barnum and Bailey. Unfortunately, membership went down to 3641.

1938 – Harrison J. Hart – Nile's Thirtieth Anniversary

In 1938 President Roosevelt began a $5 billion spending program to try to bring the economy out of its recent down turn. It was partially successful in that it infused massive amounts of new money into the United States economy and stimulated financial activity. Outside the United States, world conditions were more ominous. Germany annexed Austria with no reprimand from the world powers and made claim to the Sudetenland. Japan took over a major Chinese port city at the Battle of Wuhan and skirmished with Russia at Lake Khasan. At Nile, Potentate Hart guided Nile through another year of dances and bridge parties at the Country Club, together with balls, ceremonials, and special events. New headquarters for the Band, Chanters and Legion of Honor were opened on the second floor of the new Nile headquarters building located at 1613 Second Avenue across from the old Gowman Hotel. More rehearsal room and storage facilities were available for these three units at this new location. A Grand Opening was held on March 14. A significant event of the year was the Fortune's Frolic show at the Civic Auditorium on April 30. It was designed to raise funds to entertain Shriners who would soon be passing through Seattle on their way to the Imperial Council Session in Los Angeles later that year. Snappy drills and performances by Nile's Uniformed Units, a huge dance and eight professional vaudeville acts highlighted this showy fund raiser.

But the real highlight of the year was the Thirtieth Anniversary (1908-1938) Ceremonial held May 28 at the Shrine Auditorium. A large class of 43 new nobles crossed the hot sands of the desert that day. On June 4, 238 Nile nobles and their ladies left by train for Al Malaikah Temple in LA for the Sixty-fourth Imperial Session June 7-9. Again, Nile's Band, Chanters, Patrol and Legion of Honor performed excellently and stood out against the myriad of other Shrine Temple units. The Annual Picnic, the Fall Ceremonial and the Kiddies Christmas Party were staged without fail and were very successful because of the great efforts put into these events by Nile unit nobles. And mention should be made that Illustrious. Sir Paul H. Watt (Past Potentate 1930) passed away in September. Nile completed 1938 with a new membership of 3,521.

1939 – Charles W. Maryatt – World War Two Begins

Potentate Maryatt began the Nile Shrine year of 1939 with a joint public installation of the officers of Nile, Afifi, Al Kader and El Katif Temples at the Civic Auditorium in Seattle on February 4. This year, in addition to the monthly dance and bridge parties and the balls, Nile sponsored an Indoor Shrine Circus (Polack Brothers Circus) at the Ice Arena from April 17-22. It was well attended and was a huge success. A Summer Ceremonial on May 27 brought in several new nobles. The Pacific Northwest Shrine conference was held at El Katif in Spokane on June 10-11. Imperial Session in Baltimore at Boumi Temple followed on June 27-29. At both events the now renowned Nile Patrol, Chanters and Band made excellent showings.

A nineteenth pilgrimage to Alaska took place from August 19-September 24 during which ceremonials were held at Juneau, Fairbanks, and Anchorage. And in the October issue of Smile With Nile, the editor publicly apologized for taking to task the federal Works Public Administration (WPA) for being too slow in accomplishing its public projects. Several readers wrote in to take the editor to task and to tell him that the WPA employed hundreds of Masons and Shriners as project workers and that WPA had aided thousands of other out of work persons during these tough economic times by giving them a job. The Fall Ceremonial on November 25 and the Ninth Annual Ice Carnival on December 14-16 featuring renowned ice skater Miss Erma Anderson of Norway rounded out the 1939 Nile year. The year almost ended too gloomily with the passing of Nile's first potentate Ernest Bertrand Hussey (Past Potentate 1908) and the news of Hitler's invasion of Poland with France, England, and the Commonwealth countries' declaring war on Germany, the Soviet Union's invasion of Finland and subsequent invasion of Poland from the east and Italy conquering Albania. But the United States was not involved and had no binding military alliances with any of the participants. On the other hand, a letter from Imperial Sir Kneeland Kendrick (Past Imperial Potentate 1919-20) made Nile's year. After reading an account of the launching (by Mrs. Kendrick) of the ship SS Nile in 1919 in the November 1939 Smile With Nile, issue,

Kendrick wrote back:

> Nile Temple will always be in the vanguard of the affections of Mrs. Kendrick and myself and the cheers of the vast multitude (Nile Shriners and the all-Masonic shipwrights of the Ark and Anchor Association employed by the Skinner and Eddy Shipyard which built the ship) that witnessed the launching of the Nile still ring in our ears as does stay with us the memory of the novel and beautiful scenery (wooden camels with fezzes) which was arranged along that really triumphal march.
>
> Nile ended the decade with a net membership of 3,601.

In the next issue we will explore the Fighting Forties at Nile, the causes and effects of World War II and the new world order created by post-war governments.

Chapter Five

THE FIGHTING FORTIES

Out of a population of 132 million, over 8 million were unemployed in 1940. The National Debt was $43 billion and the minimum wage was 43 cents per hour. The 1940's were dominated by the lingering effects of the Great Depression, by food and materials rationing caused by the World War Two, by fear and anxiety over the safety of our fighting men and women in the armed services and by concern over the security of our country. Scrap drives, victory gardens, and bond purchases were the ammunition that the bulk of the population used to keep the war effort going strong. Single women came into the work forces in droves and, once that supply was exhausted in 1943, married women entered the work force as well. The post-war 1940's were marked by the baby boom, the threat of communism, the Cold War and nuclear nightmares. The GI Bill of Rights gave many who would never have had the chance otherwise to obtain a college education, buy a home or open a business.

Although the TV was perfected during the 1940's with commercial broadcasting starting in 1947, and the first computer, ENIAC, completed in 1945, radio remained the public's mainstay communication device along with print newspaper. But radio was more than just a news media. It was entertainment and a reliable companion during long nights of anxiety and depression. Soap operas, quiz shows, mystery theater stories, sports broadcasts, as well as pop bands and singers filled the airwaves with an escape to fantasy and a much-needed lifeline to the future. The Shadow, Firestone Mystery Theater, the Lone Ranger, Gun Smoke, and the Green Lantern provided intense suspense for the careful listener while Arthur Godfrey and Kate Smith were comfortable and friendly radio hosts. Meanwhile the Jitterbug dance craze allowed more individual expression than had been seen in centuries on the dance floor.

Mothers in the work force demanded and got the invention of the frozen dinner (Clarence Birdseye) now housed in the new refrigerator freezer compartment. The invention of Tupperware and aluminum foil made food storage more convenient and last longer. In fashion, the zoot suit was popular until the War Production Department put a limit on the amount of material that could be used for a single garment. Ladies as well were affected. The women's convertible suit (jacket, short skirt, blouse) came into common use because it could be used for a variety of occasions. The movies were another staple of the 1940's. Casablanca, Citizen Kane, Guadalcanal Diary and Destination Tokyo were some of the bigger hits. Walt Disney Studios produced the animated films Fantasia in 1940, Dumbo in 1941 and Bambi in 1942. After the war, the television slowly made its way into American homes. Top radio shows became television shows with Ted Mack's Original Amateur Hour, Milton Berle's Texaco Star Theater and Ed Sullivan's Toast of the Town leading the way.

In sports, things did not go well until after the war. During the war years many professionals went into the military service. The shortage of wood made bats and bowling pins scarce. The lack of rubber made balls soggy and unresponsive. The Indianapolis Racetrack was closed during the war allowing it to severely deteriorate. One interesting anecdote from the war era is worth passing on. Baseball became the single best morale booster during the war years so much so that the Japanese tried to jam broadcasts of baseball games to the troops overseas in the Pacific Theater. In response, President Roosevelt issued the Green Light letter giving formal government support to the playing of baseball games by the troops. After the war, sports took off. Baseball, basketball, boxing, and hockey were reorganized and league management ensured their post-war success. In 1947, President Truman integrated the army while Jackie Robinson became the first African-American to play for a white professional baseball team.

And Nile had many of its own war and post-war stories to tell. Some of these will be recounted here as we look at Nile nobles, their ladies, and families during the Fighting Forties.

1940 – Stephen W. Brethorst – War Rages in Europe.

Attorney Steve Brethorst came into office at a most auspicious time. Many Americans were very apprehensive about the war in Europe and did not want their country to get involved, although many felt that it was their duty to support the peoples of England and France who were absorbing the brunt of German military efforts. In April, Germany invades and conquers Norway and Denmark. In May, the Lowland Countries are invaded and the battle of France begins. In June, France falls. Air raids are then conducted over Britain and the massive bombing of several cities occurs.

At Nile, Imperial Potentate Walter Dearing visits on January 10. The Polack Brothers Circus runs from April 8 to 13 and draws thousands of patrons. A Ceremonial on June 1 nets 46 new nobles. But on July 19, Walter F. Meier (Past Potentate 1925 and Past Grand Master 1927) passes away. A Thanksgiving Ceremonial on November 23 brings in 31 more new nobles. And Nile's Tenth Annual Ice Carnival December 5-7, starring Swedish skater Vive-Ann Hulten proves to be a great success. The Patrol moved from the Masonic Temple to its new quarters on the upper floor of the building located at 1618 Broadway (between Pine and Olive) and the Chanters created a sensation at the Luncheon Club with their rendition of the Opera of Cleopatra.

Yet there are ominous stirrings. In October, the United States government starts a military draft affecting as many as 16 million young men. And on November 7, Galloping Gertie's 600-foot center span across the Tacoma Narrows plunges 190 feet to the water killing only Tubby, a black male cocker spaniel. In the midst of increasing apprehension over world affairs, Nile closed 1940 with a net membership of 3,551, a net loss of 60 from 1939.

1941 – Lewis J. Dowell – War Comes to The United States

While German bombing raids over Britain intensified, British troops were at work attacking German and Italian forces in North Africa. In May, the Bismarck sinks the HMS Hood, the pride of the British Navy. Later that month, Royal Air Force aircraft and British ships sunk the Bismarck as it was trapped in open water following a hit by a torpedo bomb that jammed her rudder. In April, Germany invaded Greece and Yugoslavia, eventually taking over all of the Balkan countries.

Potentate Dowell's year started out innocuously enough. The usual balls, dances, luncheons, and ceremonials were held. On May 24th, a Joint Ceremonial with all 10 temples of the Northwest Pacific Shrine Council was held at the Civic Auditorium. One thousand uniformed nobles performed in line at this huge event. Nile brought in new nobles that day. Nile's twentieth pilgrimage to Alaska, a 1700-mile round trip, went very well. Ceremonials were held in Juneau, Fairbanks, Anchorage and Ketchikan throughout the month of August. A Fall Ceremonial on November 22 brought in several more nobles and the Ice Carnival on December 4-6 was another sell out set of performances. Then came December 7! At 7:48 AM Hawaiian time 353 Japanese planes in two waves attacked the island of Oahu, concentrating their bombs first on Hickam Field and Wheeler Field, then Bellows Field near Kaneohe on the windward side of the island and then Ford Island right in Pearl Harbor Bay. The result was catastrophic. Five battleships were sunk and three more damaged. Two destroyers were sunk and one damaged. Three cruisers were damaged. Several other ships were sunk or damaged. 188 United States aircraft were destroyed and 155 were damaged. Most distressingly, 2,402 military and civilian personnel were killed and 1,282 wounded. Upon hearing of this event, Potentate Dowell gave this parting message to Nile nobility at the end of his term:

> We are confronted with the huge task of defending our homeland. Regardless of our political affiliations, we must stand solidly together with one objective – Total Victory – that Democracy shall never perish. Labor and capital stand shoulder to shoulder and let all Masons be in the forefront of patriotism.

On December 8, America declared war on Japan. On that same day, China and the Netherlands declared war on Japan. On December 11, Germany and Italy declared war on the United States and our country responded in kind. On December 12, Hungary and Romania declared war on the United States and India declared war on Japan. Amidst the growing world war, Nile ended 1941 with a net membership of 3,575.

1942 – J.W. Arch Bollong – the World War Is ON!

As part of his incoming message to the nobility of Nile, Potentate Bollong had this to say:

> It is trite to say that prior to December 7 all of us were sitting smug in life and complacent. Today Nile Temple and Shrinedom as well as the nation are united as never before in our history. From now on things move swiftly. The first month and a half have passed and calmness, thoughtfulness and action have moved in. This is the sign that this organization and the American people are awake to their responsibilities. This calmness, thoughtfulness, action and determination will see us through to Victory.

And carry on they did! Numerous nobles volunteered to serve in the armed forces. Fund raising to support the troops was undertaken by all units, clubs, the Daughters of the Nile, and the Ladies Oriental Shrine. The war seemed to bring on a galvanizing effect to membership recruiting efforts. An International Ceremonial was held in Vancouver, B.C. on May 30, 1942, attended by the then 12 temples of the Pacific Northwest Shrine Council.

Hearing of General MacArthur's solemn "I shall return" as he left Corregidor on March 11, 1942, Nile's class of candidates was named the General Douglas MacArthur class. Later that year General MacArthur was made a Life Member of Nile. (Note: General MacArthur was made a Shriner at a special ceremonial put on by Nile Temple at Manila, Philippine Islands on September 7, 1936. Nile Potentate Tom Holman personally supervised that Ceremonial.) The International Ceremonial was a great success. See the special tribute article about MacArthur in Chapter 13.

Since Canada was at war, special permission was obtained from the Canadian federal government to hold a parade in connection with the ceremonial at Vancouver, B.C. And guess who was the hit of the Grand Parade – Nile's Uniformed Units! Gizeh's Color Guard, divan, uniformed units, and candidates led the parade. Then came Nile! Marching with great precision right behind the Nile Divan was Nile's 62-member Band playing majestically the anthems of various Allied countries. After them came the Nile Legion of Honor bearing the flags of the United Nations and

Subjugated Nations. Following them came the mighty Chanters with their portable sound equipment, each Chanter wore a microphone so that their singing could be heard for blocks away. Then came Nile's Peerless Patrol – 48 of the finest marching men under the command of Captain James H. Fletcher. Their drill evolutions utterly delighted the thousands of spectators along Georgia Street. Finally, Nile's 109 candidates, all in colorful Arab dress, brought up the rear, all hanging onto the rope under the watchful eye of Noble Sergeant Lewis Graham.

In the world, Bataan fell to the Japanese on April 9. The Battle of Midway is fought on June 4-6. Guadalcanal falls on July 3. But the battle to retake Guadalcanal begins in November of that year as does the Battle of Stalingrad in Russia. Despite the clouds of war and many Nile nobles joining the armed services, Nile finished 1942 with a net membership of 3,686.

1943 – James W. Woodford – The War Effort Continues

Under the leadership of Potentate Woodford, Nile soldiered along pretty much as usual in 1943. A Patriotic Roll Call was established and published in each Smile with Nile issue to track our nobles in uniform. The January 1943 issue described the roll call purpose as follows: "Wherever you are in the service of your Country, Nile is proud of you and salutes you sending greetings and best of wishes in the new year and with the prayer that you will return safely to your loved ones; Furthermore, we pledge to the utmost of our ability, our efforts to help you, and all of your Brothers in Arms to carry on." War bonds and stamps were purchased. Rationing was in effect. Extensive travel was curtailed. The nation's resources needed to be conserved because it was unknown how long this world wide conflict would last.

But a funny thing happened along the way. During one of the worst crises in American history – more and more men were joining the Shrine! In 1943 Nile gained 605 new members and had 19 affiliations and 95 former members restored for a total of 750 new additions to Nile Temple. A Victory Ceremonial was held on May 29 and brought in 195 new nobles. Then the Harvest Ceremonial on November 27 brought in 305 more new nobles. The remainder came from Alaska, notable Ketchikan, Juneau, Fairbanks, and Anchorage. The Nile Family Picnic drew 2,200 nobles and their families on July 24. The Imperial Potentate Morley E. MacKenzie visited Nile on September 4 and spoke at a joint United States –Canada war effort rally in Victory Square (University St. between 4th and 5th) in Seattle. The Ice Carnival went on as planned on December 1-4.

On the battlefronts, the Russians defeat the German Sixth Army and win the Battle of Stalingrad in early February. And American forces defeat the Japanese at the Battle of Guadalcanal that same month. In August, General George S. Patton leads the 7th Army into Sicily to secure the liberation of that island. And in the Pacific, the 503rd Parachute Regiment, under the command of General Douglas MacArthur invades Papua, New Guinea to start the campaign to regain control of the Pacific Islands. Italy surrenders to the Allied Powers that year and on December 24, General Dwight D. Eisenhower is named Supreme Allied Commander in Europe. Nile ends this momentous year with a net gain of 597 and a net membership total of 4,283.

1944 – Ray L. Eckmann – Another Turning Point Occurs

Nile's growth continued in 1944. The Spring Ceremonial that year (Victory Ceremonial on June 3 at which over $5 million in War Bonds was raised by Nile) brought in 443 candidates and the Fall Ceremonial (Frank B. Lazier Ceremonial on November 25 honoring Frank's 33years as Recorder) brought in 376 more. Add to that the 122 new nobles gained in Alaska from the 18th Alaska pilgrimage to Fairbanks-Anchorage-Juneau that year and almost 1,000 new nobles were added to Nile that year. The November stated meeting was attended by 850 nobles, 21 of which were the surviving members of the original 1908 Patrol. Also, that year, Hatasu Temple No. 1 of Daughters of the Nile embarked on a project to raise money to buy a B-29 Super Fortress Bomber for the war effort. By the end of the year, they succeeded in selling enough bonds to buy two of them!

On the battlefronts, American forces charged through the Solomon Islands and then landed in the Marshall Islands liberating them in early February. The Russians pushed westward and defeated German troops in several battles. American and British forces pushed upward through Italy. But the biggest military event was the Allied Forces invasion of Normandy, France on June 6. Known as Operation Neptune, which was the initial invasion phase of Operation Overlord, it was the largest land invasion in history with close to 160,000 troops landed that day on five separate beachheads codenamed: Omaha, Utah, Gold, Sword and Juno. By the 4th of July over one million men had been landed. The invasion fleet had been drawn from eight navies and included almost 7,000 vessels. Once the beachheads were secured and fortified, Operation Cobra or the march inland began on July 24. On August 25, Paris was liberated and on September 3, Brussels was freed from German occupation. It was the beginning of the end for the German regime.

And at Nile, the nobles and their ladies continued to buy war bonds and otherwise support the war effort. The 14th Annual Ice Carnival again took place in early December and the Kiddies' Holiday Party went on as scheduled on December 22. At year's end Nile's net membership total was 5,119.

In the next issue we will look at how the war ended and at Nile's first few years of post-war activity.

THE FIGHTING FORTIES

The middle and late 1940's brought many changes to all aspects of American society. The year 1945 was especially noteworthy because it marked the demarcation point when the United States became a true world power and eventually a superpower. It was still a year of war and death, but consider what happened that year. General Douglas MacArthur, our stalwart Nile noble, returned to the Philippines on February 7. The Soviets started liberating the Nazi concentration camps. Corregidor and Bataan were recaptured in February. The Battle of Iwo Jima was fought on February 19. In April, the Battle of Okinawa began and would last until June 21. Holland was liberated by Canadian troops on May 4. On May 8, Victory in Europe (VE Day) was declared. In early August, the bombings of Hiroshima and Nagasaki led to Victory in Japan (VJ Day) on August 15. And on September 2, Admiral Yamashita and the Japanese Navy formally surrendered. A delegation led by Mamoru Shigemitsu presented the surrender papers to General MacArthur and Fleet Admiral Chester Nimitz aboard the USS Missouri. On October 24, the United Nations comes into existence as a forum to peacefully prevent further world wars.

On a lighter note, bikinis are introduced and sold for the first time in Paris, France on July 5, 1946. Also, that year, Tupperware is invented by Charles Tupper and sold in department and hardware stores. In 1947, Raytheon invents and markets the first commercial microwave oven. But that year the Cold War begins. And the United States Air Force is created out of the Army Air Force and some components of the Navy Air Force.

n 1948, the State of Israel is declared and almost immediately a war ensures with neighboring Arab states. Israel is victorious and several nations recognize the new Israeli nation, among them the United States Also, that year, President Truman signs Executive Order 9981 formally ending segregation in the armed forces. In 1949, Israel is admitted to the United Nations as its 59th member and a peace treaty is signed with Syria ending the 19-month Israeli-Arab War. And in 1949, the Vatican announces that it has found in subterranean catacombs what it believes are the bones of St. Peter, the first Bishop of Rome. It would take another 19 years before Pope Paul VI confirms that they are indeed the bones of St. Peter after rigorous scientific research and study.

1945 – Harold E. Gray – The War Ends

1945 marked the return of many Nile servicemen from the war and, of course, the end of hostilities both in Europe and in the Pacific. In particular, Manila was liberated and many Nile nobles (estimated at up to 60) who had been interned at the Santo Tomas Internment Camp in Manila were freed. Their letters concerning their three-year internment and treatment fill a large section of the April 1945 issue of Smile With Nile. Noble Frank D. Jones wrote:

> Was recently released from torture and starvation in a prison camp, 40 miles from Manila, on February 23, in what was a most thrilling and dramatic rescue by Paratroopers, amphibian tanks and Filipino guerillas. We, 2,140 in number, were scheduled to be executed at 8 AM that morning. We were rescued at 7 AM.

Unfortunately, several Nile nobles, including Noble John Arthur Cropper, and Noble Paul Whitacre who had been incarcerated in that same camp, died earlier that month before the American army liberation. And Noble Walter Murray Croasby died in the Muntinlupa internment camp before it could be liberated in March of that year. In 1945, Nile had 418 of its nobles in uniform, including General Douglas MacArthur, Major General W. F. Marquat, Rear Admiral Fred A. Zeusler, United States Coast Guard, and Rear Admiral R. W. Dempwolff, United States Coast Guard. And overall, more than 50,000 Nobles of the Mystic Shrine from all over the country served in the armed forces during World War II.

The September 1945 Smile with Nile proclaimed on its cover: "Nile Temple is deeply grateful that peace has come at last to a troubled world." Potentate Harold E. Gray held a Spring Ceremonial on May 19 and a Victory Homecoming Ceremonial on December 1 of that year in addition to a pilgrimage to Ketchikan, Alaska with Imperial Potentate Alfred G. Arvold in attendance. Total new nobles that year: 993. In other news, Dr. August Werner, Professor of Music at UW, who had just become a Nile noble the preceding November, took over as Director of the Chanters, who put on one of the best Kiddies' Christmas Parties ever witnessed at Nile on December 21. And the Legion of Honor hosted an Open House for all other Uniformed Units, the first time that such a thing was done at Nile. The newest unit of Nile was the Nile Bowling unit which had 40 members in 1945. The 15th Annual Ice Carnival on December 5-8 was another outstanding success. Nile ended 1945 with a net membership of 6,143.

1946 – W. Hal McDowell – Nile Marches into the Post-war Era

1946 was relatively calm. Frank B. Lazier retired to become Recorder Emeritus after 35 years of service as Nile Recorder and Frank T. Ostrander took over as Recorder. The Imperial Council met that year in San Francisco on July 23-25 hosted by Islam Temple. A Past Potentate's Ceremonial on June 1, an Imperial Council Ceremonial in honor of the visit of Imperial Potentate William Woodfield, Jr. to Nile on June 25, a Coast Temples' Ceremonial on November 23 and another pilgrimage to Alaska (Fairbanks, Nome, Anchorage and Juneau) occurred and 1,145 new Nile nobles were created that year.

The Annual Nile Picnic on August 1 was attended by the staggering number of 5,361 nobles, ladies, and family, an all-time high up to that time. The Polack Brothers Shrine Circus on August 30 –September 8, the

Annual Nile Halloween Party on October 26, the 16th Annual Ice Carnival on December 11-14, the Kiddies' Christmas Party on December 15 (1500 kids and 2900 total attendance) and a Holiday Shrine Dance on December 28 closed out a fine year of merriment and celebration after the exhausting tension of the war years. Nile ended 1946 with a net membership of 7,190.

1947 – Jo Dudley Cook – Amidst the Cold War, Nile Prospers

Sad news opened the year of 1947. On February 5 at 7:15 am, Miss Nile the beloved camel passed away from old age and peritonitis. Brought from China in 1922 by Potentate Hugh Caldwell, Miss Nile was a favorite visitor at Nile Temple. She shared her home at Woodland Park Zoo for many years with Potentate, a male camel that was obtained by Nile Temple in 1923. Together they produced an offspring, Outer Guard. Both Outer Guard and Potentate preceded Nile in death by several years.

Potentate Jo Dudley Cook, an attorney, had a terrific year. Besides being a 33rd Degree Mason, he was a top west coast trial lawyer and for many years was lead counsel at Unigard Insurance Co. The ceremonials that year, a Spring Ceremonial on May 24, and a Fall Ceremonial on November 22, brought in another thousand new nobles. At the Fall Ceremonial, Past Potentate Daniel Trefethen presented Frank Lazier with a bronze bust of Lazier designed and cast by August Werner who, it turns out, was not only a remarkable musician but also a very fine sculptor and painter. The Annual Nile Picnic was attended by 5,400 people. The grounds had been improved that year to allow for more picnic tables. The sports field had been leveled, a large area had been cleared of underbrush, new restrooms were added and the swimming beach had been enlarged. The Sixth Annual Indoor Polack Brothers Shrine Circus was held from August 29 to September 7. And the 17th annual Ice Carnival took place on December 3-6.

Renton Shrine Club started up that year and the annual Kiddies Christmas Party, sponsored by the Nile Chanters was another great success. Amidst the start of the Cold War, a term coined by United States Presidential Advisor Bernard Baruch in an April 16, 1947 speech and popularized by Walter Lippman in his 1947 book "Cold War," and increasing international tension with the Soviet Union, Nile ended 1947 with a net membership of 7,849.

1948 – George G. Rogge – Nile's Fortieth Anniversary

In 1948, Nile celebrated its Fortieth Anniversary at its Spring Ceremonial in honor of its 1908 charter members. The flyer proudly stated:

"Granted its dispensation by the Imperial Council in St. Paul, Minn., July 15, 1908. (Its) Petition was signed by 467 nobles, largest number on any petition up to that time. Now, Nile is 12th in membership of 159 temples."

As part of the anniversary celebration Nile nobles' tributes to these charter members were to be made by securing candidates whose candidacy was to be credited to a living and active charter member of their choice.

At the Spring Fortieth Anniversary Ceremonial on May 22, 22 of the 47 living charter members were present and accorded special honors for their pioneering effort in forming Nile Temple. A class of 413 new nobles was inducted. 254 more new nobles were created in the Fall Ceremonial held on November 20 in honor of Nile's 19 Shrine Clubs. And 129 were added from the pilgrimage to Alaska from September 30 to October 14. On July 31, 5,754 people attended Nile's Annual Picnic, which was getting bigger with each passing year.

Two new units and the North Kitsap Shrine Club came into being in 1948. The Nile Golf Club was organized that year and the new drum and bugle corps held its organizational meeting on September 20th at the Gowman Hotel. And, through the efforts of Nobles Art Hughes and Cliff Smith, a Nile Mounted Patrol was formed and had its organizational meeting on April 19th. This latter unit was formed in response to the thrilling sight of the 20 Palomino horse patrol of the King County Sheriff's Office, which performed at the 1947 Nile Picnic. At the 1948 picnic, an eight horse Nile Mounted Patrol delighted the Nile Picnic attendees.

Of particular note, in the February 1948 issue of Smile with Nile, the editor (Frank Lazier) apologized for perpetuating the myth that Past Potentate John McLean invented the "Smile with Nile" slogan in 1915. The editor now admitted that research shows that the slogan was submitted in 1914 by Noble Herbert A. Schoenfeld, the 1915 Chairman of the Publicity Committee. Several slogans were submitted and his was chosen by the Publicity Committee. McLean, as Potentate that year, merely announced and popularized the new slogan to the world. Nevertheless, this was another banner membership year for Nile which ended 1948 with a net membership of 8,433.

1949 – Kendall L. Howe – Smile with Nile Editor Finally Retires

Potentate Kendall Howe enjoyed a good post-war year. The usual ceremonials (Spring, May 21 and Thanksgiving, November 26) and pilgrimages occurred adding another 800 nobles to the Nile. At the Annual Nile Picnic on July 30 attendance swelled to 6,678. The beautiful Palomino horses with their silver saddles of the Nile Mounted Patrol under the direction of Noble Arthur C. Hughes were greatly appreciated by the picnic crowd. And guess what? The drum and bugle corps, in its first public appearance, performed admirably at the picnic under the direction of Captain Walter C. Pittson. They later performed at the Thanksgiving Ceremonial and at the 19th Annual Nile Ice Carnival on November 30 of that year. This year also marked the retirement of Frank Lazier, age 90, who voluntarily tendered his resignation as Editor of Smile with Nile after 37 years at the helm.

Finally, Nile hosted a General MacArthur Ceremonial in Tokyo, Japan just four years after V-J Day. Participating were nobles from 103 sister temples. The 161 novitiates were all serviceman or service-connected civilians, most sponsored by the Torri Shrine Club. Major General C. A. Willoughby, a featured speaker, remarked that Torri Shrine Club of Tokyo and Nile should be closely affiliated because "Seattle has always rightfully been the Gateway to the Orient" for Shrinedom. The Kiddies' Christmas Party on December 18 sponsored by the Chanters together with the Patrol and Legion of Honor once again made a great hit with the several hundred youngsters in attendance. The decade of the Fighting Forties came to a close with Nile's net membership standing at 8,830.

Thus, the Fighting Forties ended in relative calm after a tumultuous beginning and after fierce battles with the Axis powers to save the world for democracy. The 1950's would present a different type of problem for America as new would-be world powers jockeyed for position around the globe, especially in the Far East. Hot war in Korea and the Cold War in Europe. Could the Marshall Plan and the United Nations hold the countries of the world together and prevent another world war? Or would disaster come from nuclear bombardment from the United States new arch enemy, the Soviet Union which exploded its first nuclear bomb in 1952 or, as some feared, from so-called death satellites (Sputniks) in the sky? Nobles and their ladies had much to think and pray about during the 1950's as they went about the business of fund raising for the 15 Shriners Hospitals for Children in existence at that time.

Watch for the next article – – The Fabulous Fifties.

Chapter Six

THE FABULOUS FIFTIES

The Fabulous Fifties 1950 - 1954

The 1950s, dubbed here the Fabulous Fifties, were a time of social, economic, and political retrenchment. After the devastating effects on the American psyche of the Great Depression and World War II, Americans, generally, were going to practice normality and conformity. An emphasis on national security and the development of infrastructure and resources would allow the United States to evolve as a world leader and eventually a superpower, a role it was thrust into by the recent global conflict. Although the Korean Conflict, the Cold War and the Sputnik Scare beleaguered American patience, to a great extent the 1950s were a fortunate interlude between global conflict and the social revolution which was to come in the 1960s. All in all, America grew strong and prospered during the 1950s and that growth and prosperity gave it the strength and stamina to survive the rest of the millennium.

As background, consider that following the great victories in Europe and in the Pacific theaters of war, the post-war peace was short lived. The Soviet Union had caused an Iron Curtain to fall across Eastern Europe in 1947, juxtaposing an array of communist party dominated countries against the NATO allies. The Cold War had begun. The United Nations had been formed but was still in its infancy. Japan was occupied by American forces, but the Soviet Union had forced a division of Korea across the 38th parallel, essentially dividing that country in half. The Cold War now was to grow into international tension throughout the world. The first flare up of this heightening tension began on June 25, 1950 when the army of the Democratic People's Republic of Korea (North Korea) invaded South Korea.

The United Nations received its first test. It responded by authorizing (without the veto of the Soviet Union which had walked out during discussions over the proposed substitution of Red China for Taiwan on the Security Council) an international force to intervene and defend the South Koreans. Since this force was mainly made up of United States troops, an American Commander of the United Nations Peacekeeping Command was appointed. And who better than anyone at that time to take such a command? None other than Master Mason and Nile Noble General Douglas MacArthur!.

But the 1950's were much more than the Korean Conflict. Rock and roll music, suburbia, the Interstate Highway System, the Beat Generation, and the advance of television broadcasting were just some of the hallmarks of the 1950's. The biggest social effect was the domination of Americans' attention by the TV. Not since the invention of the radio had a mass medium so captivated the American mind. In the 1950's, the amount of viewing time escalated rapidly as many radio and vaudeville stars made the transition to television. News broadcasting, through the development of the coaxial cable and microwave relay, became much more hypnotic as "anchormen" such as Edward R. Murrow and Walter Cronkite dramatically told Americans the news as a story instead of just reading monotonous script.

Variety shows, such as The Ed Sullivan Show and Disneyland, and sitcoms, such as Ozzie and Harriet, Father Knows Best and the Honeymooners (Jackie Gleason Show) filled the airwaves at night. During the day, live "soap operas" engaged the attention of housewives and retirees. And in 1954, color television made its debut, further entrancing American eyes and mind.

In the field of education, the Supreme Court decision of Brown v. Board of Education made it clear that separate but equal facilities for whites and blacks were not enough. The nation's educational districts had to integrate. Despite Little Rock, Arkansas and Governor Orval Faubus, the main battles of educational integration would be fought in the 1960's.

In fashion the gray flannel suit was popular among most businessmen and women wore dresses with pinched in waists and high heels. For the kids, blue jeans became popular with the boys and poodle skirts for the girls. Saddle shoes and blue suede shoes were obligatory footwear.

Individual ownership of automobiles increased substantially through mass advertising and sharp design as now seen on TV commercials. The creation of the Interstate Highway System fueled the motoring mentality: recall the Dinah Shore jingle, "See the USA in your Chevrolet," and indirectly gave rise to the drive-in restaurant and drive-in movies. Centralized marketing areas outside congested downtowns were now possible and the rise of shopping malls (Northgate in Seattle among the first in 1950) began.

Housing starts zoomed off the chart. Many returning GI's wanted their own homes to start a family, and with the GI Bill, tens of thousands hit the housing market with a bang. In response, suburban housing complexes were created, the first and most notable of which was Levittown, built by William Levitt in suburban New Jersey for returning servicemen and their families.

And the music scene became enriched with the sounds of Elvis Presley (a gospel singer when he started), Bill Haley and the Comets, Jerry Lee Lewis and the many Doo Wop singer groups who crossed over from the rhythm and blues genre. Big Band music continued to be popular, but many of the big bang singers became crooning stars on their own, such as Frank Sinatra, Perry Como, Dinah Shore, Peggy Lee, and Rosemary Clooney.

All in all, the 1950's were a special time in American life as they were at Nile. As we shall see, Nile nobles and their ladies were as patriotic, philanthropic, and peripatetic as any other social group and grew in size and stature to almost the zenith of Nile's status as a fraternal organization.

1950 – James H. Fletcher – Korean Conflict Begins

In 1950, Nile Temple membership surged over the 9000 mark. The Spring Ceremonial on May 20 honored the great screen actor Harold C. Lloyd, Imperial Potentate that year, who traveled to Seattle for the Ceremonial. Potentate Fletcher led another pilgrimage to Tokyo where 137 new nobles were created on Armistice Day (November 11). The class was named in honor of Noble Lt. General Walker, Commander of the UN Armies in Korea. Due to the outbreak of hostilities there, General Walker could not attend the Ceremonial. However, Nile Noble General Douglas MacArthur welcomed his Nile brothers at his private quarters in Tokyo. Potentate Fletcher and the Divan then traveled to Manila where another 92 nobles were initiated at the Bamboo Oasis Club in that city. A Thanksgiving Ceremonial was held on November 25. All in all, 10 ceremonials were held that year bringing in 703 new nobles.

Over 800 Nile nobles traveled to Los Angeles for the Imperial Session where many of Nile's units won plaudits and praise. Especially striking was the Mounted Patrol with its 18 beautifully matched Palomino horses parading down the streets of LA. The Annual Nile Family Picnic under the direction of the Veteran Patrol played host to 6000 nobles and their families on July 29. And the Children's Christmas Party hosted by the Chanters drew over 1500 children.

Nile finished 1950 with a net membership total of 9,357.

1951 – H. Dan Bracken, Jr. - Truman Recalls MacArthur

In April, 1951, President Truman recalled MacArthur from Korea and relieved him of his command. MacArthur had just recently executed one of the most brilliant tactical maneuvers in military history.

In order to stem the advance of the North Korean Army in South Korea, MacArthur conceived and launched the amphibious assault on the city of Inchon deep in N. Korea. Violent tides at this location and a strong enemy presence made this a dangerous operation, which was opposed by the Pentagon. However, on September 15, 1950, the attack was launched and proved to be decisively successful. The North Koreans were caught off guard. The North Korean Army advance in South Korea was cut off from its supply lines and began a fast retreat back into North Korea. The United Nations troops pursued the invaders back into North Korea across the North Korean border and right to the border of Red China. In Washington, D.C., this was judged to be a violation of the United Nations peacekeeping charge which was simply to defend the South Korean border and keep the peace. MacArthur, however, argued for extending the conflict not only through North Korea but across the Yalu River into China where there were bases supplying the North Koreans with munitions and other supplies.

China appealed to the Soviet Union for help, which responded with supplies and air power, but with little manpower. Truman, alarmed that this conflict could turn into a Third World War, and perhaps a nuclear one, ordered no further advance. In the meanwhile, the Chinese Volunteer People's Army (composed of mostly Red Chinese Army regulars) stormed across the Yalu River to aid the North Koreans and caused the United Nations forces to retreat back across the border. MacArthur wrote to the Republican House majority leader, Rep. Walker, expressing his concerns about the course of the war and, in effect, asking Congress to take appropriate action. Truman blew up over this perceived attempt to set the Legislative Branch against the Executive Branch over this issue and promptly recalled MacArthur in April 1951.

Nile Temple, of course, strongly supported its outspoken Noble General. As a result, an outstanding event of 1951 occurred in connection with the Nile November stated meeting to which Potentate Bracken ad invited Nile Noble MacArthur. 4000 Nile nobles attended that meeting! After General MacArthur finished speaking in which he strongly defended his actions, Noble Judge William J. Wilkins gave a heartfelt response which said in part:

> Moreover, history will record that you demonstrated your true greatness as an American when, upon your return to these shores-unselfishly and without rancor-you gave freely of your time, as you did last night, in bringing forcibly to the American people the true conditions, both at home and abroad, as they confront us today and you have revived our spirits and our will to fight. But, General MacArthur, we are proud of you because you typify and represent, better than anyone else, the high ideals of Masonry and Shrinedom. You possess to a high degree great moral courage, sterling honesty, a sincere belief in fair play and in your fellow man and, in the words of our Shrine Ritual, you have given us an example of a clean, honorable, wholesome and manly life.

Under Potentate Bracken's leadership, the Nile Temple Holding Corporation was incorporated as a non-profit corporation in 1951 to hold title to the Country Club property at Lake Ballinger. This was done to relieve a conflict with Imperial Bylaws that no temple incorporated under the laws of their State could exist and as such hold title to real property. Also, land was acquired near the Seattle Civic Arena to build a new headquarters building.

The Nile Uniformed Units were on display and in great form in Vancouver, B.C. that year for the NW Shrine Conference. And the First Ceremonial in Okinawa was conducted by Nile Temple at the Okinawa Masonic Temple, courtesy of Aloha Temple, which had jurisdiction over that island. Other nobles were created during that pilgrimage to the Orient at the Torii and Dragon Shrine Clubs in Japan and Hong Kong respectively.

Nile's membership at the end of 1951 was 9,692.

1952 – Glenn H. Carpenter - Director's Staff Unit Created

In 1952, Potentate Carpenter welcomed the Director's Staff as an integral part of Nile's units. Director's Staff evolved out of the old Wrecking Crew, which had conducted the Second Sections of ceremonials for many years. The Second Section Wrecking Crew members historically came from the Arab Patrol (later just Patrol) because it was the Patrol, as the only organized unit of Nile in 1908, which conducted the first Second Section at that historic Ceremonial on December 2, 1908 at the Moore Egyptian Theater in Seattle. The Director's Staff would now be a separate unit performing this essential task.

Aside from the tensions created by the Korean Conflict, which by now was rapidly escalating, Nile nobles and their ladies had a fairly normal year. The highlight was probably the election of General Dwight D. Eisenhower as President in November of that year. The Intermountain Shriners Hospital was opened in Salt Lake City in September and Nile made another pilgrimage to Tokyo, where the featured speaker was General Mark Clark.

The year ended with a net Nile membership of 10,117, making Nile one of only a small handful of temples to break the 10,000-member mark.

1953 – Ruben E. Lovegren – Korean Conflict Ends

Potentate Lovegren presided over another relatively quiet year at Nile. The Korean Conflict (not "war" because there would have had to have been an official declaration of war by the United States Congress) came to a rather inglorious end with the Armistice that took effect on July 27, 1953.

That year, Chanters Director August Werner made quite a hit singing one of the lead roles in the Seattle Opera production of La Boehme, which toured the Northwest that year. And from May 20-23, 1953, the Nile Legion of Honor hosted its first national conference. Nile noble John H. (Jack) Wait, Nile Legion of Honor Commander in 1940 and 1952, was installed as National Commander. Nile would have had a National Commander come from its ranks several years earlier, but three Nile nobles who had been in the National line never made it to top (Colonel Watkins resigned due to ill health when he was first Lieutenant Commander and both Bert Snyder and Julius Anderson died while coming up the line).

With the October issue of Smile With Nile, came a change in publication size. The magazine had been published in 6" by 9" issues for almost 30 years. The October issue was 8-1/2" by 11."

The Nile Annual Family Picnic in July, again hosted by the Veteran Patrol, drew over 7,000 nobles, ladies, and children. Ceremonials on May 23 and November 21 and a pilgrimage to Alaska brought many nobles into Nile and Nile ended 1953 with a net membership total of 10, 523.

1954 – Hal N. Snyder – Frank Lazier Passes

In January, 1954, Nile suffered a great loss when longtime Recorder, SWN editor and P.P. Frank B. Lazier passed away just 10 days short of his 95th birthday. Frank was a 1908 charter member of Nile and was elected as Nile's first Oriental Guide. He served as Potentate in 1911 and was elected Recorder in 1912. He held the post of Recorder for 35 years, retiring from that post in 1946 to become Recorder Emeritus. He also edited Smile with Nile for 37 years, retiring from that post at the end of 1949 at the age of 90.

On happier notes, Potentate Snyder presided over an All State DeMolay Night, which was attended by Imperial Sir Frank S. Land who would become Imperial Potentate later that year. Land is the acknowledged founder of DeMolay and was "Dad" to over 1,700,000 DeMolay boys at the time. In June Nile hosted the Pacific Northwest Shrine Convention attended by 14 temples and over 10,000 nobles from their respective temples. And from what we can tell from Smile with Nile records, the Greeters unit marked its first appearance as a Nile unit this year.

A most amusing incident occurred in connection with that Pacific Northwest Shrine Council. Emperor Haile Selassie of Ethiopia was visiting Seattle at the same time. While the Emperor was at the Bremerton Naval Shipyard walking along a pier to inspect a Naval Honor Guard, a man in a black tasseled red fez waved at him and yelled: "Hi, Emp"! Selassie was confused by this man in a fez and asked his interpreter for help. The interpreter could only respond with a shrug of the shoulders. Later that week, the Shriners held a pageant at High School Memorial Stadium to which Emperor Selassie was invited. After he was suitably briefed on Shriner history, behavior, and dress, Selassie told the assembled Shriners, through his interpreter, that he greatly admired the colorful dress of the Shriners as well as their enthusiasm for their cause.

And talk about ball attendance during the 1950's: The Potentate's Ball that year was graced by over 3000 nobles and their ladies (the ball was held at the downtown Seattle Civic Auditorium). A new innovation and the highlight of the evening was the fezzing of new nobles by Deputy Imperial Potentate Frank S. Land. Later that year, in July, Imperial Sir Frank would become the Imperial Potentate of the Shriners of North America.

Also, in 1954, a District Grand Lodge was constituted in Japan by the Most Worshipful Grand Lodge of the Philippines and Nile Noble William J. Eichorn was appointed as District Grand Master. Spring and Fall Ceremonials and pilgrimages to Alaska and the Orient kept Nile's membership up over the 10,000 mark during these "Golden Years" of Nile Temple. Nile's membership at the end of 1954 was 10,749.

You can see from the previous issue of Smile with Nile, this issue and the next issue that starting from the mid-1940s through the mid-1960s, Nile enjoyed robust growth, great activities, and widespread acclaim as one of the leading temples in all of Shrinedom. These are the Glory Years or Golden Years of Nile Temple when membership remained at all-time highs and there were many hands to do its work and to work for the hospitals. In the next issue, we will explore the continued growth of Nile through the rest of the 1950's. We will also study the explosive growth of Shriners nationally and internationally and watch the development of more hospitals and a change in patient caseloads (owing to the Salk vaccine) from polio to orthopedic pediatrics in general.

THE FABULOUS FIFTIES

The mid-fifties linger in the minds of most Americans as an idyllic reprieve from the ravages and tensions of war and civil strife. It was an era of benign self-indulgence and rapid scientific and technological development. The Salk vaccine was introduced on April 12, 1955. This vaccine would lead to the eradication of polio in the world and prompt Shriners Hospitals for Children to move in other directions of pediatric care. Recreationally, Disneyland opened in Anaheim, California on July 17. And for the growing number of television kids, the Mickey Mouse Club premiered on television station ABC on October 3. However, as a precursor to the turmoil listed in the Sizzling Sixties chapter to come, Rosa Parks was arrested on December 1, 1955 for refusing to give up her seat on a Montgomery, Alabama city bus to a white person.

On March 12, 1956, the Dow Jones Average hit a milestone and rose above 500 for the first time. On the national front, patriotism abounded. President Dwight D. Eisenhower, authorized the addition of the phrase "under God" to the Pledge of Allegiance on June 6, 1956. Later, on July 30 of that year, Congress, by unanimous Joint Resolution, adopted the phrase "In God We Trust" as the National Motto.

Elvis Presley appeared on the Ed Sullivan Show for the first time on September 9, 1956. In 1957, American Bandstand premiered on the ABC TV network. And on February 17, 1958, in a tribute to the TV as an international media, Pope Pius XII declared St. Clare to be the patron saint of television.

But the end of the 1950s held new concerns for Americans and Nile nobles. On October 4, 1957, the first Sputnik was launched into orbit around the Earth prompting security concerns and a race to put the United States' own "spy satellites" into orbit. Unfortunately, the United States space program was woefully behind the technological advances of the USSR and effort after effort to launch a satellite failed. On November 3, the Soviet Union launched its second Sputnik with the dog Laika aboard, an astounding technological development that caused the United States media to dub the new artificial "moon" in the sky, "Muttnik." In 1958, on January 31, the United States would finally have its own orbiting satellite with the successful launch of Explorer 1.

However, a Pacific Northwest company by the name of Boeing would launch an even more valuable aircraft with the flight of the Boeing 707, one of most commercially successful airplanes ever. The year of 1959 closed the decade of the 1950s with the admission of Alaska and Hawaii as the 49th and 50th states respectively. 1959 was also the premier year of the St. Lawrence Seaway, Rod Serling's Twilight Zone on TV, and pantyhose for the ladies.

America was on a roll and so was Nile. If having a temple with over 10,000 members was not enough, Nile reached higher, for 12,000 members, and almost made it!

1955 – Leslie W. Eastman – New Nile Temple Headquarters

In 1955, plans for the new Nile Temple Headquarters building at Third Avenue North and Thomas Street were approved. The cost was to be $200,000 and was financed in part by 2.5% Debenture Bonds issued by the Nile Temple Holding Corporation. The new temple headquarters would include administrative offices, a large auditorium with stage and practice rooms for the musical units, committee meeting rooms, a large lounge, locker rooms for the nobles, a large vault for records storage and a parking lot for the members. 1955 also marks the first evidence of a Temple Guard unit at Nile, although they may have existed for a few years previously as an outgrowth of the Provost Guard.

The Potentate's Ball on February 5 drew over 3000 to the downtown Seattle Civic Potentate Eastman held a Shrine-Masonic Festival on March 12, a predecessor to recent All Masonic Nights, to which all Master Masons, York Rite and Scottish Rite Masons were invited. A pilgrimage to Hawaii occurred on March 25. The Ice Follies Shrine Night was held on May 12 and PNSA occurred on June 10-12 in Spokane with a fine turnout by Nile's Units. On July 30, Nile's Units participated in the Seafair Grand Parade and two of Nile's units won sweepstakes awards – the Mounted and Marching unit, and the Nile's Band won the top award in the Musical Division.

Ceremonials held on May 21 and November 26th brought in many new nobles, as did another pilgrimage to the Orient in November. The year concluded with another fabulous two-hour Kiddies Christmas Party put on by the Chanters with the assistance of the other units.

By the end of 1955, membership had reached the astounding number 11,111 members (Note: Nile's Temple number was No. 111).

1956 – Frank B. Donaldson - New Nile Headquarters Building

In January, 1956, the City of Seattle issued the Building Permit No. 1 that year for the new Nile headquarters building. A groundbreaking ceremony was held on January 6. The Nile Temple Building Committee Chairman was Noble Roy Taylor. Nelse Mortensen & Co. (Nelse was father of Cliff Mortensen, a future Nile potentate) was the general contractor, Navarre Plumbing and Heating, the Mechanical Contractor, and City Electric and Fixture Co., the Electrical Contractor. Of important note is the principals of all of these companies were Nile nobles! Imperial approved the building finance bonds and they were issued in February. Construction went rapidly and the building was finished in October. A move from the old Masonic Temple headquarters took place in November, and on November 24, 1956, the dedication ceremonies were held at the new headquarters building located at 229 3rd Avenue North in Seattle.

Earlier that year, nearly 6000 people attended the Nile Picnic. Potentate Donaldson held ceremonials on May 26 and December 8 again bringing in many new nobles. Nile's divan and nobles once again traveled to the Orient creating new nobles at Manila, Hong Kong, Taiwan, and Japan. Nile's Shrine activity overseas reaped an unexpected dividend when the Ali Shan Oasis Shrine Club of Taipei, Taiwan presented Nile with a colorful pedicab to be used by Nile in parades. The Shipstad and Johnson Ice Follies on May 9, the Polack Brothers Circus on September 12-16 and a production of the musical "Old King Cole" for the Kiddies' Christmas Party by the Chanters on December 23 rounded out a fun year of activities. There was now 17 Shriners Hospitals in operation and Nile's membership total continued to swell to 11,376.

1957 – Thomas N. Fowler - Year of the Sputnik

This year is remembered for a couple of disturbing events. In the fall of 1957, the World's Fair commission decided that to successfully stage a world's fair in Seattle (Century 21 Exposition) it would be necessary to condemn Nile's brand-new headquarters building and property. In November, 1957, Nile offered to lease the building and property to the World's Fair Commission for the duration of the Exposition. Not only was this offer turned down, but the World's Fair Commission further stated that it would be necessary to tear down Nile's HQ building so that a more "spectacular" building could be put up on the Nile's lot and adjoining property. Nile was served with a condemnation lawsuit by the State and Nile promptly responded with its own lawyers who consisted of both attorney Nobles and outside counsel.

The next year, on March 6, 1958, Judge Malcolm Douglas of the King County Superior Court granted the State's petition to condemn the Nile property and also that of some adjoining landowners. Nile and the adjoining owners promptly appealed to the State Supreme Court. Nile was represented by Nile nobles Thomas Fowler (P.P. 1957) and Ford Q. Eldridge (HPP). Another offer to lease was made to the World's Fair Commission, but again this offer was turned down. Eventually the condemnation would be stayed until the early 1980's when the City of Seattle would finally be successful in taking Nile's Seattle headquarters property and paying dearly for it.

On October 4, 1957, the Soviet Union launched Sputnik I (literally Sputnik means co-traveler or traveling companion). Of great concern was that the R-7 booster rocket, which had put Sputnik into space, was capable of carrying nuclear warheads. Observing a Cold War enemy's spy in the sky orbiting over North America unnerved people. Many in the United States saw this event as a failure of our educational system in the areas of science and mathematics. The United States' Vanguard efforts to launch a satellite failed miserably, with booster after booster blowing up on the launch pads. Sputnik II was launched on November, 3, 1957, carrying a live dog, Laika. This incredible feat caused humorists in the United States to rename the satellite, Muttnik.

Potentate Fowler, an attorney with a downtown Seattle law firm, had his hands full that year. Besides attending to his law practice and helping to prepare and argue Nile's appeal of the condemnation order, he conducted ceremonials on May 25 and November 23 which again netted many new nobles and he led the Nile delegation of units to Pacific Northwest Shrine Association PNSA, formerly the Pacific Northwest Shrine Council in Tacoma. Nile's peerless units, resplendent in both looks and performances at association meeting, also appeared in full regalia and formation at Nile's Annual Picnic, which drew over 5000 people, and at the Seafair Parade where they were very well received. A pilgrimage to Alaska in the company of Imperial Potentate Thomas Melham and his lady, where Nile conducted ceremonials in Anchorage, Kodiak, and Fairbanks, secured several new nobles for Nile. The Ice Follies, Circus, and another fabulous musical production for the Kiddies' Christmas Party, "Christmas in Disneyland" by the Chanters, completed Potentate Fowler's busy year.

Ending 1957, Nile's net membership stood at 11,459.

1958 – James M. Cain – Nile's 50th Anniversary

In 1958, Potentate Jimmy Cain combined Nile's 50th Anniversary with the "Shrinerama," a spectacular pan- Masonic event, honoring the Red Cross of Constantine's United Grand Imperial Session held in Seattle, on July 25-26. At this event, Ford Q. Elvidge, Nile's High Priest and Prophet was installed as the Grand Sovereign of the United Imperial Council of the Red Cross of Constantine. This event also honored all other Masonic organizations and was attended by numerous Masonic dignitaries from all over the country. A feature of the event was a performance by the First Section's operetta, "On The Road To Mecca," directed by Noble George T. McGillivery who wrote the script. Three hundred local Knights Templar (many of them Shriners) marched in the Grand Parade alongside Nile's Uniformed Units. Also, that year, Nile was given exclusive jurisdiction over Alaska by the Imperial Council. And the West Seattle Shrine Club Oriental Band was making news by winning two sweepstakes awards and one novelty prize during parades that year. That West Seattle oriental band would later become the nucleus of the Nile Oriental Band.

Potentate Cain was the only known person to both play in and later referee a Rose Bowl football game. With a fun-loving Potentate in office, it is no wonder that the first big event of the year was a Gay 90's Revue on February 12 with nine big acts and starring Steve Pease and his Gay 90's Troup. Ceremonials held on May 24 (honoring 1909 Potentate Ralph Stacy) and December 6 (honoring 1912 Potentate Daniel Trefethen) brought into Nile what was getting to be its usual 100 plus new nobles. On a somber note, Past Potentates Howard M. Findley (P.P. 1933) and Jo Dudley Cook (P.P. 1947) passed away that year. Both were attorneys (Howard Findley was also a judge at King County Superior Court) and both were very active in the Seattle legal community. Another pilgrimage to Alaska where a hundred new nobles were created, the Shipstad and Johnson's Ice Follies on June 5, the Pacific Northwest Shrine Association in Portland on June 5-7 and the Shrine Circus on September 11-14 augmented and amplified the fun year that Nile nobles and their ladies enjoyed in 1958. The year ended with another sparkling performance by the Nile Chanters with their Kiddies' Christmas play "A Christmas Secret Told," attended by over 3000 children and parents.

During Nile's glory years, Nile's net membership increased again to 11,500.

1959 – Lloyd X. Coder – State Takes Nile Land for I-5.

Potentate Lloyd X. Coder's year was marked by the State's first attempt to condemn 35 acres of the Nile Country Club property for a new freeway to be built across that land. The price proposed by the State was $35,000. Now, both the downtown headquarters building and property and a significant chunk of the country club property were in the condemnation sights of the State. As mentioned above, Nile would obtain a stay of the condemnation of its downtown headquarters property. The State's demand for the proposed freeway property could not be derailed. However, astute legal work by Nile attorney nobles and hard negotiation allowed Nile to "sell" those 35 acres for almost a quarter million dollars, a very large sum of money in those days.

Ceremonials on May 23 and December 5 again garnered almost 200 new nobles. PNSA in Calgary, Alberta (Al Azhar Temple as host) highlighted Nile's Uniformed Units' proficiency and pizazz. Potentate Coder hosted Imperial Potentate Clayton F. Andrews in August and took him and his lady for a memorable voyage aboard Noble Horace McCurdy's luxurious yacht, "Blue Peter," followed by a salmon barbecue that evening at the Country Club grounds attended by over 800 nobles. Imperial Potentate Dr. Andrews, M.D., spoke to Nile nobles about the slowing of gains in total Shrine membership and urged them to spread the word to Blue Lodge Masons about the benefits of being a Shriner and the prestige of being an integral part of the Shriners Hospitals for Children.

Yes, the balls, the circus, the Ice Follies, the ceremonials, the Kiddies' Christmas Party, and other special events still occurred. The divan went on another pilgrimage to the Far East visiting Hong Kong, Taipei, Tokyo, and Manila and creating more nobles over there (217 that year). An interesting development occurred at Imperial Council Session in Atlantic City that year. Afifi's Past Potentate Chester A. Hogan was elected to the position of Outer Guard of the Imperial Divan. Later, in 1969, "Chet" Hogan, as Imperial Potentate, would bring to Seattle and Nile Temple the hosting of its third Imperial Session (the previous two occurring in 1915 and 1936).

Many of Nile's other units, such as the Mounted Patrol, the Bowlers and the Golf Club presented activities, participated in parades, and contributed to Nile's support of the Shriners Hospitals in Spokane and Portland. There were far too many events occurring during Nile's glory years of the 1950's to mention in this article, but they are remembered and appreciated by all of Nile. Nile was at its zenith during these years.

Nile finished the 1950's with 11,612 nobles. Nationally, the Shrine had grown to 166 temples with well over 800,000 nobles. But how would the Nile and the national Shrine fare in the 1960's? Would Nile forfeit its property to the State and become a renter once again? Would Imperial Shrine ever reach its stated goal of one million members? Tune in again next month when Smile with Nile will bring you the "Sizzling Sixties." The term "Cold War" was coined by diplomat Bernard Baruch in 1947 and popularized by columnist Walter Lippman that year in his book of the same name.

Richard M. Kovak

Chapter Seven

THE SIZZLING SIXTIES

In the last installment we looked at how Nile nobles and their ladies reacted to the Cold War events of the 1950's – the Korean Conflict, the race to dominate the upper atmosphere with satellites and the growing tensions with the Soviet Union and Red China. In November, 1960, John F. Kennedy, a Senator from Massachusetts edged Vice President Richard Nixon in one of the closest elections in presidential history. Kennedy was the only Roman Catholic and only Pulitzer Prize winner ever elected President. His administration would witness several defining events of this decade: The Bay of Pigs invasion, the Cuban Missile Crisis, and the building of the Berlin Wall. Later in the decade, his successor, President Johnson would have to cope with the Space Race, the modern American Civil Rights movement, and the Vietnam Conflict. Now we will see how Nile Temple and its nobles and ladies coped with one of the greatest cultural and social change eras in American history – The Sizzlin' Sixties.

1960 – LaVerne Foote - Nile Temple
Membership at Its Zenith

Although Nile noble membership kept growing through the 1950s and may have exceeded the 12,000-member mark during some of those years, the annual net membership, due to deaths, demits and suspensions, always seemed to keep Nile's year-end net membership at just under 12,000. For example, on December 31, 1958, net membership was 11,500. In 1959, there were a total of 668 creations, affiliations and restorations which would have given Nile a total of 12,168 members, However, demits, suspensions and deaths numbered 556, leaving Nile with a net membership of 11,612 on December 31, 1959. That number probably went up in early 1960 as a result of the 1960 Spring Ceremonial, but as we shall see, Nile's membership numbers leveled out and then started to decline from that year onward. Nile would never reach the 12,000-member mark at the end of a calendar year, though it was not from lack of trying.

But that does not mean that Nile nobles and their ladies, with Potentate Dr. LaVerne Foote in the lead, did not continue to enjoy themselves, support the hospitals and put on great events. In 1960, the Spring Ceremonial on May 28th and the Fall Ceremonial on November 26th brought in 200 new nobles. The 25 Shrine Clubs of Washington and Alaska were duly saluted in a special two page spread in the May issue of Smile with Nile. Nile went to the Imperial Session in Denver and thoroughly distinguished itself through its fine units. Over 4,500 nobles and their families frolicked at the Nile annual picnic in July. Imperial Potentate George A. Mattison and his lady visited Nile on August 22 and then accompanied journeyed the Divan on Nile's Annual Pilgrimage to Alaska. Seven ceremonials were conducted: Anchorage, Sitka, Kodiak, Cordova, Juneau, Fairbanks, and Nome. On October 1, the Nile Band performed at the cornerstone laying for the new Seattle Valley Scottish Rite Temple on Capitol Hill. Unfortunately, the Kiddies Christmas Party had to be canceled that year due to the ongoing renovation of the Shrine Auditorium at the Seattle Masonic Temple.

By the end of 1960, Nile was the 10th largest temple in all of Shrinedom with a year-end net membership of 11,469.

Note: The 25 Shrine Clubs of Nile Temple during the 1960's were: Ballard-University; Bremerton; East Side; Enumclaw; Green River; Jefferson; Lake Ballinger; Northwest; Olympic; Renton; Skagit; Snohomish; Snoqualmie Valley; South Kitsap; Whidbey Island; West Seattle; Anchorage; Cordova; Farthest North; Juneau; Ketchikan; Kodiak; Nome; Petersburg; Sitka.

1961- Ford Q. Elvidge – The Kennedy/Khrushchev Cuban Missile Crisis – The Berlin Wall

In 1961, Ford Q. Elvidge, lawyer, former Governor of Guam, past Grand Master of Washington, and past Grand Sovereign of the Red Cross of Constantine reigned as Potentate while Nile Noble Alfred J. Ring reigned as Grand Master of Washington. Nile's legal beagles successfully stalemated the attempted condemnation of its downtown headquarters building by the City of Seattle and, in a negotiated deal, the HQ building was leased to the Century 21 Corporation to use for the upcoming Century 21 Exposition (1962 World's Fair). Nile's offices were moved to 603 Second Avenue North in Seattle for the duration of the exposition. Ceremonials were held on May 27 and December 2, but fell short of accumulating the desired number of new nobles to offset the number of demits, deaths and drops for that year. Imperial Potentate Marshall Porter attended the Nile Picnic in July and Nile's contingent of 250 Uniformed unit men, led by high strutting Drum Major Walt Woodburn, were the hit of the Seafair Grand Parade. The Nile Bowlers hosted the PNW Shrine Bowling Congress that year with 98 Shrine bowling teams in attendance. The championship was won by the Farthest North Shrine Club of Fairbanks who promptly donated their cash winnings to the Shriners Hospitals.

And as for that 35 acres that the State coveted for its freeway and was offering only $35,000? Sold and deeded to the State for $241, 961, a princely sum in those days. The severed 14 acres on the other side of the eventual freeway were sold in 1964 for $151,000, creating an additional extraordinary income for the temple coffers.

On the international front, the United States inspired Bay of Pigs invasion went sadly awry. Conceived as a way to remove Fidel Castro from office, following his assumption of power after Fulgencio Batista was chased out of Cuba, miscommunication and misplaced secrecy scuttled the operation. First, the landing site for the invasion was moved at the last minute from the port of Trinidad in Cuba, a haven of anticommunist fighters, to Bahia de Cochinos (Bay of Pigs) which had the effect of isolating the invaders from the homeland insurrectionists.

Second, Adlai Stevenson, United States Ambassador to the United Nations had not been briefed about the operation and was still denying to the United Nations that the United States was in the process of fomenting an insurrection in Cuba. When the first wave of United States air strikes occurred on April 15, 1961, an embarrassed and angry Stevenson contacted McGeorge Bundy about this turn of events. Bundy, not realizing the importance of the second and third waves of air strikes to the success of the mission, canceled them after Stevenson dressed him down. Bad weather hampered the invasion landing force (Exile Brigade 2506) and Castro's soldiers (Castro was aware of the invasion from loose talk and sources in Miami) were waiting for them when they landed.

Third, given this embarrassing scenario, United States military advisors told Kennedy to drop the whole scheme and to provide no follow up nor rescue support. As it turned out, despite Castro's advance warning of the invasion, the Cuban Air Force planes were sitting on the ground and could have been wiped out if the second and third waves of air support had occurred. In the aftermath of the bungled invasion, hundreds of Cubans were executed by Castro between April and October 1961.

Kennedy would also have to deal with the building of the Berlin Wall by the Soviets that same year. The Iron Curtain had since 1952 closed the East German border from West Germany. But because Berlin was occupied by the Four Allied Powers (United States, United Kingdom, France, Soviet Union) and divided into four zones East Berliners and East Germans could travel freely to West Berlin and from there seek emigration to West Germany. By 1961 emigration of the young and the smart had become so large that it was an embarrassment both to East Germany and the Soviet Union. Khrushchev suggested to East German Council Chairman Walter Ulbricht that a wall be built to stop the flow of emigrants to the West.

In early August, such a wall, consisting at that time of barbed wire, concrete blocks, and guard posts, was put into place around the three western sectors and between East and West Berlin. American General Lucius Clay suggested to Kennedy that this was the start of a total closedown of Berlin to the West and perhaps the prelude to an eventual takeover of all of Berlin by the Communists. Kennedy responded by authorizing a mission to reassure West Berliners that the West would protect them. On August 19, Clay and Vice President Lyndon Johnson flew into West Berlin. Three brigades, one each from the United States, the United Kingdom, and France were present to greet them. Kennedy ordered them to be reinforced.

On Sunday morning August 20, the United States First Battle Group, 18th Infantry under the command of Col. Glover Johns, Jr., convoyed from West Germany to East Berlin. A column of 491 vehicles with 1500 troops in full battle gear stretched out for 100 miles along the Autobahn into West

Berlin. East German police could only hold their breaths and watch from behind trees along the road. At noon the convoy reached West Berlin and was met by Clay and Johnson. A parade through the streets of West Berlin, passing right by the Brandenburg Gate, reassured West Berliners that the United States would not forsake them. Afterward, fresh troops would be rotated into West Berlin every three months. But the Berlin Wall would remain in place until 1989.

At Nile, the only bad news was that the net membership count fell slightly to 11,290.

1962 – Cliff Mortensen – the Seattle World's Fair

General Contractor Chief Executive Officer Cliff Mortensen took over as Potentate in 1962 and the pace of life at Nile picked up. Nile redeemed the 2-1/2% debenture bonds used to finance the acquisition of the land and the construction costs of building the downtown headquarters building. The 1962 World's Fair (Century 21 Exposition) opened using Nile's headquarters building as the Flag Pavilion. And a questionnaire was sent out to all nobles to determine how to develop the country club property to better serve the nobles and their families. Among the many choices on the questionnaire were: tennis courts, lawn bowling, outdoor archery, swimming pool, bowling alleys (in the basement of clubhouse), and a golf course! Guess which was the most preferred by a majority of nobles! The ceremonials that year were held in the Opera House. The Polack Brothers Shrine Circus performed at the Civic Ice Arena in September, and that same month a call went out to form a Nile Oriental Band with an organizational meeting to be held later that year. As it turned out, Nile wound up adopting the West Seattle Shrine Club Oriental Band as its own, and the legend of the Nile Oriental Band, already award winners as the West Seattle Shrine Club Band, began.

The best news of the year was the vote by the representatives of the more than 830,000 Shriners at the 88th Imperial Session in Toronto to fund up to $10 million the building and operation of the Shriners Institutes for Children's Burns – in effect, the creation of the Shrine Hospital Burn Centers.

However, the news that held America in stark terror that year broke in October 1962. Called the Cuban Missile Crisis in the United States, the Caribbean Crisis in Russia and the October Crisis in Cuba, it began when

United States reconnaissance photographs taken October 14, 1962 by a U-2 spy plane revealed offensive nuclear missile bases (vs. previously known defensive non-nuclear missile placements) being built in Cuba (probably in response to United States missile bases built on the Turkish-Soviet border). Kennedy called a meeting of the Joint Chiefs of Staff to deal with this situation. The United States had no contingency plan to deal with a nuclear threat only 90 miles from the United States because Kennedy had been convinced (and reassured by Khrushchev) that the USSR would never attempt such a bold move. The JCS recommended an immediate invasion and destruction of the bases and missiles! They agreed that the Soviets would not stop the United States from taking Cuba. Kennedy, however, believed that if the United States invaded Cuba, the Soviets would have an open invitation to take over Berlin. Kennedy ordered a naval quarantine to be set up around Cuba, that all United States personnel be removed from Guantanamo Bay and that the United States military be put on a worldwide Defense Readiness Condition or DEFCON 3 alert. After much posturing on both sides over the next few days, a compromise was struck on October 28, 1962 whereby the Soviets would remove the missiles from Cuba in exchange for the United States removing all offensive missiles from the Turkish-Soviet border. However, the removal of missiles from Turkey was not made public and it looked like the United States had won a major Cold War confrontation hands down. In any event, Nile nobles and their families could relax and once again pursue Shrine activities.

Nile's net membership took only a slight dip to 11, 244.

1963 – Aurie J. Thompson – The Nile Oriental Band Debuts

Potentate Thompson pledged to move the development of the Country Club property along. He appointed a Standing Committee to spearhead development of the property. A preliminary land development plan showing the layout for a 9-hole golf course and the site of a new clubhouse, in addition to the drill and sports field and picnic grounds which were already there, was presented to the nobility for approval.

The new Nile Oriental Band performed in a variety of events, including the ceremonials, PNSA in Billings, Montana, the Hi Yu Parade in West Seattle, the Waterland Festival in Des Moines, the Nile Picnic, and gave a concert for the residents of the Masonic Home in Zenith. But this is not to imply that the other units were not active. They performed in many of the same events and more. Nile now had close to a full complement of units: Patrol, Band (Charley Decker became the new Director that year), Temple Guard, Legion of Honor, Greeters, Mounted Patrol, Chanters, Drum & Bugle Corps, Motorized Squadron, Bowlers and Golfers. All they needed was a Clown unit! And so, the call went out in October 1963: "Wanta Be A Shrine Clown?" The Clown unit was organized that year and went on to become one of the most respected and competitive units at every PNSA competition.

The Boston Shrine Hospital was awarded the first burn treatment unit. And Astronauts Gordon Cooper and Virgil "Gus" Grissom became Shriners at Bahia Temple in Florida.

Unfortunately, 1963 came to a sad close with the assassination of President Kennedy by Lee Harvey Oswald on November 22, 1963 in Dallas, Texas. Two days later, Oswald was gunned down and killed by Jack Ruby before Oswald could be put on trial.

Nile's net membership took another slight dip to 11,109 still keeping it as the 11th largest temple in America.

1964 – Arthur T. Bateman – Noble
General MacArthur Gone

1964 brought new wind to Nile's sails. On January 21, the Clown unit held its first regular meeting. 1963 Potentate Aurie Thompson passed the gavel to the new potentate, lawyer Arthur T. Bateman. Potentate Bateman sent out a call to form a Floating or Sea Patrol, later to become the Nile Yacht Club. Fourteen Temples came to Seattle for the PNSA Convention hosted by Nile at the Seattle center grounds. The Nile Divan traveled to Alaska on the 42nd Pilgrimage to that state where they were met by Imperial Potentate O. Carlyle Brock and his lady. They visited all of the Alaska Shrine clubs and held several ceremonials with Imperial Sir Brock delivering the Inspired Charge. Nile was able to retake possession of its HQ building at 229 Third Avenue and held a Homecoming Ceremonial at its old digs. Work continued on the development of the Country Club property and remodeling began on the Country Club building to build a new kitchen, dining room and lounge instead of building an entirely new clubhouse elsewhere on the property.\

On April 5, 1964, beloved Nile Noble General Douglas MacArthur passed away shortly after his memoirs had been published. He had been living the last few years with his second wife, Jean Faircloth, at the penthouse of the Waldorf-Astoria Hotel in New York City. He was buried in Norfolk, Virginia, his mother's ancestral home. In memory of MacArthur, Noble Owen Martmel donated the first flag flown over Tokyo by MacArthur. That flag is on display to this day over the lobby of Nile Temple.

On the national Shrine front, burns treatment centers were built that year in Boston, Galveston, and Cincinnati to fulfill a need that Imperial had recognized the year before and had voted into existence.

This year was full of the usual Nile Shrine events – the annual picnic, the circus, the pilgrimages, and the ceremonials. In addition, Nile had formed a Third-Degree Team, consisting of proficient nobles from 12 different lodges that would perform the Masonic third degree for lodges requesting it. Nile held a fundraiser at the Masonic Temple on October 21, 1964 to raise funds to renovate and make major improvements to the Temple. The featured speaker was Nile Noble Senator Henry "Scoop" Jackson. A call went out to form a Motor Squadron unit. And the Nile Oriental Band donated funds and bodies to construct the barbecue building (Picnic Area A) on the Country Club grounds.

In Berkeley, California, the Free Speech movement (Jack Weinberg and Mario Savio) began on the UC Berkeley campus, a movement that would later coincide with the Civil Rights movement and forever change the way that Americans engaged in social change processes.

However, although Nile membership stayed over the 11,000 mark for the past six years, it was clearly starting to fall. Nile ended 1964 with a net membership of 10,916.

The remainder of The Sizzling Sixties are full of fame, intrigue, and surprises as well as tragedy. See how Grand Lodge tries to shut down Nile and how Nile responds in the next issue.

MORE OF THE SIZZLING SIXTIES

The 1960's continued the trend of youth and change. More than 70 million teenagers populated the 1960's and their influence on education, clothing, music and politics is still felt today. The Civil Rights movement took off in a big way in the mid-1960's with race riots in Watts in 1965, the Black

Richard M. Kovak

Power movement of Malcolm X, the women's movement spearheaded by Betty Friedan, Pauli Murray and Gloria Steinem, and the Hispanic labor movement under Cesar Chavez. The Civil Rights Act of 1964 was amended by Congress to include gender. Many young people dropped out of mainstream society and became hippies from Haight Ashbury in San Francisco to the East Village in New York. And the buildup of troops in Vietnam using the draft created both heroes on the battlefield and draft protests in the streets with draft dodgers fleeing to Canada. It was a decade of angst, adulation, astonishment, and apathy. So much was happening so fast on so many different fronts that, as one wag put it, "If you remember anything from the 1960's, you really weren't there."

1965 – William E. Parker – Redone
Country Clubhouse Opens

Potentate Parker, a registered civil engineer and land surveyor served as Seattle's City Engineer from 1953-57. He took over control of a refurbished Nile Country Clubhouse and Grounds.

On March 20, 1965, the remodeling of the Country Club building was completed and the eastern section looked very much like it does today. A grand reopening celebration was held on that date with 170 nobles and their ladies being welcomed by Manager Knut Yttervik. The Club House facilities were open Tuesday through Saturday for dinner service and on Sundays, a Prime Rib Buffet Dinner was available for $3.25. The other big news was that a contract had been awarded for the construction of a 9-hole golf course on the Country Club grounds.

Imperial Potentate O. Carlyle Brock visited Nile on May 4 which was designated an All Masonic Night with various concordant bodies invited to attend. The highlights of the evening were a concert by the Nile Band and a presentation of Nile's famous First Section drama "On the Road To Mecca." Ceremonials, held on June 5 and December 4, and the Polack Brothers Shrine Circus were great successes. In October, a Nile Masonic Fund-Raising Dinner was held with Noble Senator Henry Jackson as its featured speaker. At the Enumclaw Parade, Nile's Patrol again won the Grand Sweepstakes Award and the drum and bugle corps took first place in its category. Nile golfers won the Shrine International Golf Tournament for the first time in six years and took home Low Gross honors. Nile's

16th Pilgrimage to the Orient took place in October with the Nile Divan welcoming into Nile 163 new nobles from Manila, Tokyo, Hong Kong, and Taiwan.

Nevertheless, Nile's year-end net membership slipped down to 10,850.

1966 – Llewellyn S. Jordan - Grand Master Bovingdon Becomes a Noble

In 1966, Washington Grand Master George Bovingdon became the first new Nile noble of that year. Lobbying efforts were made by the Nile Divan to Imperial to locate the proposed fourth burn treatment center in Seattle. A Joint Ceremonial was held with Afifi Temple that was attended by Imperial Potentate Barney Collins. Development of the golf course was coming along well. And the Clown unit had a great year, appearing in the Tacoma Daffodil Parade, PNSA in Tacoma, the Imperial Shrine Session in San Francisco, and elsewhere. Of note was the formation of a Boeing Masonic/Shrine Club open to all Boeing employees, whether members of the Craft or not.

1967 – Wharton T. Funk – Grand Master Closes Nile's Bars

1967 brought more fame to Nile. Noble Ford Elvidge was named an Honorary Commander of the Most Excellent Order of the British Empire by Queen Elizabeth. Word came out that Seattle and Nile Temple would host the Imperial Council Session in 1969 where Chester A. Hogan, an Afifi noble from Puyallup, WA would preside as Imperial Potentate. New Bylaws were adopted by Nile creating for the first time a Board of Trustees and a Country Club Board to help manage Nile's property concerns. The Hospital Supply Corps set new records for the provision of food and groceries for the Portland and Spokane Hospitals. And report came that the new golf course had finally been seeded after numerous problems had to be overcome. Play was expected to start in 1968.

But every year has its adverse news. Grand Master Audley Mahaffey decided that it was unseemly and un-Masonic for Nile to be selling intoxicating liquor at its Country Club facility despite the fact that Nile had a legal Class H license issued by the State to do so. He therefore enjoined any Mason from attending or participating in any activity held at the Nile Country Club because it would constitute un-Masonic conduct and lead to charges against that Mason. In response to this ruling, the Nile divan, at its meeting held December 18, 1967, decided that to comply with the Grand Master's Order, it was necessary to close the Country Club which was done with the concurrence of the Board of Trustees.

1968 –C. Noel Caldwell - Nile 9-Hole Golf Course Opens

Play did finally begin on the new course on May 1, 1968 after a golf pro (Bob Tindall) and his assistants had been chosen. A formal ceremonial opening was held on May 11 with the Chanters, the Band, and other Uniformed Units in attendance. On July 31, 1968, the first hole-in-one was recorded on the new course. Mr. Bill Crisp, a guest of Noble Jerry Marpel, accomplished that feat on Hole #9 and was witnessed by Noble Marpel. Nile continued to show solidarity with the other Masonic bodies by performing its operatic drama, "On The Road To Mecca" as the entertainment feature of the Masonic Service Bureau's fundraising event, Hour of Music and Dance. And, after the change in Grandmasters at Grand Lodge, the Nile Country Club reopened! The usual Nile activities continued unabated as preparations were being made for the Imperial Convention to be held at Nile the following year.

Unfortunately, 1968 also witnessed the murders of Robert Kennedy and Martin Luther King, Jr., two events which further galvanized the American Civil Rights movement into political and social action.

1969 – Vernon E. Bell - Men On The Moon
and Imperial Shriners in Seattle

1969 is memorable to Nile nobles for two great events: the Imperial Council Session held at Nile Temple July 29-July 4, and the first manned landing on the moon by United States astronauts July 20. Vernon Bell presided as Potentate that year and what a year it was! The first public installation ever held of Nile officers and the ensuing program was presented on January 11 at the Opera House. The pageant "Look To The West" was performed and narrated by Nile Noble Judge John Cochran. Imperial Potentate Chet Hogan was the

Installing Officer. The big event of the year was the Imperial Convention. Over 100,000 Shriners attended the various events that comprised the Convention. Beginning with the Chester A. Hogan Ceremonial held June 28, through the Grand Parade with over 200 Shrine Units participating on July 1, and ending with a closing session on July 4, the 96th Imperial Session was a great success in large part due to the organizational and management skills of Nile Director General, Aurie Thompson, P.P.

Later that month came one of great events of all time, not only for Nile and America, but for the world. Throughout history humankind had speculated about the moon, the closest celestial body to Earth. From poetic notions to pretty shrewd guesses about its composition, man has longed to journey to its nearest celestial neighbor. The Soviets were thought to be well in the lead in achieving this goal through their Luna series which photographed the never-before seen back side of the moon and actually landed (probably crash landed) a human made object on the moon's surface for the first time. But the United States, under spurring from President Kennedy in the early 1960's, rushed to catch up. Americans watched in awe as first the Mercury, then the Gemini and finally the Apollo series of launches brought the United States closer and closer to that age-old goal. The climax came on July 20, when after the Apollo 11 space capsule landed on the moon, the commander of the Apollo 11 mission, civilian Neil Armstrong, stepped out of the lander and walked on the moon. He was ably backed up by command module pilot Mike Collins and lunar lander pilot Buzz Aldrin, a noble of Arabia Temple in Houston. However, Armstrong's first words: "That's one small step for a man, and one giant leap for mankind" came out as "That's one small step for man..." because of radio difficulties. Nevertheless, the 500 million people watching this historic event rejoiced that the impossible had been accomplished. Most social commentators acknowledge that this lunar landing and walk is one the defining moments in human history.

And life at Nile went on. Over 6000 attended the Nile Picnic. A great time was had at the PNSA Convention in Calgary (Al Azhar Temple). The Ringling Brothers Circus was a smash hit for Nile and the Oriental Band completed the construction of the barbecue shelter. The year ended with another successful ceremonial and a resplendent Holiday Ball.

In next month's article we will look at the problems that beset Nile as falling membership starts to create financial problems. We will also witness the institution of more units, the difficulties over the sale of the Masonic Temple and the effects of the Vietnam War on Nile and its nobles.

Chapter Eight

THE SCINTILLATING SEVENTIES

We left off the 1960's with two great events that stirred the hearts and emotions of Nile nobles and their ladies: the 96th Imperial Council Session in Seattle and the first steps by United States astronauts on the moon. The 1970s continued the changes that started sweeping the United States and the world in the 1960s. The anti-war, the Black Power, the gay rights, the feminist, the sexual freedom, and the anti-establishment political movements would reach their heights during this decade. For many though, the social activism of the 1960's would evolve into social activities for one's own pleasure in the seventies. In fact, author Tom Robbins was moved to dub these years the "Me Decade." Major social institutions, such as the family, religion, and government, lost the confidence of this generation, which slipped more and more into individual hedonism to escape the crises and the hectic social movements occurring during this decade. Such crises as the Vietnam war, the Nixon resignation in 1974 over Watergate, the oil crises of 1973 and 1979, and the economic recession (stagflation) drove people to abandon their faith in our government, religious and fraternal leaders and to seek pleasure in the world before it disintegrated. The lunar exploration program ended in 1972 with Apollo 17 in 1972 due to lack of funding. Iran turned from a pro-Western monarchy to an anti-Western Islamic theocracy. Economic recession and stagflation would greatly affect the economies of the Eastern bloc nations and pave the way for a massive political shift in the 1980's.

Not everyone lost faith and hope during this time. The environmental movement started raising the awareness of people to the fragility of our planet. Action to save the planet was advocated. The Green Revolution in many Asian countries offered the promise of feeding the world through modern scientific agricultural techniques. A new world of sensual wonder was being promised by technology (personal computers and microwave ovens), a different kind of music (disco, New Wave, punk rock, heavy metal) and cinematic extravaganzas (Star Wars and Close Encounters of the Third Kind). Spurred by these sci-fi epics the United States launched the Voyager series of unmanned spaceships in 1977 to find life in outer space. And the first full facelifts on women were done in the 1970s!

At Nile, the nobles and their ladies were at ease and seemingly uncompromised by the large changes engulfing our society. After all, their work was to raise funds for the hospitals and to support the temple activities.

1970 – Walter M. Woodburn – Mayor Wes Uhlman Becomes a Noble and the Shurtah unit Starts Operations

In 1970, longtime Nile Band Drum Major Walt Woodburn took office as potentate. Nile membership at the start of 1970 was just a shade under 11,000 (10,909). One of the newest nobles was Seattle City Mayor Wes Uhlman who joined at the previous December Ceremonial. Noble Art Nelson, a Chanters charter member in 1920, was recognized for 50 years membership in that unit. 1970 also marked the startup of operations of the Shurtah unit, chartered in late 1969 (Shurtah means police in Arabic). Shurtah was to be a social unit of active, retired, or ex-law enforcement officers, not a drill team unit. Its first members were Ed Marion and Ted Fonis. An enthusiastic response from the Nile nobles guaranteed the success of this proud unit. Later that year, a group of Nile Shurtah members traveled to Calam Temple in Lewiston Idaho to help organize the second Shurtah unit in the United States.

Another unit formed that year, the Mini-Bike unit, was active in summer parades. The Nile Temple Clowns were a hit at the annual Seafair Parade as well as many other parades, including the PNE (Pacific National

Exhibition) parade in Vancouver, B.C. where they joined with Gizeh Clowns to form a spectacular 32-clown unit. And the Shrine Circus (Ringling Brothers/Barnum & Bailey) had its best financial year up to that time.

On the national front, the first Earth Day was celebrated on April 22. It was the brainchild of Senator Gaylord Nelson of Wisconsin to have a teach-in on the environment. He first preached this idea in 1969 in Seattle and later that year in Atlanta. Organizers were found to contact various groups dealing with pollution control, pesticides, loss of wilderness and wildlife. Universities and then whole cities agreed to participate. The day of April 22 was chosen primarily because it was the birthday of one of Nelson's organizers, Julian Koenig, a public relations executive who also suggested the name "Earth Day." Coast to coast rallies were held attracting 20 million people. The idea was well received by various conservation groups and Dennis Hayes formed the Earth Day Network which has been a prime force in propelling Earth Day to become and remain a global event.

However, despite well intentioned efforts, net Nile membership fell to 10,679, the start of an overall declining trend that would last until the present day.

1971 – Victor W. Haskell - Calliope unit Formed

Potentate Vic Haskell granted the charter for a Calliope unit at Nile during this year. As the Pote would later remark: "It's the only kind of music you can hear above the conversation." Charter members were: Ed Meserly, President, Ken Miller, Vice President., Bill Gloeb, Secretary-Treasurer, Ernie Lenke, Gene Walsh, Carl Schneider, Charlie Rice, Joe Wiltham, Hank Doolittle, and Bob Chaffer. PNSA at Vancouver, B.C. was a tremendous success with Nile's Drum and Bugle Corps and Oriental Band taking home first place trophies and the Motor Squadron and Legion of Honor Drill Team taking home second place trophies. Also, that year, the second Shrine Bowling Congress was hosted by Nile with the Nile Fares team winning first place with a record setting pinfall. And a successful pilgrimage to the Far East netted 322 new Nile members, including Major General Blakefield, Chief of Staff of the United States Eighth Army.

On the national front, a new stock market index, geared to technology stocks, the National Association of Securities Dealers Automatic Quotations

System (NASDAQ), starts up on February 8. The 26th Amendment to the United States Constitution is certified, lowering the voting age from 21 to 18. Disney World opens in Orlando, Florida. And on November 24, D.B. Cooper parachutes over southwest Washington from a Northwest Orient Airlines Boeing 727-100 plane that he hijacked carrying with him a briefcase containing $200,000 in ransom money. The flight (NWOA Flight 305) began in Portland. During the flight to Seattle, Cooper informed the stewardess that he had a bomb in his briefcase and that he would detonate it if he was not given $200,000 and four parachutes when the plane reached Seattle. After the plane landed at Seattle-Tacoma International airport, the FBI complied with his request and all of the passengers and most of the flight crew were released. The plane then took off toward Reno, Nevada trailed by Air Force fighters. But Cooper had ordered the plane to be flown at a low speed of 170 knots, flaps at 15 degrees with landing gear down and at an altitude under 10,000 feet. Also, the passenger cabin was to remain unpressurized. Shortly after takeoff, the rear passenger cabin door exit light flashed indicating the aft airstair had been launched and Cooper was gone. Because of darkness and a heavy rain storm occurring at the time and no light from the ground due to cloud cover, the Air Force pilots did not see the parachute. The Air Force jets trailed the Boeing 727 to its landing at Reno where the FBI, to its chagrin, found Cooper not on board. To this day, it is the only unsolved commercial aircraft hijacking in aviation history.

Net Nile membership at the end of 1971 stood at 10,775, a net gain of almost a hundred!

1972 – Kenneth F. Grimes - 100th Anniversary of the Shrine

In 1972 Kenny Grimes took over as Potentate and immediately set about preparing Nile nobles for the Western Shrine Association Convention (WSAC) hosted by Al Malaikah Temple in Los Angeles celebrating the 100th Anniversary of the founding of the Shrine (1872 in New York City). But first came the Oriental Band's Second Annual Crab Feed in January ($3 per dinner)! In June, nearly 800 Nile nobles and their ladies traveled to LA for the WSAC. Nile won five major trophies : Legion of Honor Drill Team, Capt. Don Wright – first place; Drum and Bugle Corps, Capt. Merle Claflin – first place; Mounted Patrol, Capt. Albert Galante – second place;

Chanters, Director Fred Sethmann – second place and the overall Director General's Trophy for first place showing among all temples. Unfortunately, despite a spirited effort, the Oriental Band finished out of the money, a loss that would inspire them to new heights of glory in later years as we shall see. And the Greeters received their first trophy from Greeter Bill Boon's lady, Pauline, for making it all the way around the LA Coliseum track on their first venture as a marching unit.

At another venue, though, the 1972 Olympics in Munich were marred by the deaths of 11 Israeli athletes and coaches and one West German police officer killed by militant Palestinian Arabs of the Black September movement. Five of the terrorists were killed by West German police during a botched rescue attempt. The three surviving terrorists were eventually released in exchange for the passengers of a Lufthansa airplane captured and held hostage by Black September. Later, the Israeli Operation Wrath of God found two of the terrorists and killed them. The sole remaining terrorist is still alive today and believed to be hiding out in Africa or Syria.

At Nile, the decline in membership resumed when Nile's net membership at the end of 1972 fell to 10,594, a loss of almost 200 with deaths accounting for almost half of the loss.

1973 – Maury Sughroue - Past Masters Club Formed

Nile under Potentate Maury Sughroue was a slightly quieter place during this year. However, unit activity continued in full swing. The call went out to form a Nile Club for Past Masters who are Nile Shriners. 35 Nile Shriner Past Masters representing 23 different lodges attended this organizational meeting. Nile's units once again proved their superiority over the competition at PNSA in Billings, Montana that year. The Nile Band took first place honors (as well as first place in the Skagit County Fair Parade and second place at Oak Harbor). The MiniBikers and the Motor Squadron took first places in their respective categories. The Oriental Band bounced back from their devastating loss in 1972 at the WSAC to defend their first-place championship at PNSA. The Legion of Honor Drill Team took second place, but lost the first-place trophy to a dubious amalgam of a combined Al Azhar-Al Shamal Drill Team consisting of two full drill teams, two massed color guards and their drum and bugle corps! A question arose as to whether this was a fair competitive entry in the drill team competition.

Nationally and internationally, 1973 was a hot year. On October 6, Egyptian forces crossed the Suez Canal and invaded Israeli held Sinai Peninsula, thus precipitating the Yom Kippur War. Simultaneously, and as part of a secret strategy with Egypt, Syria launched an all-out attack on the Israeli occupied Golan Heights. For three days the combined Egyptian and Syrian forces achieved victories which looked like payback for the Israeli victories in the 1967 Six Day War. But the Israelis quickly regrouped pushing Egypt back across the Suez and repelling the Syrians. As Israel once again marched on both Cairo and Damascus, the Soviet Union flexed its political muscle and instigated a forced diplomatic halt to the Israeli advances. A ceasefire was eventually brokered by United States Secretary of State Henry Kissinger. At the end of the war, Israel gained more territory in the Golan Heights and Egypt was once more relegated to its side of the Suez Canal. However, Egypt's Anwar Sadat proclaimed October 6 a national day of victory in Egypt because it showed that Egypt could strike back and hold its own against Israel (at least for a time).

The Yom Kippur War was partially responsible for the oil crisis of 1973. Because the United States had begun to resupply Israel with arms during this conflict, the Organization of Arab Oil Producing Countries (OAPEC) imposed an oil embargo on oil sold or shipped to the United States and to other countries supporting the Israelis (chiefly the United Kingdom). The oil embargo lasted until March, 1974, not so much on account of the Yom Kippur War, which had ended on October 26, but because the Arab oil countries wanted to stabilize the amount of income derived from their oil production. In the United States, gas prices rose drastically and rationing had to be imposed because of limited oil supplies. In turn, the oil crisis was a major impetus to the stock market crash of 1973-4.

Nile's net membership at the end of 1973 was 10,606, a surprising result and the last time that Nile would show a positive increase in net membership.

1974 – Warren H. Ploeger - Al Aska
Temple Formed – Nile Nobles Demit

During Potentate Warren Ploeger's year Nile continued its activities unabated. The big event that year was the PNSA hosted by Nile Temple in Seattle May 23-25. Imperial Potentate Jacob Wingerter showed up to give Imperial's blessings to this outstanding event. But news from the Imperial Council Session in Atlantic City was both sweet and sour. A new temple, Al Aska, was formed in Anchorage, which would divest Nile of much of its jurisdiction in Alaska. (Nile would retain concurrent jurisdiction for the time being with Al Aska in southeastern Alaska, southeast of Cape Fairweather). While celebrating the birth of the new temple, Nile would also experience about 700 demits (almost all from the Alaska Shrine clubs) that year in favor of the new temple. Nevertheless, another successful pilgrimage to the Far East brought in many new nobles to almost offset the demits. And the Nile Oriental Band struck back again winning the World Champion Oriental Band trophy in Reno, Nevada! The World Champion trophy means that the Nile Oriental Band was not only the best in its Big Band class, but the best overall in all band classes. Rumor has it that the Nile Oriental Band played so beautifully that thousands of people chose to watch it march by instead of gawking at a multi-million-dollar casino robbery that took place nearby during the parade competition.

Nationally, the country went through a political wringer with the resignation of President Richard Nixon over the Watergate scandal. With imminent impeachment pending, a public trial of the president in the Senate was averted when now President Gerald Ford pardoned Nixon to ease the nation's angst over this event. The break in at the Democratic National Committee's offices in the Watergate office complex in 1972, was aimed only at finding some information about Nixon's dealings with Howard Hughes. It resulted in a cover up by the White House, lying, perjury, the convictions of numerous political staffers, the firing of top officials at Justice, and ultimately, the resignation from office of one of most powerful presidents in United States history.

Nile's net membership at the end of 1974 was 10,063 primarily due to the demits to Al Aska Temple.

Tune in next month to read about more new units formed at Nile, the battle over the Seattle Masonic Temple – would Nile get its fair share of sale proceeds, the dawn of the age of the personal computer, the Seattle Mariners, the Supersonics, and Walt Odom's challenge to membership declines.

THE SCINTILLATING SEVENTIES

1975 – J. Frank Platt - Fun on Wheels Formed; Teeny Wins National Clown Title

During Frank Platt's year as potentate, the Nile divan formed a Long-Range Planning Committee consisting of the Elected Divan, the Junior Past Potentate, the Chairman of the Board of Trustees, the Chairman of the Country Club Board and five nobles appointed from the nobility. Its purpose was to map out plans for Nile's long term needs and to assist the present boards with their planning work. On the lighter side, Washington State University coach Jim Sweeney was the featured speaker at the Knights of Columbus/Nile St. Patrick's Day Lunch, and Louis Long, "Teeny" of the Nile Clowns, won a national clown competition at the National Clown Convention held at Cedar Rapids, Iowa that year.

The call also went out to form a recreational vehicle group called Fun On Wheels. The pro shop doubled in size and new additions were made to the clubroom and locker area. And although the Oriental Band was not able to retain its "overall" world champion status (edged out by the unlimited size band from Long Beach), they won the first-place trophy in the large band competition.

This year saw the advent of the world's first personal computer, the Altair 8800. Developed by Ed Roberts of Micro Instrumentation and Telemetry Systems (MITS) in 1974, it first appeared for sale to the general public as a hobbyist kit in the January issue of Popular Electronics. Although Roberts thought that he might sell a couple of hundred of these kits, the demand for them came in the thousands. The onset of this marketing phenomenon did not escape the attention of two Harvard engineering students who promptly developed a basic programming language interpreter for the Altair to make it more useful to hobbyists. Roberts agreed to have them produce the interpreter for the Altair and the legend of Bill Gates and Paul Allen grew from there. They later formed a company in Albuquerque, New Mexico called Microsoft to make interpreters and software for other personal computer manufacturers, eventually moving it to the Seattle area and renaming the company Microsoft.

Nile's net membership at the end of 1975, 9896, was the first time since 1951 that the net membership fell below the 10,000 mark.

Richard M. Kovak

1976- Robert C. Kercheval – United States Bicentennial Year

In the Bicentennial Year of our country's Declaration of Independence (despite the Declaration in 1776, independence was not assured until the defeat of General Cornwallis at the Battle of Yorktown in 1781 followed by the Treaty of Paris in 1783, and the present United States government was not formally created until the adoption of the Constitution in 1787), Potentate Bob Kercheval held an Interfraternal Luncheon on February 16 at the Eagles Hall. Eagles, Elks, Moose, Knights of Columbus, and Shrine nobles all got along together well despite the barrage of competing petitions to join each other's clubs. By Resolution that same month the Savings In Nile (SIN) fund was created to generate capital for the Nile Building and Grounds Capital Improvement Fund. The Shrine Yacht Club was organized and formed this year. And the nobles and their ladies had a good time at the Kingdome watching international soccer star Pele (at the time the highest paid athlete in the world) play for the New York Cosmos against the Seattle Sounders. The Nile Temple Bowlers honored and learned their history from P.P. Ray L. Eckman who had started the Bowling Club when he was Potentate in 1944. The Bowlers also organized and held the First Annual Youth Bowling Jamboree for the DeMolay, Job' Daughters and Rainbow Girls. The stated purpose of the event was to show the Masonic Youth groups that Nile and the Shriners were interested in them and supported their activities.

Nile's net membership at the end of 1976 was 9,707.

1977 – Douglas W. Vicary - New Portland Hospital

During Doug Vicary's year as Potentate, substantial additions to the grounds were made. The picnic area was built up with hardwood tables and benches on concrete slabs. The 10,000 square foot maintenance and First/Second Section shed was built. And the Mobile Camper area for the Fun On Wheels campers was started. Three Shurtah unit members (Morrie Deming – Occidental 72; Walt Evans Jr. – Ravenna 275; Al Petty – Damascus 199) served as elected Masters of their respective lodges that year. Other Nile units took home trophies from the PNSA competitions in Edmonton that year. First Places were won by the Nile Band, Nile Drum

& Bugle Corps, Legion of Honor Drill Team, Mini Bikes, and Motor Squadron, and the Nile Chanters took second place. Based on these wins, Nile also won the Overall Trophy. Not to be outdone, the Oriental Band won the Champion's Trophy for medium size bands at the Western States Association of Oriental Bands. And, at the 103rd Imperial Council Session in New York City, the nobility voted to construct the new Portland Hospital building.

The Seattle Mariners, an expansion baseball team franchise, played their first game on April 7 in the Kingdome, losing to the California Angels 7-0. The Mariners were Seattle's payback from Major League Baseball for losing the Seattle Pilots in 1970. In 1969, Seattle was awarded a Major League Baseball (MLB) franchise under ownership by a consortium led by William Daley (former owner of the Cleveland Indians). Beset by financial problems after its first year of play, MLB caused the franchise to be sold to Milwaukee in 1970, where it was renamed the Milwaukee Brewers. The City of Seattle, King County and the State of Washington filed suit against MLB for breach of contract. At trial in 1976, MLB offered Seattle one of the 1977 expansion teams if it would drop its lawsuit. A consortium of local owners headed by entertainer Danny Kaye paid for the franchise and the ownership rights to start the new team in Seattle. Unfortunately, the Mariners did not have a winning season until 1991 and are one of only two teams never to have played in the World Series.

Net Nile membership at the end of 1977 was 9,650.

1978 – G. Warren Averill - Loss of Downtown Headquarters

G. Warren Averill took over as potentate in 1978, just in time for the King Tut Exhibit at Seattle Center which Nile nobles and their families attended in droves. Nile's fortunate proximity to the Tut Exhibit allowed it to earn valuable revenue through renting space to the Tut Exhibit promoters and selling tickets to the exhibit. However, the passage of the Center Improvement Bond Issue by the voters doomed the old headquarters building. After fighting off a condemnation action by the City of Seattle two decades ago, the headquarters building succumbed to a forced purchase under the Bond Issue. The Long-Range Planning Committee now had to double up its efforts to find a new home. Of the two possibilities, remodeling the

Seattle Masonic Temple or constructing a new building elsewhere, the latter seemed more appealing to Nile nobles. When the proposed gift of a parking garage at the Masonic Temple fell through due to lack of action on the part of the many Masonic owners, a new building was the obvious choice. But where was it to be located?

Land was getting very expensive in downtown Seattle following the rebound from the "Boeing Bust" years of the early seventies. Why not the Country Club property? And indeed, it was to be. At the October stated meeting, Nile nobles voted 5-1 to locate the new temple building on the Country Club property. In other news, the recreational vehicle area at the Country Club property was completed, the Drum & Bugle Corps started its successful barbecue beef concession at the Monroe Evergreen Fair, the Zem Zem unit was created to do bar tendering work at official Nile Temple functions, and Nile units won many awards at PNSA in Portland, including first places by the Drum & Bugle Corps, Band, Chanters, Mini Bikes, Motor Squadron and the Truckers. Nile again won the Overall Trophy. And Teeny the Clown won several first places at the International Shrine Clown Association Convention in Macon, Georgia.

1978 was also the year of Three Popes. Paul VI, on the Vatican throne since 1963, dies in August. His successor, John Paul, dies after only 33 days in office. On October 16, Karol Wojtyla, a Cardinal of Poland is elected as Pope John Paul II, the first non-Italian pope since 1523.

Just prior to those events, in September, the Camp David Accords were signed between Egypt and Israel which in turn led to the Egypt-Israel peace treaty of 1979. Appropriately, the leaders of those two countries, Anwar Sadat and Menachem Begin, shared the Nobel Peace Prize for 1978.

Net membership at the end of 1978 was 9,236.

1979 – Walter L. Odom - A New Headquarters Building

Walt Odom's year as Potentate was marked by substantial progress toward building the new Nile Temple building. An architectural firm was selected and preliminary plans were drawn up. Three locations were thought to be possibilities for the new building, including the pro shop area, the rubbish area near the side of fairway No. 10 across from the clubhouse kitchen, and a two-story addition on the north end of the existing building. The latter location prevailed. Walt held a public Ceremonial at the Seattle Center

Arena "Salute To Shrinedom," the first public ceremonial in many years. Attending that Ceremonial were Most Worshipful Grand Master Toby Johnson, a longtime Nile noble and Grand Orator Walt Woodburn, P.P. Eight units won trophies at the PNSA in Boise and Nile was awarded the Overall Trophy. On the national Shrine front, the first Spinal Cord Injury Center, an 8-bed ward, opened at the Philadelphia Shriner Hospital.

In September, the Seattle Times published an article by Paul Andrews on the decline of fraternal societies, especially the Masonic fraternities. The article was responded to by Harry Lehrbach, a Nile noble who was the editor of the Masonic Tribune and who was also the Smile with Nile editor. After acknowledging the factual accurateness of the declining membership numbers cited by Andrews, Harry went on to detail the positive side of Masonry, that is, all the good charitable and philanthropic work done by the lodges, the rites, and the Shrine. He concluded his article with the following words:

> And if you still think Freemasonry is dying on the vine because of TV or other special pressures, remember that every day of every year, Masons are meeting in friendship and fellowship in a sincere effort to make the world a little better place for everyone.

It should also be noted that the Seattle Supersonics won the National Basketball Association Championship this year, defeating the Washington Bullets 4 games to 1. Led by Coach Lenny Wilkins, the championship team consisted of forwards John Johnson and Lonnie Shelton, center Jack Sikma, guards Gus Williams and Finals MVP Dennis Johnson, together with key reserves Fred Brown and Paul Silas.

Nile ended the decade with a net membership total of 9,080.

Potentate Odom, who was most concerned about the decline in Nile Temple membership (from just under 11,000 at the start of 1970 to just over 9000 in 1979), had a slogan that year which read: "Rise and Shine in '79." He said: "Nile Temple did not become as great as it is through the efforts of any one individual - it became great through the desires and efforts of a great many individuals. We can reverse the present downward trend if you as an individual will join hundreds of others in helping Nile Temple to "Rise and Shine in '79.""

As we shall see, Nile nobles did rise and shine, not only that year but during the next decade too! Join us next month as we witness the move from the old headquarters building to the new headquarters at the Country Club, more championships for Nile's units and a Masonic hassle over the sale over the Seattle Masonic Temple. On the international front, we shall see massive political changes that changed the balance of power in the world. And technology marched on to new and innovative heights.

NOTE: The highest recorded year-end net membership at Nile was 11,612 on December 31, 1959. This number made Nile the 10th largest temple in North America. Nile stayed above or right around 11,000 net membership for the next 10 years, but dropped to 10,063 on 12/31/74 after a record 700 demitted that year following the formation of Al Aska Temple in Anchorage that year. By the end of 1975, Nile net membership dipped below the 10,000 mark and steadily declined ever since. National Shrine membership never did reach the one million mark, the stated goal of Imperial. In 1979, membership reached 941,799. It declined thereafter to approximately 200,000 as of the date of this book.

Chapter Nine

THE EXCITING EIGHTIES

For Nile and the Northwest, the 1980s were bookended by the volcanic eruption of Mt. St. Helens on May 18, 1980 and by the Loma Prieta earthquake during the World Series in the San Francisco Bay area on October 17, 1989. In between these two natural disasters, a tremendous amount of social, cultural, and political change occurred. This was the decade of the baby boomer and the yuppie, the Reagan Presidency, and his campaign against the "Evil Empire," the fall of the Berlin Wall and the rise of mega billionaires like Trump, Gates, Buffet, Boesky, and Helmsley. Technology would run rampant with the development of Gates' Microsoft Disk Operating System (MSDOS) software and Steve Job's Macintosh, the first computer to use a graphical interface. In science, the moon was once more a forlorn object in the sky for poets to speculate about, while the Space Shuttle became the darling of NASA. The end of the decade would see revolutions occurring in one Iron Curtain country after another eventually leading to the breakup of the USSR in the 90s.

Styles in music, art, fashion, and personal grooming all went "over the top." Despite double digit inflation, binge spending became so common that author Tom Wolff dubbed these years the "splurge generation." On the other hand, this decade saw a sort of religious revival in America with an emphasis on "Family Values." And a new conservatism held sway in political circles, led by Ronald Reagan in the United States and Margaret

Thatcher in the United Kingdom, which lasted up to the Clinton years in the 90s.

One very interesting fact about the 1980s is that it was the decade of the highest birthrates in history, surpassing those of the 1960s and 1970s. The omen of this for Masons and Shriners is that the large number of children born during this decade would become the 20 and 30-year-olds of the twenty-first century and thus eligible for membership in the various Masonic bodies. In today's world, the largest and fastest growing segment of new members in Masonic bodies is the so-called Millennium Generation, those born between 1981 and 1999.

At Nile in the 1980s, our nobles and their ladies kept their heads down and their shoulders to the wheel continuing to avidly fundraise for the Shriners Children's Hospitals and to enjoy each other's company in a variety of social settings. But the swirling social, political, and cultural changes of this era would prove to be too daunting a set of obstacles to membership growth and development during this decade.

1980 – John W. Bolenbaugh - Mt. St. Helens Blows Its Stack

During John W. Bolenbaugh's year as Potentate in 1980, Mt. St. Helens erupted. On May 18, at precisely 8:32 AM, a magnitude 5.1 earthquake at Mt. St. Helens triggered the most violent and destructive volcanic eruption in United States history. Destroyed by the lateral blast and by the volcanic mudflows (lahars) were almost 250 homes, 27 bridges, 15 miles of railway and 185 miles of highway. 57 people were killed or never found. 4 billion board feet of timber were blown over by the lateral blast, which peaked at 300 miles per hour. The resulting landslide traveled 14 miles down the N. Toutle River Valley burying it to an average depth of 150 feet. At noon, plumes of hot ash, pumice, and gas (pyroclastic flows) poured out of the crater traveling only 5 miles northward, but 250 miles eastward to completely darken Spokane at midday and then around the world driven by the prevailing easterly winds. The mountain's elevation was reduced from 9,677 feet to 8,365 feet.

Things were much calmer at Nile Temple. The PNSA at Vancouver, B.C. took place and a successful pilgrimage (celebrating the 100th Anniversary of the birth date of Noble Douglas MacArthur) was made to the Orient which brought in 133 new nobles. A Grand Lodge Dinner was held at the temple attended by Grand Master Toby Johnson, a Nile noble. The Cornerstone Fund was established to raise funds for the new mosque to be built at Nile. (Recall that in 1979 the City of Seattle did a forced purchase of Nile's downtown (Seattle Center) headquarters building and the nobility voted 5-1 to relocate the headquarters administration offices out to the Nile Country Club).

To the north of Nile, the Quebecois Movement in Canada reached its peak with a countrywide vote on the issue of secession (or independence if you were a Quebecois). The move was defeated in a national referendum 59.56% to 40.44%. Back in the United States, Ronald Reagan defeated Jimmy Carter for the Presidency, ushering in a new era of conservative politics. The1980 Summer Olympics in Moscow were boycotted by the United States and 64 other countries over the 1979 invasion of Afghanistan by the Soviet Union. And the Winter Olympics featured the "Miracle On Ice," in which the college hockey stars of the United States defeated the heavily favored Soviet Union Red Army team in the semifinals. The United States hockey team went on to defeat Finland for the Gold Medal.

Unfortunately, 1980 ended with the shooting death of Beatle John Lennon on December 8 in New York City.

And no miracle of membership was in the offing for Nile as membership slid to 8,817.

1981 – Wayne Sherbon - National Shrine Membership Takes Hit

Wayne Sheirbon's year as potentate was marked by continued planning of the new headquarters mosque. At the August stated meeting the nobility approved a 2-million-dollar capital building budget. The contract would be let on a design build basis (in other words the building had to be designed and built to fit the budget allowed for it). Although there was much controversy, the nobility eventually agreed that an addition to the north end of the existing building would provide the most bang for the buck.

On the national Shrine front, it was acknowledged by Imperial that national Shrine membership had taken its first big hit. Total Shrine membership had decreased by 5,660 nobles in 1980. Imperial inaugurated its national membership program in 1981, the first of what would be a series of unsuccessful attempts to stem the decline of Shrine membership. Ironically, this major decline in membership occurred during the same year that Imperial opened its new 48,000 square foot glass and steel office headquarters in Tampa, Florida on 6.7 acres of prime land with its 12 domed skylights, garden atrium, large corporate office pods, cascading waterfall, and lush tropical gardens.

Back at Nile, performing unit success at the PNSA in Billings, Montana was modest, although the Nile Band took home the first-place trophy for big bands (no other bands competed), and the drum and bugle corps won first place in its category despite the heart attack of Music Director and Acting Drum Major Jim Day during the night parade.

Nationally, music took a giant leap forward with the debut of a music video TV station, MTV. Started as an outlet for teasers and advertising for new songs, it soon became an American institution featuring almost all the new and emerging music pop stars and bands from 1981 forward. Yet, despite the predominance of hard rock and heavy metal music during this era, Nile's soft and easy music style prevailed at the Pote's Ball and other dances held by the various units.

The year had one big scare when President Reagan was shot on March 30 by John Hinckley, a mentally disturbed man who was subsequently incarcerated for the rest of his life. President Reagan made a remarkable recovery and went on to serve two terms as president. His Secretary, James Brady was not as lucky and his shooting by Hinckley confined him to a wheelchair for the rest of his life. He became an ardent advocate for gun control.

Nile membership decreased that same year to 8503.

1982 – Peter F. Woeck - Noble Scoop Jackson Leads The Shrine Parade - The Falkland Islands War.

In 1982, Peter F. Woeck was elected potentate and Noble Al Cox came aboard as Oriental Guide. It was rumored that Al served his first year on the divan as a deckhand on Peter's 85-foot yacht, the Sea Star. PNSA was held at Nile that year on June 2-5 and was "Major League" with a Shrinerama pageant and a parade Grand Marshaled by Nile Noble Henry M. (Scoop) Jackson, United States Senator of the State of Washington. The parade ran from Stewart Street all the way down to the Kingdome where the Shrinerama took place. Uniformed unit competitions took place at the Seattle Northgate Mall.

Plans and architectural drawings (Balzhiser Architectural Group) for the new headquarters building were received and approved that year. Imperial approved the move of the Nile headquarters from Seattle to Lake Ballinger during the Imperial Council Session held in Orlando. And the new Portland Shriner's Hospital building was dedicated by the Grand Lodge of Oregon with Nile and several other temples and Masonic bodies in attendance.

A most amusing international incident occurred this year when Argentina decided to invade the Falkland Islands, which they called the Malvinas, a small group of islands off Argentina's South Atlantic coast. Britain had been in possession of these islands since colonial times, but a new military junta in Argentina had taken control of the government the year before. They decided to strengthen their tenuous political status and flex their military muscle by reclaiming these islands which most Argentinians considered to be part of their country.

The junta led by General Leopoldo Galtieri figured that the United Kingdom would not spend the time, effort, and risk to retake these small islands of very limited strategic value almost 7000 miles away from the United Kingdom. The actual offensive was started by the group of Argentine scrap metal dealers raising the Argentine flag on South Georgia Island on March 19. In order to dissuade Britain from reinforcing its small garrison on the island, an amphibious assault led by junta Admiral Jorge Anaya landed in the Falklands on April 2 and quickly overwhelmed the British garrison forces. However, the junta underestimated the resolve of United Kingdom Prime Minister Margaret Thatcher. Her Conservative Party was facing elections soon, which they were not favored to win, and the loss of the Falklands without taking retaliatory action could have been seen as a sign that her government was weak and indecisive, a sure precursor to an election loss.

After skirmishing in the press with each other, (London tabloids likened the three junta leaders, Galtieri, Lami Dozo and Anaya to an Argentine version of the Three Stooges and the Argentine press portrayed Thatcher with an eye patch over one eye and labeled her a "pirate, a witch, and an assassin"), Thatcher immediately dispatched a large naval and air support force to retake the Falklands. The first significant naval encounter was the sinking of the Argentine light cruiser General Belgrano by the British nuclear-powered submarine HMS Conqueror. London tabloids screamed "GOTCHA" and Newsweek's cover read "The Empire Strikes Back."

After 74 days of fighting, Britain retook the Falklands and Argentina surrendered the islands on June 14. Despite the loss of life (255 British deaths vs. 649 Argentine deaths), it was a decisive British victory and Thatcher's Conservative Tory Party went on to win the elections. For the Argentines, it was their first war since the 1880's and it ended badly. After a bout of fervent patriotism during the invasion, Argentinians turned their attention back to their country's disastrous economic situation and awaited another turn of events in Argentina's internal politics. General Galtieri disappeared from the junta three days after the surrender.

At Nile membership totals dipped again to 8,314.

1983 – John G. Jones III - Nile Celebrates Its 75th Anniversary – New Headquarters Building Is Dedicated

During John G. Jones III's year as Potentate the new Nile two-story addition to the existing ballroom and country club facilities was built, dedicated, and occupied. Groundbreaking actually took place on December 20, 1982 with Potentate Woeck turning the first shovelful of dirt. But the construction by the general contractor, Hugh Ferguson Company, occurred during the first six months of 1983. By July, the building was completed and ready for dedication.

On July 30, 1983, Nile held its 75th Anniversary Ceremonial, commemorating its formation in 1908. A Banquet, Ball and Dedication with Imperial Potentate Richard B. Olfene in attendance took place with several hundred nobles and their ladies present. Also attending were the Imperial Oriental Guide, Edward McMullan and Washington State Grand Master C. Donald Brons who laid the plaque for the occasion. All assisted in dedicating the new building as well as celebrating Nile's Diamond Jubilee. Imperial Potentate Olfene expressed his feelings about this grand occasion in these words:

> On behalf of the more than 912,000 Shriners of North America it is with great pleasure that I congratulate all of you on this very special occasion – your 75th Diamond Anniversary (1908-1983) and the dedication of your new mosque. Nile Temple has made many significant

contributions to the growth and success of the Shrine and its great philanthropy, Shriners Hospitals for Crippled Children. Nile Temple has a long and illustrious history, one that you can all be extremely proud of.

Nile's performing units won five first places, four seconds, two thirds and the Overall Trophy at PNSA held in Spokane that year. 600 nobles and their ladies attended that historic event. The one sad note was the passing of Nile Noble Senator Henry Scoop Jackson that year.

Despite these stellar successes, Nile membership continued to slide to 8,032.

1984 – Robert Stephen - Year of the Penguin

Bob Stephen's year as potentate began as the Year of The Noble but quickly became the Year of the Penguin owing to as Director of the Second Section he had subjected many candidates to allegedly 'sadistic' initiation tests and that his year was to be a "Year for the Birds." Birds became penguins and during his rump installation all of his aides sported 2 inch high penguins on their shoulders and he was repeatedly dogged by a six foot plus penguin who constantly chastised him to "never let go of the rope" as he repeatedly failed all of his "bird tests" in true Second Section tradition.

As proof of his "sadistic" nature, Bob's motto for the year was "Work Your Way To PNSA" scheduled for Calgary, Alberta because Nile was not going to pay for anyone's expenses to go. On a more serious note, the new headquarters offices were furnished with new drapes and office furniture. A new unit, the First Aid unit, was created, chartered, and installed. The unit was organized to provide immediate emergency care on a temporary basis until a regular aid car comes on the scene, for any sick or injured persons at Nile Temple functions, especially parades and large gatherings. June 8 marked the installation of Nile Noble Fred E. Clyne as the 53rd National Commander of the Legions of Honor. The installation was held in Oklahoma City and attended by Potentate Stephens, three Nile past potentates and 72 Nile Legionnaires plus their ladies. On July 31, 1984, at a special noon luncheon, the final payments were made to the new building architect and building contractor at a final figure slightly below the capital budgeted amount.

Working your way to PNSA apparently did not take its toll on the units because Nile was awarded the Grand Overall Trophy at the Calgary PNSA that year. Led by a first place in drill competition won by Nile's Peerless Patrol and the Oriental Band's first-place finish in its division at Pacific Northwest Shrine Oriental Band Association (PNSOBA), first-place trophies were also won by the Clown unit, the Mini Bikes and the Truckers. The Legion of Drill Team took a second-place trophy as did the Chanters. All in all, it was a great showing for the "Illustrious Penguin." However, Nile's membership count at the end of 1984 was 7,667.

Tune in again next issue when we will learn about the personal computer revolution, the space shuttle program, the return of Haley's Comet and the beginning of the end of the Soviet Union and its communist revolution. What significance did these events have for Nile Shriners and their ladies and for all Americans? You will just have to wait another issue to find out!

THE EXCITING EIGHTIES

Like the 1960s, the 1980s were a watershed decade in American life. The personal computer revolution revved up into high gear with IBM, Microsoft Windows Operating System and the MacIntosh graphical interface system leading the way. Prisons overflowed as crime rates tripled from the levels of the 1960s. In politics, Geraldine Ferraro became the first woman to be on a presidential ticket and Jesse Jackson became the first black presidential candidate. Sandra Day O'Connor became the first woman appointed to the United States Supreme Court on September 21, 1981 when the Senate confirmed her appointment. She served on the Supreme Court until 2006 when she retired. In 1988 the Human Genome Project was funded and work began on mapping the whole genetic structure of the human body, a project that would not be completed until the 2000s.

Cable TV was born during the 80's and by 1989 60% of American households had cable service. Sneakers (or athletic shoes) became so expensive that the Los Angeles Police Department accused shoe manufacturers of cashing in on drug money "earned" by inner city kids who bought these shoes more for the look than the play. Nike responded that it was the high cost of technology that made the sneakers so expensive, even though labor costs (five-year-old through 12-year-old laborers in

Asian countries) were relatively low. The fall of the Berlin Wall in 1989 capped this historic decade.

At Nile, the large pilgrimages to the Orient and the fabulous ceremonials were diminishing in number and size. Yet, the primary purposes of Nile, to enjoy clean, wholesome family fun and to support the Shriners Children's Hospitals were further advanced by Nile Shriners and their ladies and continued unabated. The new headquarters building, grafted onto the old ballroom and country club, was proving to be a great success. Plans would soon be in the works to expand the golf course. And the sale of the old Seattle Masonic Temple would bring new funds into Nile's coffers. It was truly an exciting time in Nile's history!

1985 – Robert J. Hoefer - National Legion of Honor Convention at Nile

Roland J. Hoefer's year as Potentate was marked by several interesting events. On March 26-29, Nile hosted the 54th annual meeting of the National Association of Legions of Honor. Nile Legion of Honor Past Commander Fred E. Clyne made it through the eight-year line of the national LOH leadership to become National Commander. Special guests at this gala event were Governor Booth Gardner, Seattle Mayor Charles Royer, Imperial Potentate Gene Bracewell, Admiral Herb Bridge, and Seattle historian and author Bill Speidel. Earlier that month Noble Mel Blanc appeared at a Nile Supper Show.

Capital improvements accomplished that year were a new fan exhaust system, new sound system, and oak paneling for the ballroom. Construction of a Library and Memorabilia Room next to the Scimitar Room, took place under the direction of Historian Freddie Hayden. New stacking chairs, new furniture for the Ladies Lounge were bought and extensive improvements to Picnic Area B were also done. Portraits of Nobles Henry Jackson and Douglas MacArthur were presented and unveiled in the presence of Mrs. Jackson and Imperial Potentate Gene Bracewell (Mrs. MacArthur was too ill to travel from New York). They were eventually incorporated into a panorama with the MacArthur flag that flew over Tokyo and hung above the lobby in the new mosque (where it can be found to this day). A bus was purchased from Gizah Noble Ken Smith's company and a Transportation Corps created to run it. The Viking Shrine Club was organized and chartered that year and a Camera Club was organized. The drum and bugle corps came home with two first-place trophies from competition at PNSA in Casper, Wyoming. And Danny Thomas became a Shriner at Al Malaikah Temple in Los Angeles. Ceremonials were held on June 15 and December 7 attracting a surge of new candidates.

At the end of 1985 Nile's net membership was 7,440.

1986 – Albert Cox - Year of the Shrine Mason and Enthusiasm

In 1986, Al Cox took over as Potentate and promoted enthusiasm as his motto. Don Linderoth took over that year as Recorder from Harold Foster. Enthusiasm must have been endemic throughout the Units because from Imperial Session and PNSA they came away with a slew of trophies. At the Imperial Session in Los Angeles the Nile Band won first place trophies in competition and parade marching, the drum and bugle corps took second in music competition, the Oriental Band second place for medium sized bands and the Mini Bikes first in unit competition and second place in obstacle course. But it was at PNSA in Tacoma that our units really shined. The Band took first-place trophies in Music Competition and Parade Marching. The Patrol took first-place in drill competition. The Chanters scored second place in competition singing. The Legion of Honor won third place in parade marching. The Oriental Band won second places in Class B competition and parade marching. Truckers placed third in 4-wheel competition; Second Section took second place for hot sands Ceremonial stunts. The clowns won several awards including first place in balloon competition, third places in Gimmicks and Auguste Clown and second place in parade. The Mini Bikes received third place trophies in competition and parade. With all these trophies it is no wonder that Nile Temple was awarded the Grand Overall Trophy.

During Potentate Cox's year, the Oriental Band received the distinct honor of being appointed Tong No. 31 of the Illustrious and Ancient Mandarin Degree. The first degrees were conferred on May 29 and June 24. Ceremonials on June 7 and December 6 brought in a substantial number of new nobles, but, as was becoming the case on an annual basis, not quite enough to offset the passage of the Black Camel through the temple. An interesting design for several apartment/condominium units proposed for the lakeside property adjoining the old 7th fairway was circulated that year. Yet the cost and objections from golfers doomed this proposal.

Also, that year, Imperial designated 1986-7 as the Year of the Shrine Mason in another attempt to stem the decline in membership. The new temple Library opened for business and visitors (it is currently occupied by the Hospital Supply Corps as its offices) but the display of fezzes from all 191 temples and its fascinating memorabilia can still be viewed. Imperial launched its major Donor Recognition Program at the Shriners Hospitals. Master award centers, consisting of oak and mahogany wall boards, were constructed in each of the hospitals to display large gold and silver medallions presented in honor of major donations to that particular hospital. And Past Queen of Hatasu Temple #1, Janet Dash, was installed as Supreme Queen of the Daughters of the Nile at Supreme Session in New Orleans.

This was also the year of Halley's Comet. In February, 1986, the comet was supposed to be seen from various parts of Earth. However, the comet and the Earth were on opposite side of the sun at this juncture and the viewing of the comet was the worst in several thousand years. Moreover, light pollution from the vast urbanized areas of the globe made viewing nearly impossible in the northern hemisphere. Several comet probes, dubbed the Halley Armada, were launched by the European Space Agency, a Soviet Union/France joint project and by Japan to intercept the comet in early March. About all they ever found out, despite the flurry of photography, was that the comet was more like a "snowy dirtball" instead of a "dirty snowball" as had been previously thought. For your convenience, though, the comet will return for a much better viewing on July 28, 2061.

In the meanwhile, Nile's net membership rocketed down to 7,168.

1987 – Fred A. Sethman - A Sad Year for Nile

Fred Sethman took office as Potentate with high hopes of continuing the resurgence of Nile. His program, Re-dedication, and Active Participation (RAP), was a follow up of Al Cox's enthusiasm program. Potentate Sethman wanted every noble to rededicate himself to the work of the temple and to give their active participation to the tasks that they would be called on to do by the Directors of Units and the Directors and Deputy Directors of the Shrine Clubs. In particular, attention would be given to the new screening clinics program, which was inaugurated that year. Active participation in the membership program was also emphasized. Membership column writer Pat Roney wrote impassioned pleas to the nobles in Smile with Nile regarding the need to curb the precipitous fall in membership that Nile was experiencing.

A promising year would be dimmed by the untimely passing of Potentate Sethman on July 18 due to complications arising from a surgery that he had undergone the previous year, ironically almost exactly 60 years to the day that another potentate passed away in the middle of his year – Fred R. Harrison July 22, 1927. By the end of the year Pat Roney was gone too. But Nile nobles carried on. At PNSA in Portland, Oregon, our Truckers and Mini Bikes captured first places in their respective categories. Our clowns took first place in the 5 Man Skit. Individual clowns won first places in Individual Balloon (Ken Plowman), Multiple Balloons (Dick Speidel) and Carl Bortel took seconds in Multiple Balloons and Costume and Makeup. The Band took first place in Marching. The Chanters, Legion of Honor and Director's Staff won second places. Although our fabulous Oriental Band had to settle for second place in their specialty, the Oriental band Director, Bernie Press, won the Outstanding Director award. Alice Kennedy (mother of 2007-8 Queen Kathy Ramich) was installed as Queen of Hatasu Temple #1.

And Nile did find time to celebrate the Centennial of the United States Constitution, September 17, 1987, Constitution Day. Ceremonials occurred on June 6 and December 5 netting many new nobles, but at the end of 1987, Nile's membership total was 7,056.

1988 – Gordon Anderson - The Seattle Masonic Temple Sale

Gordon Anderson had to take over the leadership of Nile in July 1987 while still Chief Rabban. He brought Nile to a successful close of that year and followed up that difficult task with a great performance during his year as Potentate.

The major issue that came to a head that year was the controversy over the Seattle Masonic Temple (SMT). The temple building was owned by a corporation consisting of several Masonic groups. Several lodges as well as Nile Temple held significant amounts of shares in the corporation by virtue of their contributions of money back when the it was being built (It was dedicated in 1916). Other Masonic bodies contributed smaller amounts. The Washington Grand Lodge had no significant stockholder interest in the corporation. But in 1984 Grand Lodge made an offer to buy the SMT. The Chair of the SMT Board, without consulting the shareholders, responded that the SMT was not for sale, but the promise of significant amounts of money caught the stockholders' attention. Now the existing corporation bylaws were somewhat ambiguous as to how the ownership of SMT was to be construed. Rival sets of amended bylaws were proposed to clarify this ambiguity. A legal fight ensued between Grand Lodge and significant shareholders, which included Nile Temple and several prominent lodges, over whether the SMT was owned by proportional representation based on the amount of buy in money contributed both when the SMT was first built and thereafter (and thus number of shares issued and held by the contributors), or whether it was owned on a one group/one vote basis as proposed by Grand Lodge. The difference was staggering as to the amount of money that a group would receive depending upon whether it was an equal or a proportional shareholder. Not only that, but Grand Lodge would have received a huge windfall from the sale when it had only a minimal financial interest in the SMT. After litigation broke out and threatened to destabilize relationships between Nile and Grand Lodge and between certain lodges and Grand Lodge, Potentate Anderson and his attorney eventually won the day with a compromise made with the new Grand Master and his attorney, the final details and agreement of which were finalized during Potentate Ed Davidson's year in 1989. Nile would eventually receive a significant share of the proceeds from the sale of SMT based on its ownership of a large number of shares.

Potentate Gordy also instituted a Membership Watch that year and called for a minimum of four new nobles from each unit. The June 11 and December 3 ceremonials were successful follow-ups to the Membership Watch program. The picnic grounds were extensively remodeled courtesy of a gift from the Snohomish Shrine Club. And the brand-new restrooms at the picnic grounds were dedicated on June 10, 1988. Because of the pouring rain most of the spectators and dignitaries had to huddle inside the restrooms for the dedication whether they had to go or not. Only at Nile! The Nile Band, Chanters, Oriental Band and Legion of Honor Flag unit combined to perform a Patriotic Salute To America at both the Monroe and Puyallup Fairs. It was so popular that Gordy held an open stated meeting in October where it was again performed. On Ivy League Day at Nile, 143 ladies from all units at Nile planted 7000 ivy plants on the banks of the golf course. And President Ronald Reagan was made an Honorary Shriner by Imperial Potentate Voris King at a special ceremony held in the Oval Office.

Yet despite all the publicity and determined efforts, Nile's net membership total fell to 6,881.

1989 – Edgar Davidson - Earthquake Halts World Series – the Berlin Wall Falls

During Edgar Davidson's year in office as Potentate, after almost six years of disagreement, a new set of Seattle Masonic Temple bylaws were agreed upon which would ensure a very satisfactory outcome for Nile when the SMT was sold. It turns out that the alternative bylaws proposed by Grand Lodge, proposing one vote per organization, could not trump Washington State corporation law which made it clear that ownership of a corporation was based upon the number of shares owned by a shareholder.

The San Juan County Shrine Club was formed and chartered. Nile took the Overall or Grand Aggregate Trophy at PNSA in Vancouver, B.C. that year owing to the award-winning performances of many of its units. First-place trophies were won by Second Section, Chanters, Clowns, Oriental Band, Mini Bikes and Truckers. The Patrol took home a second-place trophy while the Legion of Honor Drill Team and the Concert Band contributed with third place trophies to the overall standings. Later that year, Potentate Davidson led Nile in the 75th Pilgrimage to the Orient which once again allowed Nile to gain new members in Hong Kong, Taipei, Manila, Tokyo, and Singapore. Home ceremonials were held on June 19 and December 2. Several successful screening clinics were held and, in Spokane, bids were received and a contract let for the construction of a new Spokane Hospital unit.

But in October, the Loma Prieta earthquake struck. And although, Seattle only felt a slight physical ripple, it was emotionally and deeply moved by the extent of destruction caused in the Bay Area. The quake, which measured 6.9 on the momentum scale had a 7.1 surface magnitude reading. It was the first earthquake to be broadcast on live TV, courtesy of the Goodyear blimp, because it occurred during the warm-ups for the third game of the World Series at Candlestick Park. Uncannily, the earthquake had been predicted both by Baltimore Sun columnist Kevin Cowherd in an article appearing in the San Jose Mercury News that morning: "An earthquake could rip through the Bay Area before they sing the anthem for Game 3" (which is when it occurred) and by retired geologist Jim Berkland in an article titled "Is a World Series Earthquake Coming" published in the Gilroy Dispatch four days earlier. Unfortunately, the earthquake killed 63 people, injured 3,757 others, and left homeless another 12,000. The damage was estimated at $6 billion. The collapse of the double decker Cypress Viaduct in West Oakland (part of the Interstate-880 Nimitz Freeway) was the most visible symbol of the disaster. Shown many times on TV and in the newspapers, it brought home to Seattle residents the possible collapse of the Washington State Route 99 viaduct running through the heart of Seattle if a similar event occurred there.

But the most stunning event of 1989 and the one which eventually led to the breakup of the Soviet Union and to the present world configuration was the fall of the Berlin Wall on November 9, 1989. As background, Ronald Reagan made a 1987 speech at the Brandenburg Gate to then Communist Party General Secretary Gorbachev which included the line: "Mr. Gorbachev, tear down this wall." Gorbachev in 1989 repealed the Brezhnev Doctrine in favor of non-intervention in the internal political affairs of the Iron Curtain countries. Poland's internal affairs had already been destabilized by the rise of the Solidarnosc labor movement led by Lech Walesa. Hungary would soon follow. The Hungarian government removed its physical barriers with Austria on August 23, 1989, paving the way for thousands of East German tourists in Hungary to now escape to Austria. Alarmed at this mass exodus, the Hungarians removed the rest of the East German tourists to Budapest where the tourists stormed the West German embassy there and refused to return to East Germany. East German authorities immediately forbade any more visits to Hungary. A similar incident occurred in Czechoslovakia with a similar travel ban. Mass demonstrations took place in October in East Germany over the travel restrictions.

By November 4, the demonstrations had multiplied and in East Berlin over half a million East Germans demonstrated at the Alexanderplatz. Erich Honecker, the East German Communist Party leader resigned and the new leader, Egon Krenz tried to mollify the people by allowing refugees to exit directly through crossing points between East and West Germany with proper permission (aka "show me your papers"). The new regulations were to go into effect on November 17. However, the East German Politburo spokesperson, Gunter Schabowski, had not been briefed on this procedure and its timing, and when queried on November 9 by the West German media about this, he replied that he assumed some sort of relaxed exit procedure would be effective immediately without delay. That afternoon, the West German TV station, ARD, broadcasting an incomplete version of the Schabowski interview, intoned and exaggerated Schabowski's remarks as follows: "This ninth of November is a historic day. East Germany has announced that, starting immediately, its borders are open to everyone."

Upon hearing the broadcast, tens of thousands of East Germans gathered that evening at the Berlin Wall demanding that border guards immediately open the gates. The East German guards, caught off guard, called for instructions to their superiors, but everyone had heard the broadcast and nobody in command was willing to give an order to use lethal force to stop the onrush of humanity at the wall. Greatly outnumbered, the guards opened the checkpoints and gates with almost no identity checking. The flood of East Germans going through the checkpoints that night was met by an equally ecstatic flood of West Germans on the other side. Celebrations continued all through the night with people climbing the wall and starting to chip away at it with hammers and chisels to obtain souvenirs. The nickname "Mauerspechte" (wall woodpeckers) was coined to commemorate these zealous souls. The East German regime recognized the irony of all this and reluctantly opened 10 more border crossings the following weekend and ordered bulldozers to remove barriers and open the old German roads to free travel. With the "fall" of the Berlin Wall, the decline and fall of the Soviet Union would not be far behind.

At the end of this historic decade Nile's membership total stood at 6,664.

And so, the Exciting 1980s ended. What would the 1990s bring? More earthquakes, volcanos, hurricanes, and political upheaval? And how about Nile? Any new and dramatic events to occur there? Watch for the next installment where we will analyze the disintegration of the USSR, the Bill Clinton years, the social happenings at Nile and the building of the second nine holes of the Nile Golf Course.

Chapter Ten

THE NOBLE NINETIES

The 1990's were a time of great sociological, cultural, political, and technological change. Rapid globalization of markets after the reunification of Germany in November 1989 and the collapse of the Soviet Union (USSR) in December 1991 resulted in the creation of huge mega-companies (the Merger Decade) and the amassing of immense wealth that in turn gave rise to an unprecedented amount of disposable income spending. Discoveries of oil and gas in the former republics of the USSR formed the basis for free market economies in those countries. Newly liberated Iron Curtain countries, such as Poland, Hungary, Lithuania, and Estonia witnessed robust economic growth rates in the 1990s. The formation of the Economic Union (EU) in Europe and the adoption of a single currency (euro) in its member states meant much freer movement of goods, labor, and services throughout Europe. The North American Free Trade Agreement (NAFTA) allowed the free transfer of goods, labor, and services throughout North America. The United States stock market boomed so much in the 90s that Alan Greenspan, the Fed Treasury czar deemed this economic period one of "irrational exuberance." The advent of personal computers in many homes allowed the World Wide Web and the Internet to morph into the biggest change in world culture since the inventions of the automobile and the airplane. Computerized Internet trading came into existence to further increase the volumes of business being transacted during this period. Other electronic innovations premiering during this decade include email, MP3 players, mobile phones, digital cameras, compact disc burners, compact disc-Read Only Memory drives and the DVD media format.

At Nile, the steady progression of fund raising for the Shriners Hospitals and of staging fun activities for the nobility and their ladies continued despite ever declining membership numbers. It was hard to believe that a temple that had almost 12,000 members in the early 1960's was now down to less than 5000 by the mid-1990's. The end of the decade would see a possible solution to Nile's recruiting problems in the opening of the country club golf course to the public and the building of a second nine holes.

1990 – Howard S. Olson -Fun with
A Purpose – The Gulf War

Potentate Howard S. Olson's theme was Fun With A Purpose by which he meant having a good time while still pursuing funds for the care and transportation of Shriner children. The highlights of his year included a Joint Ceremonial with Al Malaikah Temple of Los Angeles at the Nile on August 11 (69 new nobles for Nile were created) and a September pilgrimage to southeastern Alaska (18 new Nile nobles). PNSA took place in Spokane on May 23-26. The Band won first place. The other Nile units participating in competitions won enough places and shows to force a tie with Gizeh Temple for the Overall Award. But at the awards banquet when it was suggested that a coin toss determine the Overall Trophy winner, Potentate Olson stood up and graciously declared that Gizeh should be awarded that trophy based on their fine showing in most of the events. A very successful Food Caravan to the Portland Hospital took place. The Hospital Supply Corps, aided by five Nile Shrine Clubs (Northwest, Snohomish, Eastside, Kitsap, and Ballard-University) delivered in excess of $25,000 worth of food and products. And the Nile Car Club was officially chartered at Nile on December 12, 1990.

Internationally, Iraq invaded Kuwait on August 2. As a pretext for the invasion, Iraqi President Saddam Hussein accused Kuwait of flooding the world market with oil, thus lowering the price of oil, and coincidentally, depriving Iraq of oil money it desperately needed to erase the enormous debt it had accumulated during its disastrous war with Iran. The United

States reacted by sending two carrier groups to the Gulf under codename Desert Shield ostensibly to protect nearby Saudi Arabian oil fields, which were of tremendous strategic importance to the United States. In November, the UN passed a resolution (Resolution 678) condemning the invasion and authorizing the formation of a coalition force, led by the United States, to be sent to the Persian Gulf to repel the invaders. In January, 1991 Operation Desert Storm began with an aerial bombardment that destroyed most of the Iraqi air and ground equipment. In February, the UN Army (mostly United States troops) launched its ground assault and drove the invaders from Kuwait in four days despite Saddam's heroic claim that this would be the "mother of all battles." The UN force penetrated Iraqi territory and drove almost to the outskirts of Baghdad before a ceasefire was declared ending hostilities. The land portion of the Gulf War had lasted a mere 100 hours.

Back at home, Nile's net membership on December 31, 1990 stood at 6,248.

1991 – George Jurgich - Give Me A Hug! - Collapse of USSR

How many Potentates start their year out with a beautiful poem written to them by a Washington Supreme Court Judge on the front page of Smile with Nile? Only George Jurgich who was lavishly praised by Retired Supreme Court Judge Bill Goodloe in just such a manner. George hugged everybody he came close to. His theme that year was The Heart of the Shrine – Masonry. He created three new appointed divan positions: Executive Aides (now Ambassadors) to liaison on Nile's behalf with Grand Lodge, Scottish Rite and York Rite. Howie Johnson took over as Recorder that year and Nile's address changed from 500 NE 205th St. Edmonds, WA 98026 to its present address of 6601 224th St. SW, Mountlake Terrace, WA 98043 without a single tree being moved! PNSA in Billings, Montana on June 13-15 netted Nile the Overall Trophy for its many trophy awards in the competitions. Longtime Band Noble Tommy Solberg celebrated his 100th birthday at Nile that year. Tommy held Card No. 1 of the American Federation of Musicians Union AFL-CIO denoting 88 years of continuous membership at that point in time. At the September stated meeting a proposal to add another nine holes to the golf course passed with a vote of 281 to 66. A letter requesting approval to go forward with the golf course expansion was sent by the potentate to Imperial Shrine and the Imperial Council replied by giving its permission. Oriental Guide John Gronlund was appointed Chair of the Golf Course Oversight Committee to supervise the progress of the expansion project. But the proposed expansion would face opposition from Mountlake Terrace City Council members as well as from the Ballinger Lake Advisory Committee. As a result, it would be a few years before construction could begin on the second nine holes.

But the biggest news of the year was the collapse of the Soviet Union, known for 73 years as the Union of Soviet Socialist Republics or USSR. In 1990, Mikhail Gorbachev was elected USSR President with the unstated goal of converting the USSR to a market economy (vs. the USSR's strictly controlled centralized economy). To achieve that objective there had to be more autonomy given to the constituent republics to develop their own resources and to encourage them to trade more freely within the Soviet bloc. However, the political independence ambitions of many of the republics would eventually supersede Gorbachev's hopes for a looser union of trade partners.

In July, Boris Yeltsin won the presidency of Russia with 57% of the vote, defeating Gorbachev's candidate Rytzin. Gorbachev tried to get the republics to sign the New Union Treaty which would convert the USSR into a federation of semi-autonomous republics. However, an old guard coup to prevent the signing of the treaty occurred and Gorbachev was placed under house arrest. Public sympathy in the various republics turned against the conspirators and in favor of Gorbachev. Led by Yeltsin, mass demonstrations took place in Moscow and other cities during which the coup leaders were condemned and vilified. Attempts by the coup organizers to arrest Yeltsin failed and the coup collapsed after three days. Gorbachev returned as president, but with little power. Now, republic after republic started declaring their independence from the USSR. Yeltsin led Russia's Declaration of Independence.

On December 8, leaders of Belarus, Ukraine and Russia signed the Belovezha Accords which declared the dissolution of the USSR and the formation of the Commonwealth of Independent States (CIS). On December 21, all member republics, except Georgia, signed the Alma-Ata Protocol affirming the dissolution of the USSR and joining in the CIS. Russia was allowed to assume the USSR's seat in the UN and on the

Security Council. On December 25, Gorbachev resigned as President of the USSR and declared the office extinct, and on that same night, the USSR flag was lowered for the last time over the Kremlin. The next day, the Supreme Soviet of the USSR completed the dissolution process by dissolving itself.

In the meanwhile, back in August, a little noticed event of worldwide importance occurred when Tim Berners-Lee posted a summary of the World Wide Web Project and its associated software (web browser and web editor) on the alt.hypertext newsgroup. British engineer Berners-Lee, now Sir Tim, is presently the Director of the World Wide Web Consortium. He developed the hypertext, URL and HTML protocols which we use every day on the Internet. (Recall that the Internet is merely the interconnected computer networks on which the World Wide Web operates. The Web is the application which allows everyone to locate, extract, share and deliver information to others throughout cyberspace.)

And the breakup of Yugoslavia began on June 25 when the republics of Croatia and Slovenia declared their independence from Yugoslavia. The ensuing Yugoslav Wars would last for another four years.

At the end of 1991, Nile's net membership was down to 5,640.

1992 – Robert Wright – Sound an Alarm!

Sound an Alarm was Potentate Bob Wright's theme in 1992. The alarm was to alert nobles to continue recruiting new members, to continue raising funds for the hospitals and to continue participation in inter-temple activities like PNSA. In several ways it was also an alarm to Nile about decreased participation in unit events and the about the declining membership. For example, for the first time, the Patrol sent out a call for nobles to join that group to learn the marching drills so that the Patrol could field a competitive unit at PNSA. Desperate calls for donations to the Transportation Fund were sent out in every Smile with Nile that year. As of 12/31/91, Nile membership had fallen to 5,640 (down from 6664 at the start of the decade on January 1, 1990) and would fall another 366 members by the end of 1992 (292 suspensions, 248 Black Camel, 69 new creations and 45 affiliations).

On the plus side Nile's participation at PNSA in Edmonton, Alberta that year turned out to be very successful. Nile won the Overall Trophy based on first places achieved by the band, the Oriental Band (medium sized oriental bands), the Clown unit and the Legion of Honor Drill Team. The Drill Team also won the first-place trophy at the First International Legion of Honor Meeting in Fresno, CA, with Bob Colton as Captain.

On May 27, 1992, at a special stockholders meeting, the sale of the Seattle Masonic Temple to Seattle Community College for $1, 500,000 was approved by 98.77% of the proportional voting membership. Nile would receive a handsome infusion of cash owing to its ownership of more than 50,000 shares in the SMT Corporation. Nationally, the Shrine of North America was selected as a Summit Award Winner by the American Society of Association Executives with President George Bush presenting the award to the Imperial Potentate, John W. Dean III, in Washington, D.C.

1992 also marked the election of Bill Clinton to the Presidency of the United States and the start of the great economic boom of the 1990's. Neither is given credit for the other, and by the end of decade, Clinton would be impeached and tried in the Senate and the boom would give way to the dot.com bust. This year is also known as the "Year of the Woman" because of the huge numbers of women elected to high state and national offices.

Nile's net membership closed that year at 5,274.

1993 – Charles H. Grove - Hopping with Harry.

Charles H. (Harry) Grove presided as Potentate in 1993. Early in that year Nile hosted a visit from Imperial Potentate Everett M. Evans and his lady Maxine. Plans for the expanded golf course passed another hurdle when the Mountlake Terrace City Council voted 5-1 to give Nile a conditional use permit within a shoreline conservancy area (Lake Ballinger shoreline). The vote went against the city planning commission's negative recommendation and the opposition from the Lake Ballenger Citizen Advisory Committee. Later in the year, a special York Rite Class Ceremonial was held. All the Capitular, Cryptic and Chivalric York Rite Degrees were conferred at Nile Temple followed by a group Cold Sands Ceremonial.

On July 18, at the Nile Family Picnic, Potentate Grove celebrated Nile's 85th Anniversary (1908-1993). Another successful Media Day, highlighting the Spokane and Portland Hospitals to the press, was held. Nile again won the Overall Award at PNSA held in Casper, Wyoming. Several units earned first-place trophies, either in competition, parade, or both, including the Director's Staff, the concert band, the Oriental Band, the drum, and bugle corps, and the LOH drill team. The Kitsap and Viking Shrine Clubs donated $20,000 to the Children's Transportation Fund from their circus efforts. Tony Volpentest, son of Shriner Bill Volpentest, was selected as Old Spice Athlete of the Month by Sports Illustrated Magazine. And the Nile bylaws were amended to make the December annual meeting the time when elections are held. Installation would be held at the January stated meeting. Up to this time the annual meetings at which the elections and installation occurred were all held in January.

Internationally that year, the European Community came into existence pursuant to the Maastricht Treaty of 1992, eliminating trade barriers among the European members of the European Union and creating a single Europe wide market. And of special note to the Czech and Slovak Shriners, 1992 was the year of the Velvet Divorce separating Czechoslovakia into two independent nations, the Czech Republic and Slovakia.

Nile's net membership that year settled at 5,129.

1994 – John G. Lien - Lien Takes Leadership Lead

Potentate John Lien's year was highlighted by Nile's hosting of PNSA in Bellevue (Meydenbauer Center) on July 20-23. Walt Odom, P.P. was Director General and Nile put on a tremendous show for the Imperial Potentate, Tony Bukey, and for the visiting temples. Nile units played the good hosts and gracefully allowed visiting units to win most of the competition and parade trophies. Nevertheless, a great time was had by all. Also that year, Grand Lodge, sitting in Wenatchee, made two momentous decisions: delegates approved the Alternative Proficiency Program, which meant that Masons would now only have to memorize the passwords and the obligation, and the age to become a Master Mason for a young man was dropped from 21 to 18!

An "All The Way in One Day" Reunion and Ceremonial was held on May 14 at Nile, cosponsored by Seattle Valley of Scottish Rite and Nile (100 new 32nd degree Masons and new nobles). A Master Mason could go all the way from Master Mason to Shriner in one day. Later that year a Sid McIntyre Ceremonial was held in Sedro Woolley which netted another 25 new nobles. On other fronts, the Building and Grounds crew did an amazing job that year installing new drapes in the Gold Room and Ballroom, new carpet in the Gold Room and Caravan Room, and renovating the plumbing in the old section of the building. The Building and Grounds unit was led that year by Bill Clendaniel, Andy Warner, and Ralph Rimple.

Potentate Lien did another remarkable thing that year. He was the driving force behind an expenditure of $10,000 to buy a huge red, yellow, and green striped tent from Puget Sound Tent and Awning Company. That tent, erected near Picnic Area A and which came to be known as "The Pote's Tent" has been the site of numerous Nile Picnic events, wedding parties and other events and to this day is a sure sign that summer fun has come to Nile when it goes up at the beginning of May every year.

Also, that year, the State allowed the Nile "Smile with Nile" sign, located at the corner of I-5 and 205th, to be renovated but not revolving. Revolving, it would be a distraction for I-5 motorists said State Department of Transportation (DOT) officials and would be punishable by a fine or order for removal. Since that time, the old sign has not revolved, although it is still capable of doing so. Considering the many glaring and garish signs flanking I-5 now, especially in the Fife/Tacoma area, one wonders if DOT might have a change of mind and allow the old sign to rotate today.

A Youth Soccer sponsorship program was started that year with many of Nile's units sponsoring youth soccer teams in a variety of leagues. The Nile bus, which turned out to be a mechanical nightmare, was sold to Wayne Peterson of Bothell who converted it to an RV motor home for his family. And, under Potentate Lien's sponsorship, the Nile Temple Belles (widows of nobles who had passed away) were formed under the leadership of Pearl Meagher and Elsie Joyce to give our nobles' widows a continuing presence at Nile. They receive complimentary copies of Smile with Nile.

In Europe, the Channel Tunnel, or "Chunnel" opened connecting England and France with the longest undersea tunnel in the world. Travel time between the two countries was now reduced to 35 minutes.

At the end of the year, the net membership count at Nile submerged below the 5000 mark to 4,864.

In the next issue, the Noble Nineties chapter will discuss, in addition to Nile's activities, the Princess Diana incident, the cloning of Dolly the Sheep, the building of the International Space Station, the return of comet Hale-Bopp after 4,200 years, the Y2K hoax and much more.

THE NOBLE NINETIES

Wars continued to dominate the overseas news in the second half of the 1990's with the First (1994-6) Chechen War in Russia, the Second Chechen War (1999), the Kargil War in Kashmir (India vs. Pakistan) (1999) and the Kosovo War (1998-9) (Albanian separatists vs. Yugoslavia/Serbia). In the United States, President Bill Clinton was weathering the political fallout from the Monica Lewinsky sex scandal. He became only the second president to undergo an impeachment trial in the Senate after he was indicted (impeached) by the House of Representatives. After a spirited vote almost strictly along party lines, he was acquitted and went on to finish his second term as president.

Nevertheless, the United States in the second half of the 1990's continued to experience unprecedented economic growth, so much so that Fed Chairman Alan Greenspan called it the decade of "irrational exuberance." Unfortunately, our neighbor to the south, Mexico, did not share in this abundance and President Bill Clinton invoked executive emergency powers to authorize a $20 billion loan to Mexico to help it stave off national bankruptcy.

But no loans were needed at Nile. Fund raising for the Shriners Children's Hospitals went on successfully and unabated. Imperial Shrine saw some of the best years of donations for the hospitals during the 1990's and used projections based on these increased donation years to plan the upgrade and/or replacement of several of the hospital buildings as well as upgrading the salaries of medical and administrative staffs.

1995 – John Gronlund - Expansion
of Golf Course Progresses

John Gronlund's year as potentate began with him welcoming in a new divan member, James (Jim) Hart, Jr., Oriental Band Director, who took over as Recorder that year. The permits for the golf course expansion were completed and contracts awarded for timber clearing and removal. Later that year a contract was awarded to the construction contractor for the installation of the new nine holes. Grand Master Milt Benson tried to make a progressive move by announcing a One-Day Class to become a Master Mason, but had to cancel it due entrenched opposition from other Masonic quarters.

Another successful combined Scottish Rite Reunion/Cold Sands Ceremonial was held bringing in many new nobles and the Shurtah conducted its first Fight Night fundraiser which proved to be a resounding success. Nile Treasurer Marion Holstine was elected to office (first Vice President) in the Imperial Treasurer's Association. Also, at Imperial, the vote to drop the term "Crippled" from the Hospitals name failed only because the requisite majority was not reached, but the requirement to include the Flag of Panama in Shrine flag presentations was approved.

PNSA in Butte was very fruitful. The Oriental Band won three first-place trophies: medium band, show and competition and Oriental Band floats. The Legion of Honor Drill Team took first place in parade and third place in competition. The Band won first place in both the small band and parade competitions. They might have won more awards but were denied entry into the Dixieland and German Band competitions because of late registration for those events even though they had been assured by the Butte PNSA administration that they could register on arrival. And the Legion of Honor Flag unit won first place for Best Marching unit at the Island County Parade. A successful pilgrimage to seven cities in the Orient brought in 78 new nobles. The one sad note that year was the passing of Nile Golf Pro Cobe Holmstad. He would have really enjoyed working the new 18-hole golf course which would be pretty much completed that year.

The World Trade Organization (WTO) is created that year to take the place of the General Agreement on Tariffs and Trade (GATT). Unfortunately, the Oklahoma City bombing on April 19 of the Alfred P. Murrah Federal Building cast a pall over the country. Timothy McVeigh, a militia movement activist detonated an explosive-filled truck which he had parked on the street in front of the building. He was assisted in the preparation of the bomb truck by Terry Nichols. The ensuing blast killed 168 people, including eight Federal Marshals and 19 children under the age of six. 680 others were injured and total damage from the blast was estimated at $652 million. Both McVeigh and Nichols were tried and convicted in 1997. McVeigh was executed by lethal injection in 2001and Nichols is serving a life term in prison. However, in another criminal trial, on October 5, O.J. Simpson was found "not guilty" of the murders of his ex-wife, Nicole Brown Simpson and her boyfriend, Ronald Goldman. When the alleged murderer's gloves did not fit Simpson's large hands, defense attorney Johnny Cochran argued successfully to the jury: "If the glove don't fit, you must acquit." Simpson was later found liable in a civil trial and had to pay millions in compensation to the families of the two victims.

Nile's net membership stood at 4,660 at year's end.

1996 – Fred G. Oliver - Golf Course Expansion Completed

In Fred Oliver's year as Potentate, construction was completed on the additional nine holes for the Nile golf course. The course, although still listed as private, was opened for public play. A dedication of the expanded course took place on August 11 as part of the Pote's Golf Tournament that year. Note: the actual opening of the new 18 holes occurred on July 1 when a special Shriners Only golf tournament was held. A new pro shop was completed in September under the direction of Bud Wheat and Andy Warner (W&W Construction Co.) who supervised numerous volunteer workers. To cover the cost of the golf course expansion, a loan in the amount of $1,500,000 was obtained across a six-year period. (Bonds would later be issued to pay off the loan).

A great Family Picnic was held that year highlighted by a live auction courtesy of the Washington DeMolay Foundation. At the 122nd Imperial Council Session in New Orleans, the term "Crippled" was finally voted to be dropped from the Shriners Hospitals for Children name. As stated by Everett M. Evans, Chairman of the Board of Trustees for the hospitals:

> The name change is intended to reflect the philosophy of the Shriners. We provide medical care for children totally free of charge, based only on what is best for the child. We focus on helping them lead more normal lives. Our new name, likewise, does not label them in any way, but simply recognizes them for what they are – children. And the mission of Shriners Hospitals for Children is to help children lead better lives.

On a more comical note, Potentate Oliver became the first potentate to ride an elephant at the circus in full clown makeup and costume! He was made an Honorary Clown by Nile's Clown unit and received an appropriate certificate declaring same, presented by Clown President Cliff Hayden. A Paper Crusade was inaugurated that year with Nile producing a four-page newspaper of Nile and Shrine news as part of a public awareness program. And, on a sad note, Aurie Thompson, P.P. 1963, known as Nile's "Mr. Shriner" passed away two days after his 90th birthday. Potentate Oliver dedicated the Fall Ceremonial to Aurie. PNSA in Portland was very successful for the band who won first place in all four of the categories in which it competed: Concert Band, German Band, Dixieland Band and Dance Band! And the Nile Car Club held a spectacular 5th Annual Car Show with 75 vehicles participating.

Apropos to Potentate Oliver's year, this was also the year of Dolly the Sheep, the world's first mammal to be cloned from an adult somatic cell. Scientists Ian Wilmut, Keith Campbell and others at the Roslin Institute near Edinburgh, Scotland used the nuclear transfer process to take a single cell from the mammary gland of an adult sheep to recreate the whole genetic makeup of the donor sheep. And since the cell originated from a mammary gland what better name for this historic sheep could be had than to be named after that buxom country western singer, Dolly Parton.

However, cloning would not be able to help the Nile membership count which was 4,449 at the end of the year.

1997 – Wayne Duke - No Challenge Too Great

Potentate Wayne Duke's year began with a strong slogan: No Challenge Too Great. By that he meant that Nile would have to rally to face the triple threat of declining membership, a shrinking financial base, and increased operating expenses which now included $42,000 per month payments on the golf course loan. Potentate Duke proposed several things to stem the tide of these threats, one of which was the hiring of a consultant to review Nile's food, beverage, and room rental policies. The consultant's report resulted in Nile taking over the food, beverage and room rental business and hiring the caterer, Steve Hofer, as a General Manager and employee of Nile Temple with Marlene Bell as Assistant Manager.

The Crown of Honor system was launched that year by Potentate Duke to give recognition by means of medallions, colored bars and jewels to those nobles who performed work for the temple, the units and/or for the hospitals. The Scimitar Room was renamed the Oasis and opened as a public restaurant. Largely through the efforts of Potentate Duke and Ed Fox, Director of Public Relations, an Ernest Borgnine Family Fun Nite was held on June 11. Noble Borgnine traveled from Beverly Hills, CA and, without charge to Nile, put on a great comedy show to help Nile celebrate the 75th Anniversary of the Shriners Hospitals and the 125th Anniversary of the Shrine. Noble Borgnine even made the trip to Seattle in his own motorhome which also provided him lodging while he was here. There was no charge for the show but Nile profited greatly from the sale of food and drink and the resulting publicity from the Borgnine appearance.

Potentate Wayne also initiated the idea and plan to sell bonds to pay off the indebtedness of the golf course expansion. This plan would be completed by succeeding potentates. And Potentate Duke was instrumental in obtaining Nile's Public Liquor license meaning that Nile was now one of the first facilities in the state to have both a public and a private license. The public license allowed for the sale of food and drinks via the ubiquitous cart on the golf course and turned out to be an important tool for raising revenue for Nile and its holding company.

Afifi Temple in Tacoma was the site of PNSA/PNSOBA and once again Nile units distinguished themselves by showing up in great numbers and winning more awards than any other participating temple. Grand Lodge, at its Annual Communication in June, finally approved the concept of One-Day Classes to become a Master Mason, two years after GM Milt Benson tried to make it happen. The first One-Day Class was scheduled for December 6 in Spokane and other One-Day Classes were scheduled for 1998 in various locations. And the Nile Family Picnic once again hosted the Washington DeMolay Auction.

1997 was also the year of another tragedy. On August 31, Princess Diana, and her boyfriend, Dodi Al-Fayed were killed in a high-speed car accident in Paris, France. The chauffeur, Henri Paul, and Fayed died at the scene. Diana died at a Paris hospital a few hours later. She had become the Princess of Wales when she married Prince Charles on July 29, 1981. However, they divorced in August 1996 on grounds of incompatibility. She left behind two sons, William, and Harry. An estimated 2.5 billion people watched her funeral procession on TV, the Internet or in person.

And that year comet Hale-Bopp passed close to the Earth after an absence of over 4,200 years. It was last seen in July, 2215 BC/BCE (Before the Common Era). It passed its perihelion on April 1, 1997 and was visible to most of the northern hemisphere for more than a year. For those who missed that awesome sight, it will return for your viewing pleasure in the year 4,385 AD/CE (Common Era), because its passage close to Jupiter's gravitational field shortened its orbital plane, thus making its return much sooner than expected.

Nile's net membership dropped down to 4,333.

1998 – Hans Lindquist - the Norwegian Solution – the International Space Station (ISS)

Potentate Hans Lindquist's biggest challenge was to refinance the bank loan for the golf course expansion. Five nobles had pledged $250,000 a piece to guarantee the six-year loan, but it became clear, after the first year of operation, that the holding company, which owned the golf course, would not generate enough revenue in five more years to pay off the loan. At the February stated meeting, the sale of debenture bonds in the amount of $1,500,000 paying 8.5% interest was approved by the nobility. This amount would pay off the remaining balance of the loan ($1,400,000) and provide some money for course improvements. The bonds would be sold in $5000 amounts. Approval for an exemption from the State Securities registration was obtained and approval from Imperial soon followed. The bonds would be retired over a 15-year period at the rate of $100,000 per year. Nile nobles immediately seized this opportunity both to help the Nile and to obtain a very lucrative investment. Thanks to the efforts of then Chief Rabban James O. Wood the program was completed, the loan paid off and interest payments on the bonds started on July 1 of that year.

In March a horde of Norwegians descended upon the Seattle area largely through the efforts of Peder Grambo of University Lodge #141. Potentate Hans immediately seized this opportunity to show his visiting countrymen some good old-fashioned Shrine hospitality. Scandinavian Night at Nile was a great success. The Sweet Adelines, the Nile Chanters and the combined male Norwegian Choruses all contributed to a splendid show for the visitors. The Nile parade season began a month earlier that year when Sultan Don Charles accepted an invitation for the Oriental Band to participate in the LaConner Tulip Festival parade which took place in mid-April. Oriental Band member Luke Long, who lived in LaConner, instigated this participation with a promise of a suitable feast if the band came.

On the distaff side, familiar names came to the helms of two of the ladies' organizations: Liz Seldon took over the Queen's crown of Hatasu Temple # 1 Daughters of the Nile (DON) and Helen Wilkinson assumed the High Priestess' white fez of Ahmes Court #41, Ladies Oriental Shrine (LOS). Sixty new nobles were created at the joint Scottish Rite Reunion/ Nile Ceremonial in the spring. And at PNSA in Boise, Nile won the Overall Grand Trophy again. The Band obtained four first place and one second place trophies. The Oriental Band came in second in PNSOBA competition, but first in parade. The Director's Staff came in second in competition and other units won awards in their areas, including the Legion of Honor Flag unit in competition, the Shurtah for their Paddy Wagon, the Mini Bikes in competition and the Greeters for their People Mover. Six nobles made the last known Nile pilgrimage to the Orient that year: Potentate Hans, John Gronlund, Rod Grosso, Bob Taylor, Don Charles and Dr. John Richardson, Nile Director of the screening clinics. Sixty-one new nobles were created at their stops in Hong Kong, Taipei, and Manila. And Nile's name was voted to be changed to Nile Shriners.

However, the most interesting event that occurred that year was the beginning of construction of the International Space Station (ISS). Conceived as an internationally developed research facility after several nations' individual space lab projects fell by the wayside, construction began in Low Earth Orbit in 1998. The first module of the ISS was the Russian Zarya launched on a Russian Proton rocket. Modules later added to Zarya include the American Freedom, the European Columbus, the Japanese Kibo, and the Russian Mir. These modules are regularly served by Russian rockets and the United States Space Shuttle. ISS is a research laboratory with a microgravity environment that allows experiments to be conducted in several sciences. The station orbits in a near circular orbit at an altitude of between 187 and 194 nautical miles above the Earth and travels at a velocity of 17,227 mph. It completes 15.7 orbits every 24 hours and is the largest artificial object in the sky that can be seen with the naked eye. Completion of the ISS has now been accomplished and it has served as both a very productive space laboratory and a model for international cooperation.

Meanwhile, the net membership count at Nile orbited down to 4,080.

1999 – James O. Wood - Walking Horse Wood – Y2K

Potentate James O. Wood's year was marked by the trademark Tennessee Walking Horse that he so proudly raised on his acreage south of Renton (he also raised American Roller pigeons and peafowl). Jerry Henning took over as treasurer from Marion Holstine and Nile's December election for Oriental Guide was thrown out by Imperial due to irregularities in the voting (more ballots cast than the number of nobles eligible to vote) and the position declared vacant. Don Pells won the subsequent election at the February stated meeting. The Marshal that year with the big "Are You Ready To Rumble" voice was none other than Noble Richard Kovak. Al "Bubba" Hendricks took over as Director of the Chanters and through the efforts of Noble Captain Ken Knight and the Drum and Bugle Corps a new public address system was purchased and installed. However, the sound system electronic equipment would later be stolen by unknown persons. Email came to Nile that year with the www.nileshrine.org website and the signature nileshrine.org appellation for Nile office staff. In the ladies' organizations, Charlotte Smith took over as High Priestess for Ahmes Court LOS. and Mary Jo Tutino took over the position of Queen at Hatasu Temple #1 D.O.N.

The PNSA/PNSOBA in Calgary in mid-August that year did not yield another bumper crop of trophies for Nile units. The Band, faced with numerous losses in its ranks via the Black Camel and demits was not able to compete. However, the Legion of Honor took first place in its competition. The Oriental Band took second place at PNSOBA (finishing 30 seconds short of the required time to perform cost them first place), although the band Director, Jim Hart, won the Best Director award. 1999 marked the loss of the Dis-Nay Characters (a unit composed of nobles dressed in Disney-like character costumes and performing for the kids at picnics, parades and in the hospitals). Hassles from the Disney lawyers and lack of interest apparently contributed to the demise of this long running unit. The potentate's trip to Branson (The Little Nashville of the West) was great fun and DeMolay celebrated its 80th year as the premier organization for young men to become better persons and leaders. Bob Tindall, Nile's first golf pro, passed away at the age of 82. He helped design Nile's original; course and served as its pro for 10 years from the course's opening in May, 1968. Jim Hart resigned as Recorder (Mike Lane would take over for two years and then Jim would be back from 2002-2007). To prevent another election debacle, Potentate Wood appointed Walt Odom, P.P. as election marshal and official ballot counter for the December election. Everything went well and Illustrious Sir Walt has been performing that duty ever since that time.

Scotsmen will cherish this year because the first meeting of an autonomous Scottish Parliament since the Acts of Union of 1707 occurred on May 12. Lance Armstrong wins the first of his seven Tour De France cycling victories on July 25. And on October 12, the world population reaches the 6 billion mark. But the weirdest thing that happened during the year was the Year 2000 problem (sometimes known as the Y2K bug). It arose as a result of the digital and non-digital use of two-digit year designations instead of a four-digit year. Space on computers was saved and many banks and computerized data storage system companies saved millions of dollars by using only a two-digit year designation. The problem was expected to occur when the millennium rolled over from 99 to 00. You would not be able to tell which century was being designated and there was supposed to be endless confusion with computers ceasing to process bank transactions and whole data storage systems breaking down.

Although recognized as early as 1958 by Bill Berners, little attention was given to this phenomenon until the last years of the 1990's. Then, security vendors, fix it geeks and the media got on the bandwagon to proclaim a coming digital Armageddon. Hundreds of millions of dollars were spent to "prepare" for the digital doom of the year 2000. However, when the clocks finally rolled over at midnight on January 1, 2000 very little happened. The second coming of the Dark Ages became the Yawn of a New Millennium. Many have questioned the overstatement of the problem and media's role in this scaremongering episode. Yet, a lot of folks made a lot of money for a fix of an essentially non-significant and perhaps non-existent problem. The Y2K "bug" was bogus.

Despite everyone's best intentions and earnest efforts, the net membership tally dropped below 4000 to 3,810.

Many other events and special happenings occurred during the decade of Nile's 1990s – too many to be chronicled here. Membership recruiting continued to be a priority, yet as seen above the declines kept coming, dropping net membership below the 4000 mark by the end of 1999. And the Bill Clinton years passed by with Nile surviving them. However, on the horizon, loomed the fallout from the big media scare over the supposed Y2000 computer meltdown, a knockdown drag-out fight between Al Gore and George W. Bush in the 2000 national elections, and the prospect of another Gulf War as terrorism reared its ugly head internationally. The biggest horror stories would come both early and late during the first decade of the 2000s and the story of the nation's recovery from those disasters are ones that bear retelling. But you will have to wait for the stories of the 2000s to be told. Suggestions have been made to devote this column in future issues to specific groups, units, persons, or topics important to Nile's development and these subjects may be explored before the History of Nile Project delves into the most recent history of Nile. Other the other hand, if readers would like to see the 2000's written up in Smile with Nile right away, please email or call the Nile office or the author.

Topics to be covered in the Incredible Oughts chapters include the dot. com bubble burst, the September 11, 2001 terrorist bombings, the many natural disasters, the Great Recession, and the Great Subsidies.

Chapter Eleven

THE INCREDIBLE OUGHTS

What I have termed the Incredible Oughts, the years 2000 to 2009, marked not only the turn of another century, but the turn of a millennium. Although there still may be some continuing discussion about the proper name for this decade, the name Oughts was selected here because many of our senior members and their ladies still affectionately refer to the first decade of the 1900s as "the Oughts" and what has well and timely served our seniors is good measure for their juniors. Proper pronunciation of the Oughts, though, should be "20 -oh-one," etc., not "two thousand one." The latter term was a movie title. Nevertheless, for the edification of our younger readers I will include plenty of references to the 2000s

This decade has received both good and bad reports. The triumphs achieved in electronics, robotics, communication devices, scientific exploration, music, and education have been said by some to have been offset by tremendous failures in economics, politics, social integration, financial deregulation, and relentless warfare.

Nevertheless, the decade of 2000-2009 contains some of the most incredible events ever to take place in human history. Consider the 9/11/2001 disaster, the War on Terror, the 2004 tsunami, the war in Afghanistan, Hurricane Katrina, the Great Recession of 2008-10, and the election of the first president of African-American heritage and you will marvel at how

Americans held their wits and pocket books together during this decade of demonic dilemmas.

At Nile, Shriners and their ladies continued their great charitable venture on behalf of the Shriners Children's Hospitals even when economic times became tough in the later years of the decade. The most important event affecting the Shrine in general occurred in 2009 when a cabal at Imperial sought to close six of the hospitals due to falling revenues and alleged lack of usage. How this challenge to the eight-decade old Shriners Children's Hospital system was resolved is a remarkable story in itself that will be told later in this series. Here then is the first half of the Incredible Oughts.

2000 – Gerald L." Jerry" Seldon – The Y2K Crisis Passes

Potentate Jerry began his year with some new faces on the elected divan. In addition to the new Oriental Guide, Don Cameron, Mike Lane assumed the post of Recorder and Jerry Henning took over from Marion Holstine as Treasurer. Potentate Jerry's theme was Recruitment, Retention, and Restoration. Two events that year would coincide to assist recruitment. Imperial Shrine at its 126th Imperial Session in Boston voted to eliminate the requirement that a Master Mason be a member of either the Scottish or York Rites before they could become a Shriner. As of August 2, 2000, Master Masons could now petition directly to a temple to become a noble. And on November 11 in Hoquiam, Washington, Grand Lodge sponsored a one-day Master Mason conferral class. Now a man, having petitioned and been accepted for candidacy by a lodge in the State of Washington, could obtain all three degrees, Entered Apprentice, Fellowcraft, and Master Mason in the course of one long day instead of the usual three or more months.

Potentate Jerry also inaugurated the Dime A Day, or DAD, fund to benefit the Nile Temple Building and Maintenance Fund. Nobles and their ladies were encouraged to contribute a "dime a day" or $36.60 a year to the fund. Mason jars were placed on each dining table at stated meetings to collect the dimes. He authorized the formation of a Nile Sword Team and held a Ceremonial on June 2 in honor of Lionel "Wally" Wallace, the founder of the Dis-Nay Characters (he played Donald Duck).

Coincidentally, Wally's passing in 1999 spelled the end of the Dis-Nay Characters as a Nile unit. A successful trip to Billings for PNSA netted several awards for Nile's units, including the usual PNSOBA trophies to the Oriental Band, but not enough to take away the Overall Trophy from the defending home town temple, Al Bedoo.

But, as presaged in the intro to this decade, tumultuous events were starting to occur. The dot.com bust that year started the mini-depression of 2000-2002. Prior to that, the term dot.com bubble was used to describe the rise of numerous companies specifically geared to merchandising and advertising via the Internet. The coincidence of rapidly rising stock prices and low interest rates during the late 1990's and the speculative entrepreneurship of get rich quick investors spiked the NASDAQ Index to an all-time high of 5,132.52 on March 10, 2000. Many of these e-companies operated at a loss to build market share while continuing to run up huge operating costs and debt. The Federal Reserve raised interest rates six times between late 1999 and March 2000. On Monday, March 13, a huge selloff occurred which dropped the NASDAQ into a downward tailspin. Many e-companies never recovered (Amazon and Google being two major exceptions) and dot.com company furniture and luxury automobile fire sales soon became common. There were also numerous reports of now unemployed programmers and systems analysts going back to school to become accountants, lawyers, or plumbers.

Yet, despite the fertile environment for membership, Nile's net tally fell to 3,573.

2001 – Carl L. Alexander – Keeping PACE in the 21st Century

Potentate Carl's theme that year was Positive Attitudes Change Everything (PACE). The big fund raiser that year, spearheaded by Men's Golf Club President Ben Webb, was the inaugural "Nile Temple Ball Drop." Anyone could "buy" a golf ball for $5. That ball would have a number on it corresponding to the purchaser's entry blank number. On August 24th at precisely 3:45 PM a helicopter from Snohomish Flying Service arrived, hovered over the 18th green and dropped 1,753 golf balls onto the green. The ball closest to the pin won $1000 for its purchaser. A Golf Day Tournament was held in conjunction with the Ball Drop with over 100 golfers participating.

Ceremonials that year included a Spring Ceremonial on June 9 in memory of Past Potentate (1970) Walter M. Woodburn who had passed away in 1996 at the age of 93, and a Joint Ceremonial with Afifi Temple on December 1. The summer PNSA in Billings, Montana proved to be a rousing success for Nile units. Nile's Legion of Honor Drill Team under Captain Walter Lain won Firsts for Marching unit Competition and Parade Best Marching unit. The Director's Staff took home second place for their Second Section skit and the Sword Team received second place for their drill team work. But the big winner was the Oriental Band which, despite Sultan Eric Busby's persistent misdirections, won four first-place awards at PNSOBA – Medium Band, Overall Band, Best Parade Band and Best Director (Jim Hart). And on October 14, a huge auction to benefit the Order of DeMolay was staged with Grand Master Robert Van Zee and his Grand Lodge officers in attendance. The auctioneer was Bob Blackburn, the voice of the Supersonics basketball team, who was ably assisted by Greg Legaris, popular anchor at TV station KIRO Channel 7.

Yet despite the good fortune at Nile, a somber tone would soon overtake the country after the tragic events of September 11 took place. These were a series of coordinated terrorist attacks by a group known as al-Qaeda. On that morning, 19 hijackers took over four commercial jet airliners in flight over the United States The hijackers, who had forced their way into the cockpits of the jets and took over the controls of the planes, intentionally crashed two of the airliners into the Twin Towers of the World Trade Center in New York City. Another airliner was crashed into the side of the Pentagon Building in Arlington, Virginia. A fourth jetliner was headed for the United States Capitol Building when the passengers stood up in revolt and overpowered the hijackers with the result that the jet crashed in a field near Shanksville, Pennsylvania. In all, there were 2,976 victims and 19 hijackers killed in these attacks. Another 6000 people were injured. Burning out of control with hundreds of gallons of jet fuel fueling the fires, both Twin Towers collapsed to the ground. A third office building in the World Trade Center (WTC) complex was so damaged that it eventually had to be razed. In later years, the destroyed buildings in what came to dubbed "Ground Zero" would be replaced by a new complex of buildings which would include Freedom Tower, the tallest building in the western hemisphere and the seventh tallest building in the world.

Although the victims inside the WTC office buildings and the Pentagon were completely taken by surprise, the passengers on the jetliner that crashed in Pennsylvania knew what they were up against. Rather than sit in their seats as doomed voyagers, several of the passengers, by a series of signals to each other, charged the hijackers at the command of "Let's Roll" from the one of passengers. They fought their way into the cockpit and in the ensuing fight to steer the jet liner away from populated areas, the jet crashed in an open field killing all on board.

In response, the United States launched the War on Terrorism on October 7 and later invaded Afghanistan to punish the Taliban which had given aid and sanctuary to the al-Qaeda masterminds behind the 9/11 attacks, namely Osama bin Laden and his chieftains.

At Nile, Potentate Carl offered his condolences on behalf of Nile Shriners and their ladies to the American people over this tragedy with these words in the October issue of Smile with Nile: "This is a very difficult time for the entire nation; one that will take a long time to heal. We will always remember the day it happened and never get over the devastation caused by these terrorist acts."

Recently elected Imperial Potentate Kenny Smith (Gizeh Temple) added:

> Shriners Hospitals share the nation's grief and are ready to do anything we can to help...Shriners Hospitals are sending medical teams to assist in helping the victims, and our hospitals are standing by in a state of readiness awaiting any request for assistance.

On November 9, Nile lost Noble Peter F. Woeck (P.P. 1982). Besides his family, Pete's pride and joy was his 85-foot yacht, the Sea Star, on which for many years he hosted the divan, Nile's bands, and other guests during Seattle's Opening Day of boating season in May on the Montlake Cut.

At the end of the year, Nile's membership count stood at 3,336.

2002 – L.R. "Dick" Wilkinson – Flying the Magic Carpet

Potentate Dick, a rug (carpet) merchant for many years, is also a private pilot and loved flying his Beechcraft Bonanza. Having been Commander of the Nile Flying Patrol, he was still active in the unit and flying every week when he became potentate. Grounded during his term at Nile, his theme in 2002 was "One for One" meaning that every member of Nile should bring in one new member. That year, Jim Hart, Jr. returned as Recorder. The Second Annual Ball Drop occurred on Sunday, July 21. In Ohio, a statewide One-Day Class was held across 10 Ohio cities resulting in the largest one-day initiation of new Master Masons in history, 8,300! At Nile an All Masonic Family Night on July 17 brought out Grand Master Jimmie Reid and sparkling entertainment by the Masonic Youth groups.

The Shrine Circus (Gatti Productions) was back as a temple fundraiser after an absence of several years. And ceremonials were held on June 1 honoring Noble George Jurgich (P.P. 1991) (PGM 1996-7) who passed away on March 13, 2002, and on December 14 honoring Noble Kenny Grimes (P.P. 1972) (still living). With Nile hosting the 2003 PNSA Potentate Dick appointed Gerry Seldon (P.P. 2000) as Director General to honcho this event.

But the most astounding Nile event of 2002 was the Oriental Band's capture of the World Championship Title for Oriental bands at the 2002 Imperial Session in Vancouver, B.C. Nile's Oriental Band won three trophies, Best Band in their class, and Best Parade Band, the combination of which made them the Best Overall Band. And this feat was achieved in the face of competition from the best bands from all over North America.

On the national and international fronts, the 2002 Winter Olympics were successfully held in Salt Lake City, Utah, the United States launched Operation Anaconda in March to clean out the Taliban rebels in the Shahi-Kot Valley in Afghanistan, and the dot.com bubble bust reached its nadir when the Dow Jones Average fell below 7,200 in October.

Nile's membership total ended 2002 at 3,127.

2003 – Dick Wilkinson Again – "You Are the Key"

At the end of 2002, Potentate Dick stood for reelection and was elected Potentate for 2003. His theme that year was "You Are the Key" meaning that each individual Shrine noble holds the key to the success of the Shrine and the Nile Shrine Center in particular. Dick Sardeson was elected Oriental Guide and Don Moore was elected Trustee to take Dick Sardeson's place on the Board of Trustees.

Potentate Dick would continue the fine work he started for Nile the previous year. Successful events included his "Midnight in the Oasis"

Ball on April 12, the June 7 ceremonial honoring Noble Ed B. Schack (passed April 30, 2003), and the Fall Ceremonial on December 13 honoring Noble Marion R. Holstine, both of which ceremonials brought in many new nobles. The 2003 PNSA was hosted by Nile and held at the Howard Johnson's Hotel in in Everett on August 13-16. It was a qualified success. Several temples were not able to send their full complement of units and usual attendees. Nevertheless, under Director General Seldon's steady hand the many nobles and their ladies who attended were treated to great Nile hospitality. Besides the usual hotel activities there was a Shrine Parade in Everett. There were tours of the Boeing 747 plant, the Everett Naval Facility, the Tulalip casino, and the Pike place market. The Third Annual Ball Drop took place on August 15 as part of PNSA and was another financial success. Nile's units won several awards, in particular, the Clown unit and the Oriental Band. Jerry Seldon Jr. (Stamps), Dan Pelletier (L'Oscar) and Dean Smith (Dazzle) all placed high in their respective clown competition categories. The Oriental Band outdid its usual self and won first-place trophies for Best Band Fantasy Competition, Best Oriental Band Float, Best Overall and Best Director (Jim Hart) at PNSOBA. And in a truly stunning upset, Ray Colby and Parker Johnston topped the competition for Best Duet.

2003 was also the Year of the Shrine Mason, beginning on June 1. It was Imperial Shrine's stated goal of bringing in 20,000 new nobles in a year's time. Much of the impetus was generated by Ohio's One-Day Class of Masonry which brought in 8,000 new Masons in one day. Unfortunately, neither Imperial's nor Nile's membership goals were able to be met.

Nationally and internationally, several unusual events occurred which make 2003 additionally memorable. On January 24, the Department of Homeland Security, a Cabinet level response to the September 11, 2001 tragedy, begins operation. Syracuse wins the NCAA Basketball Championship in April 7. The first horse to be cloned, Prometea, is born in Italy on May 28. On June 22, the largest hailstone ever recorded falls in Aurora, Nebraska (7" diameter; 18.75" circumference). Governor of California, Gray Davis, is recalled by voters on October 7 who then vote in Arnold (The Terminator) Schwarzenegger as the new governor. On October 15, the Staten Island ferry inexplicably crashes into a pier killing 11 people. October 24 marked the last flight of the Concorde jet thus ending supersonic jet travel. And on November 5, Gary Ridgeway, the Green River Killer, finally confesses to killing 48 women in the South Puget Sound area.

But the incident that wrenched the hearts of all Americans was the loss of the Space Shuttle Columbia on February 1. The shuttle disintegrated shortly after reentry into the Earth's atmosphere resulting in the deaths of all seven crew members aboard. The incident has been traced to the detachment of a large piece of foam insulation which broke off from the exterior of the shuttle's main propellant tank during launch which then struck the leading edge of the left wing damaging the shuttle's thermal protection system (TPS). The TPS was designed to protect the shuttle from the extremely hot temperatures generated during reentry. Although NASA engineers suspected that some damage to the TPS had occurred during launch, NASA managers limited the in-flight investigation on the rationale that nothing could be done about it with the shuttle in orbit. However, during reentry, the damaged area on the wing quickly allowed hot gases to penetrate the skin of the wing and to destroy the internal wing structure. The resulting crash debris was scattered across almost 1500 miles in the states of Texas, Louisiana, and Arkansas. After the disaster, further shuttle flights were halted for two years and the remaining construction of the ISS was also put on hold. Transport to and from and the reprovisioning of the ISS was left to Russian Federal Space Agency shuttles.

The Nile membership net total was 2,916 at the end of 2003.

2004 – Donald R. Cameron – Walk The Talk – Indian Ocean Tsunamis

Potentate Don won his spurs as a Seattle Police homicide detective finishing his illustrious police career as Detective Sergeant in 1999 when he retired from the Seattle Police Department. His slogan in 2004 was Walk the Talk, meaning put your actions where they can do tangible good instead of just talking about what you would do or what should be done.

That same year Merle Claflin came onto the divan as Treasurer taking over from Gerald B. Henning and Richard Kovak was elected the new Oriental Guide.

The two big fundraisers for 2004 were the Patti Gatti Circus and the Shrine Rodeo, June 25-27. The rodeo was part of the Professional Rodeo Circuit Association (PRCA) and attracted the top riders and ropers from all over the country to the Everett Events Center. However, despite a strong effort from the nobility and their ladies, the circus managed only a small positive return and the rodeo was less successful. Nevertheless, both ventures had the effect of promoting Nile Shrine Center in the public's eye and of giving nobles and their ladies a chance to work and play together in a common effort.

On April 14, Imperial Potentate Burt Oien visited Nile for the stated meeting and popular Scandinavian comedian Stan Boreson returned for a comedy show. Ceremonials were held on June 5, honoring P.P. Harry Grove and on December 4, honoring Noble Wally Brown. More than 20 candidates were brought in at each of these ceremonials.

As usual, the Nile Oriental Band brought good news back to Nile by winning Best Band in the large band category, Best Parade Float, Best Director (Jim Hart) and Best Overall Band at PNSOBA held in Kamloops, B. C. in conjunction with PNSA. Another special award, reflecting on Nile, was the presentation to Nile Noble Charles F. Deignan of the Order of the Rising Sun medal by Prime Minister Junichiro Kunizumi. The medal, the highest award in Japan to a civilian, was given for his work as the representative in Japan for Radio Spectrum Management, a builder of telecommunications systems in Japan. And the Legion of Honor and its Drill Team acquired a retired army vehicle which would be decorated with flags and be successfully used thereafter at all of the parades in which they participated.

The Nile Picnic held on July 18 was another huge success with the Dunk the Divan and the Egg Toss being two of the most popular events. And on June 25, the Pacific NW Prostate Cancer Institute held its annual convention at Nile hosted by the University of Washington School of Medicine. It was open to the public who could ask questions of leading prostate cancer researchers.

Nationally, Facebook (Mark Zuckerberg) was founded on February 4, the National World War II memorial was dedicated in Washington, D. C. on May 29, and groundbreaking for the new Freedom Tower at Ground Zero in New York City took place on July 4. But the event that shocked the world came on December 26 when an earthquake measuring between 9.1 and 9.3 on the Richter Scale occurred in the Indian Ocean just off the west coast of Sumatra. That earthquake and its aftershocks triggered a series of tsunamis which eventually killed over 200,000 people. The earthquake was the third largest ever recorded on a seismograph and had the longest duration of faulting (8 minutes) ever observed. It caused the whole Earth to vibrate a full centimeter. The energy released across the Earth's surface alone was the equivalent of 26.3 megatons of trinitrotoluene (TNT) or over 1500 times the equivalent energy of the Hiroshima atomic bomb.

Yet it was the resulting tsunamis that caused most of the damage and deaths. The tsunamis consisted of a succession of waves and recessions that took place over a period of several hours. In some places, the tsunami reached a height of between 80 and 100 feet and traveled inland for as much a mile. A reliable United States Geological Survey confirmed a death toll of 227,898 people with several thousand still missing or unaccounted.

Nile units and clubs contributed heavily to the humanitarian relief aid effort as did Imperial Shrine and other Shrine centers. Total humanitarian aid to the stricken countries amounted to more than $7 billion worldwide.

Net Nile noble membership was 2,627 at year's end.

In the next issue, the History of Nile will survey the rest of the Incredible Oughts, discuss the Shriners Children's Hospital scare, and expose the underpinnings of the Great Recession of 2008-10 and the Great Stimulus Package of 2009.

THE INCREDIBLE OUGHTS

The remainder of the Incredible Oughts brought about some of the greatest changes in the economy, living standards, lifestyles, and national moods since the Great Depression years of 1929 - 1940. Barack Hussein Obama II was elected the 44th President of the United States in November, 2008. He was inaugurated into office in February 2009 becoming the first African-American to hold that office. International terrorism continued to be the world's greatest threat closely followed by the great economic crisis of 2007-2010. The downturn in the economy resulted in another threat to Shriners – the loss of six of their beloved hospitals because of a lack of adequate funding. Natural and man-made disasters also seemed to plague the late 2000s. Hurricanes Katrina (2005), Rita (2005) and Ike (2008) as well as Cyclone Nargis (2008) claimed thousands of lives and wrecked untold billions of dollars of property damage. The Deepwater Horizon oil spill and methane release into the atmosphere from melting Antarctic ice added to the fears of many. So many wars, threats of war, economic crises, and natural and man-made disasters caused Time Magazine to declare this decade as possibly the "Worst Decade Ever." Nevertheless, the resolve of Nile's nobles and their ladies in the face of severe economic hardship and personal tragedy to persevere in their beloved Shrine center activities and in their cherished philanthropy, the Shriners Children's Hospitals, remains an everlasting tribute and testament to their generous spirit and loving nature. Here then are the rest of the Incredible Oughts.

2005 – George H. Wolleben – Kids Are Us

Potentate George, a veteran of several Nile units, in particular the Oriental Band, came to Nile with a wealth of business experience. As an insurance executive, restaurant owner and salvage broker, he came up with a business plan, published in the March issue of Smile with Nile, to keep Nile solvent and out of debt. He proposed changes in the way Nile's business operations were conducted and a plan to buy out the expensive bonds that had been issued to pay for the expansion of the golf course. To avoid a potential financial loss, the proposed Rodeo was canceled that year due to lack of sufficient sponsorship from PRCA sponsors, but the Nile Shriners/Patti Gatti Circus went forward to the delight of attendees making a small profit.

Another effort by Potentate George to secure the financial future of Nile almost came into existence. Nile had a preliminary agreement with Seattle Valley of Scottish Rite to sell them two acres of surplus land to build a new Scottish Rite Center on the Nile grounds. However, disagreements over site location, finances, access problems and opposition from other quarters resulted in a cancelation of the deal. Nevertheless, Potentate George's efforts and business acumen resulted in a year- end profit for Nile.

A $52 Raffle Ticket fundraiser sale inspired by the Oriental Band provided Nile some extra income, and membership profited from a successful Spring Ceremonial on June 4 in honor of Noble George E. Minnick, who passed away that year. The Oriental Band went to Imperial Session in Baltimore, Maryland in July with the divan and came away with first places in Best Parade Performance and Best in Class for Large Oriental Bands. PNSA in Edmonton, Alberta in August was a slightly different story. Al Shamal walked away with most of the awards, including best overall, amid a suspicion of "hometowning." Yet, Nile's nobles and ladies enjoyed themselves in the Oil Capital of Canada.

Potentate George and lady Lora hosted several interesting events that year, including A Classy Affair Potentate's Ball, the annual picnic, lady

Lora's Magic of Laughter Luncheon, their Western Caribbean Cruise, and the delightful Christmas Moments Holiday Ball.

Other nobles and units to distinguish themselves that year included Noble Steve Wilt who became Grand Assembly Dad for The Order of Rainbow Girls of Washington and Idaho, the Olympic Peninsula Shrine Club for its charitable fundraising events and Safety Fairs in the Sequim area, the various units who sponsored Shrine Hospital "bus tails," and Nile's High Priest and Prophet Richard Kovak who gave a stirring presentation of Albert Pike at the Seattle Scottish Rite Friends Night.

Murial V. Knapp of Seattle's own Hatasu Temple No. 1 was elected Supreme Princess Badoura at the 89th Supreme Session of Daughters of the Nile held in Lexington, Kentucky in June. And Ahmes Court No. 41, under the capable leadership of High Priestess Helen Wilkinson, had a record turnout of 53 members and seven performing units at the Western Area Organized unit meet in Medford, Oregon.

But the event that pulled at the heartstrings of Nile's nobles and ladies that year was the devastating effects of Hurricane Katrina which struck the Gulf Coast in late August. The eye of that Category 3 storm passed just east of New Orleans on August 29. However, the resulting wind and tide surges created more than 50 breaks in the drainage canal levees around New Orleans making it the worst engineering disaster in United States history. On August 31st, over 80% of New Orleans was flooded and some parts of the city sustained water levels 15 feet deep. Local, state, and federal officials could not cope with the mass evacuation (90% of the city population) and the whole area was immediately declared a national disaster area by President Bush making Federal Emergency Management Aid (FEMA) funds available. Since the original levee system had been expanded by the Army Corps of Engineers in 1965, a Congressional inquiry was held into the causes of failure of this federally built flood protection system. As of this date, studies disagree on causation, but the finger of fault has variously been pointed at the Orleans Levee Board, the Corps of Engineers, and the quality of work of private local contractors.

Yet, without regard to blame, Nile's nobles and their ladies responded generously to the Katrina relief effort needed to sustain those were dispossessed of their homes, their livelihoods, and their lives. As mentioned above, the Olympic Shrine Club did an outstanding job of raising funds for Katrina relief. Numerous other units, clubs and individuals contributed money, canned goods, and clothing to the relief effort.

At the end of the year, Nile's net membership stood at 2, 627.

2006 – Daryl Orseth – International Shrine Membership Year

Potentate Orseth's primary focus this year was membership. The International Shrine Membership year, which actually started in July, 2005, was into full swing in 2006. A hard push by Potentate Daryl resulted in 34 new nobles being created at the Spring Ceremonial on June 3, and later in the year, the restoration of dozens of nobles, many of them restored due to direct contact by the Potentate himself. On October 21, the full ritual ceremonial cast traveled with Potentate Daryl to Bremerton to conduct a ceremonial for nine candidates sponsored by the Kitsap Shrine Club (Noble Al Dillan, Director). The Fall Ceremonial on December 2, in honor of Past Potentate Howard S. Olsen brought in several more new nobles.

But there were several other very interesting events that year, hosted by Potentate Daryl and lady Pat, which caught the fancy of Nile nobles and their ladies. A Magic of the Night Spring Ball, a Western Night on July 22 featuring a poker tournament, and the Nile Picnic the following day featuring a Dunk the Divan event drew many nobles and ladies. But the most entertaining event of the year had to be the Christmas Luau and Concert on December 9 featuring the Langley Ukulele Band from Langley, B.C. This ukulele band, composed mostly of high school teenagers, put on a terrific show, and demonstrated that ukuleles could play Big Band music, classical music, rock/pop music and Sousa marches just as well as traditional Hawaiian melodies. Other events hosted by the Potentate and lady Pat were the trip to visit the Portland Shriners Hospital on June 15 and their Potentate's Trip to the Hawaiian Islands.

On May 13, Grand Lodge hosted a One-Day Master Mason Conferral Class at the Masonic Retirement Home in Des Moines, cosponsored by Nile and Afifi Temples. And on May 26, the All Masonic Night at Nile was a great success with Grand Master Most Worshipful Brother Al Jorgenson, a Nile noble, as the principal speaker. PNSA in Great Falls, Montana on August 10-12 did not yield as many awards to Nile units as usual. But the Oriental Band at PNSOBA took first place in Big Band competition and second place overall. Jim Hart, the OB Director, tied for Best Director and the Legion of Honor Flag team took second place for its performance in the parade.

In national and international news this year, the Nintendo Wii video game system is introduced, and Pluto (the planet not the dog), after 76 years as the "ninth" planet, is demoted to "dwarf planet" status. Our solar system is now defined as having eight planets and six or more dwarf planets which reside in the Kuiper belt, a band of ice/dirt objects circling the Sun just outside of Neptune's orbit. North Korea performs its first successful nuclear test on October 9 and the narcissism of the American nation becomes front page news when Time Magazine designates "You" as the 2006 Person of the Year.

Again, despite everyone's best intentions and efforts, Nile's net membership falls to 2, 493 at the end of 2006.

2007 – Richard E. Sardeson – Full Speed for Kids

Potentate Dick, a retired United States Coast Guard Captain, championed fundraising for the Shriners Children's' Hospitals as well as focusing on membership. His Waking Thoughts columns this year and over the past few years in Smile with Nile issues were inspiring as well as informative as he strove to highlight and examine the concerns facing Shrine Masonry and Nile Shriners in particular. Nevertheless, he and lady Diane found time to host and sponsor many exciting events, including their Guys and Dolls Potentate's Ball on March 24, their trip to the Copper Canyon of Northern Mexico in late October, and the Silver Bells Holiday Ball on December 8 where Potentate Dick and lady Diane hosted the bar during the social hour preceding the dinner and entertainment.

The highlight of the year, though, may have been Family Night on May 9 which featured Megan Johnson, Nile's special friend from Federal Way, who was a patient at the Portland Shriners Hospital for many years and who became a terrific booster and spokesperson for Nile and the Shrine in general. Also, that night, Seattle baseball legend Edgar Martinez was a special guest at Nile and gave an inspirational talk as well as many autographs. A magician rounded out the special guests.

Ceremonials on June 9 and December 1 brought in dozens of new nobles. The $52 raffle took its last turn as a fundraiser because of diminishing returns. The annual picnic on July 22 was another well attended success with the Dunk the Divan tank in operation again. PNSA in Cheyenne, Wyoming during May 31-June 2 was notable for the potentate was able, through Noble Jerry Smith, to hire a flatbed semi to transport three of Nile's parade vehicles to Cheyenne, including the Shurtah Paddy Wagon, the Legion of Honor military vehicle and the Nile Temple Calliope. Nile's Oriental Band again won its share of first place awards at PNSOBA and the Shurtah Paddy Wagon took home first place as "Best Ambulance."

On March 31 a Grand Lodge One-Day Master Mason Conferral Class was held in Tacoma and garnered many new Masons. And, at Imperial Session in Anaheim, CA on July 4, it was announced that a Professional Golf Association (PGA) accredited golf tournament, known as the Fryes. com Open would be a fundraiser for the Shriners Childrens Hospitals. After that initial year, it became the Justin Timberlake Open when that popular celebrity signed on with Shriners Childrens Hospitals to be their special representative and to put his name on the golf tournament fund raiser. It is now known as the Shriners Hospitals for Children Open and is played annually in Las Vegas, Nevada.

Another interesting note is that Noble Don Moore, editor of Smile with Nile had changed the publication software for that newspaper from PageMaker to InFocus that year. That new software made it much easier to electronically typeset columns and resulted in a stunning February 2007 issue which featured beautiful color photos of the divan and their ladies.

But 2007 took a terrible toll on past potentates of Nile claiming Howard S. Olsen (P.P. 1990) in January, Don Cameron (P.P. 2004) in April and Darryl Orseth (P.P. 2006) in December.

On the national scene, although no one really knew it yet, the economic boom bubble of the mid-2000s had burst and the start of the Great Recession began in December 2007, as calculated by the United States National Bureau of Economic Research. It was triggered by the emergence in late 2007 of sub-prime lending losses sustained by many over lending banks. Internationally, Hamas took over sole control of the entire Gaza Strip while Fatah retained control over the West Bank. This essentially divided the Palestinian Authority into two competing groups making the quest for a distinct Palestinian homeland much more difficult. Violence between the two groups broke out and had to be quelled by Israeli intervention.

At the end of 2007, Nile's net membership stood at 2385.

2008 – Richard M. Kovak – Bring Back The Glory

As an attorney, an historian, and an actor portraying historical characters, Potentate Kovak well realized the advantage of remembering the glory of the past to help prepare for the future. His History of Nile columns in 2007 and 2008 showed who Nile nobles and their ladies were and what they had accomplished in the past. Using this as motivation he sought to help present members strive to Bring Back the Glory to Nile.

Taking office that year with Potentate Kovak was Richard "Dick" Syson as the new Recorder, who took over from Jim Hart, an 11 year veteran in that position. Dick would prove to be a valuable aide to the potentate when they both sought and obtained a variance from the City of Mountlake Terrace to build a new digital sign board to be placed at Nile's front entrance. The City of Mountlake Terrace (CMT) had classified the Nile property as recreational and under the City Sign Code no electronic signs were allowed in these areas. However, the City quickly recognized Nile's value to the City as both a good neighbor and a good attraction for visitors to the City and the CMT Hearing Board had no problem granting the variance. An anecdote from that hearing involves the sole member of the public who showed up at the public hearing to comment on the proposed sign. He claimed to be a neighbor representing "hundreds of clients." It turns out he was the Manager of Holyrood Cemetery from across the street and his only comment was: "Why didn't you people do this sooner to let everyone know who you are. You folks are such a great organization. People would mistakenly drive into your property thinking that it was part of the cemetery grounds."

Potentate Kovak and his lady Carol hosted A Murder Mystery Dinner which replaced the usual staid ball that year and was very well received by the attendees. Ceremonials were held on July 12 in honor of departed Past Potentate Don Cameron and on December 13 to co-celebrate Nile's 100th Anniversary of its Formation and the Sesquicentennial (150 Year Anniversary) of Grand Lodge Masonry in the State of Washington. The latter event was attended by the Imperial Potentate Doug Maxwell and his lady Patricia and by Grand Master Doug Tucker and his lady Glynnis. Dozens of new nobles were created at each ceremonial and the Imperial Potentate himself fezzed several of the new nobles in December. Another highlight of the year was the Potentate's Trip to the Highlands of Scotland which involved trips to famous Masonic lodges and Grand Lodges in Scotland and the conferral of the Royal Order of Loch Ness Degree at Nairn, near Loch Ness. And the Traveling Golden Fez was instituted that year designed to promote intervisitation among the various Shrine Clubs. Similar to the Traveling Trowel of blue lodges, a certain number of members of a visiting Shrine Club could win the Golden Fez away from the Shrine Club currently in possession of it by attending the host Shrine Club's stated meeting.

Other events included a revamped three ring Nile Circus which turned a profit, a huge turnout for All Masonic Night on May 14 with famed Northwest pianist Walt Wagner astonishing the crowd with his virtuoso playing, a large and successful Nile Picnic chaired by P.P. Jerry Seldon, and another Murder Mystery Dinner at the annual Halloween Party. The sound system was revamped that year with new wiring and equipment thanks in large part to High Priest and Prophet Dave Ramich, who also assisted the Potentate and the First Section in reinstating the old backdrops for the ceremonials which had been lying dormant for almost 20 years.

PNSA was held in Boise, Idaho that year and as usual Nile's Oriental Band picked up some big prizes at PNSOBA. They won the Large Fantasy Band competition, Best Director (Jim Hart), Best Band Parade Float, and Best Overall. In addition, Noble Ray Colby won first place for Best Solo Musette. The Shurtah made news when one of their fight events was videotaped by Comcast and later televised via Comcast's On Demand channel. And real Operative Masons awarded fellowcraft (journeyman) honors on July 29 to their apprentices who were learning the bricklaying trade on Nile's grounds. Nile had made an agreement with the local bricklayer's union to provide outside work space and inside office space for classroom instruction for the apprentices in return for brick work to improve Nile's several picnic shelters. As it turned out the bricklayers' union donated the materials as well as providing the labor to transform Nile's aging wood shelters into brick lined masterpieces.

In other news, the Portland Shriners Childrens' Hospital broke ground for its new multi-million-dollar addition and Potentate Kovak was very pleased to confer the Nile Order of Merit on Noble Mike Mathis (a burn survivor himself) for his continuing good work in assisting severely burned children face the world in their various conditions through his Burned Children Recovery Foundation and through Camp Phoenix, a free week of recreation in Northwest Washington for severely burned children to enjoy themselves in the company of their peers.

The hard part of 2008 came later in the year when the Great Recession devastated the stock market. Right after the fall of Lehman Brothers brokerage house into bankruptcy on September 15, the Dow Jones Industrial Average fell more than 500 points that day, only the sixth time in history it had fallen so far in one session. Larger one-day losses would soon follow. Stocks continued to fall over the next several months. Despite the passage of the Emergency Economic Stabilization Act of 2008 on October 3 and other "bailout" measures to shore up financial institutions, the Dow continued downward until it reached a low of 6,549 on March 9, 2009. By then the Dow had lost fully 20% of its value. During this time many other banking houses and insurances companies either collapsed or were begging the government for financial help.

The reasons for the recession are too complex to be fully discussed here but essentially the collapse of the housing market bubble in 2008 triggered the crisis because the value of many securities were tied to real estate pricing. Easy financing credit for home purchases allowed the housing market to boom. Seeing this boom, Wall Street brokerage houses devised new financial agreements known as mortgage backed securities (MBS) and collateralized debt obligations (CDO) to allow financial institutions and large investors throughout the world to invest in the booming United States housing market. When home prices started falling many new homeowners found themselves owing more in their mortgage amounts than their properties were worth and many began defaulting on their payments resulting in foreclosures. The foreclosure epidemic eroded the borrowing strength of banks leading to bank failures and this financial distress soon spread to other sectors of the economy. Some blame the government regulators for failing to stop the "blue sky" issuance of MBS or at least to regulate it to be in tune with the actual strength of the housing market. But it was too late for that when the crisis hit in late 2008.

The crisis would continue through 2010. Hundreds of thousands of people would lose a significant portion of the value of their pensions, individual retirement accounts (IRAs), stock portfolios and mutual funds. Some would lose their homes and their life's savings. Yet, large financial institutions and insurance companies would receive collectively hundreds of billions to maintain their companies and to continue their extravagant salaries and perquisites.

Nile finished 2008 with a net membership tally of 2262

2009 – Eugene "Gene" Gilbert – Be Firm to Your Purpose

Potentate Gilbert, a retired Marine Corps Lieutenant Colonel) who spent most of his working life as a restaurateur, meant by his motto to be firm to the purpose of raising funds to support the Shriners Children's Hospitals. He and his lady Dottie worked industriously to support the hospitals. But they also had to fund raise for Nile and did so by introducing a Cash Raffle Calendar. For $25 per calendar one had the chance to win back the price of the calendar on a daily basis. Larger cash amounts were awarded once a month and on special holidays. The calendar raffle raised a significant amount of money for Nile.

Potentate Gene also wanted to recognize the 100th Anniversary of the Charter of Nile Shrine Center much like Potentate Kovak the year before held a Centennial Celebration commemorating the formation of Nile in 1908. The Charter Celebration was held on June 20 in conjunction with the Spring Ceremonial. Notably, the June 20 Ceremonial included a live presentation of the Shrine Arch in lieu of the usual Second Section. The Shrine Arch program, originally produced by Ararat Shriners of Independence, Missouri, tells in dramatic fashion the story of Masonry from the basic blue lodge degrees through the Scottish and York Rites and ending with the Shrine and its hospital system. An explanation of the Shrine's hospital charity is included. It had been presented in video format in 2008, but was performed live in 2009 by Nile nobles, in particular the Director's Staff unit.

Social events hosted by Potentate Gene and lady Dottie included a Red White and Blue Military Ball on March 14, the Annual Nile Picnic on July 22, and a Winter Wonderland Ball on December 5. Unfortunately, a proposed Heritage of America trip to the Philadelphia/Washington, D.C. area had to be canceled.

At PNSA in Billings Montana June 4-6, Nile's Oriental Band was edged out in Large Fantasy Band PNSOBA competition by the hometown Al Bedoo Oriental Band. Still the Nile OB took first in Parade for Oriental Bands and first place overall for floats in the parade due in large part not only to their superior parade performance, but also to the new parade vehicle which had been purchased from Afifi Shriners and totally overhauled with new Nile graphics and adornments.

The Shurtah unit added Ultimate Mixed Martial Arts (MMA) Boxing to its sponsored events and this type of boxing proved to be even more profitable than the Amateur Youth Boxing events that it still continued to sponsor. With encouragement and support from the Nile Shurtah unit, a Shurtah Club of Gizeh Temple was organized and officers installed with Nile's Shurtah officers in attendance at Abbotsford, B.C. on February 5.

However, the big news event of 2009 was the attempt by a cabal of Imperial Officers to close six of the 22 Shriners Childrens' Hospitals to cut costs and save money in the face of a deteriorating economy. This effort to close the Shreveport, Galveston, Erie, Greenville, Spokane, and Twin Cities hospitals was opposed by another group of Imperial Officers led by Doug Maxwell. The issue of closure came up at the Imperial Session in San Antonio and was soundly defeated by the rank and file membership. But, to solve the financial crisis facing the hospitals, the session voted to allow the hospitals to accept third party pay from insurance company and government sources to help pay for treatment. Disclosure of third party pay sources was to be optional and no collection would be attempted if the effort did not receive approval from the patient's family. A task force was set up to pursue this new funding scheme through an independent collection company.

Internationally, the outbreak of the H1N1 influenza or "swine flu" was declared a global pandemic on June 11. It eventually resulted in the deaths of almost 12,000 people worldwide. And the death of pop singer Michael Jackson on June 25 resulted in a cyber jamming fiasco to the extent of crippling Internet access for a time due to the unprecedented crush of users hitting websites and web addresses on the web for information and blogging.

2009 ended with a net membership count of 2100

2010 – Satoru Tashiro

Potentate Sat, a Boeing Manager, PhD. electrical engineer and a past Grand Master (2004-5) of the Grand Lodge of Washington immediately took up the reins of Nile Shrine Center and gave it a polished manager's hand. His slogan, "United in Heritage and Purpose" signaled to nobles that regardless of our ethnic or national ancestry, they are united in supporting the Shriners Children's Hospitals philanthropy and the Nile Shrine Center itself. Potentate Sat is a member of the Board of Governors of the Portland

Hospital and well knows the amount of dedication it takes to support this great endeavor.

Together with his lady Lorna, they hosted several successful social events, including their spring ball, A Night in the Orient, held on March 13, the All Masonic Night on May 14 and the Holiday Ball on December 11. Ceremonials on June 5 and November 13 brought in several new nobles but not as many as had been hoped. And several nobles and their ladies greatly enjoyed Potentate Sat's and lady Lorna's Potentate's Cruise through the Panama Canal.

Potentate Sat volunteered the Nile temple to put on the drama of the Master Mason Third Degree at the open-air presentation in Granite Falls. It went wonderfully well with costumes borrowed from the Seattle Scottish Rite, stage direction by the potentate, and all actors being nobles from Nile. Members of the potentate's home lodge, Lakeside No. 258, did the other ritual work.

Nile tried a new circus this year, Cindy Migley's Circus Spectacular, but despite a valiant effort on the part of the divan and the units and clubs, it failed to make a profit and its future use at Nile was in doubt. Later that year, some of the proceeds from the sale of cell tower rights helped to erase that loss. The Cash Calendar continued to bring in a modest fund-raising profit for Nile.

Of special interest is at Imperial Session in Toronto, Canada, the Session granted a charter to a new temple in Manila, Philippines (Mabuhay) and to a new temple in San Juan, Puerto Rico (Al Rai'e Saleh). It also voted to grant dispensation for a new temple (Emirate) to the Federal Republic of Germany to be headquartered in Hamburg, Germany), the first temple outside of North America. These are the first new temples chartered in the Shrine family since Masada (Yakima, Washington) in 1991. The Session also voted to officially change the name of Shriners of North America to Shriners International. In other Imperial Shrine news, NASCAR race car driver Dave Ragan agreed to sponsor the Shriners Childrens Hospitals on his race car events and to donate a portion of his racing team's proceeds to the hospitals. Imperial also set up online the Shriners Village where information and merchandise relating to the hospitals could be obtained.

PNSA in Spokane was another well attended success. The Oriental Band again won several awards at PNSOBA including Best Large Fantasy Band and Best Director (Jim Hart). And the new Olympic Peninsula Shrine Club Motorized Quad unit received a well-deserved Participation Award for making a first-time appearance in the Motorized unit competition. The Nile Legion of Honor Flag unit at the Granite Falls Parade on October 2 carried the Philippine flag in its honor guard for the first time due to the 2010 chartering of Mabuhay Temple in Manila.

In national news, the explosion at the Deepwater Horizon offshore oilrig platform in the Gulf of Mexico triggered the worst oil spill in United States history. Eleven men working on the platform died in the explosion and 17 more were severely injured. The spill caused immense damage to both land and marine wildlife as well as devastating the economic life of fisherman, processors and service industries based on the Gulf fisheries. It is estimated that as much as 180 million gallons or 4.28 million barrels of oil escaped during the whole episode. The blown-out pipe was finally capped on July 15 and declared "dead" on September 19.

Internationally, the World Health Organization declared the H1N1 (swine flu) pandemic over on August 10. The Winter Olympics were held February 12-28 in neighboring British Columbia bringing tens of thousands of tourists through Seattle on the way to Vancouver, including a few Shrine nobles and their ladies who stopped off to see Nile on their way to and from B.C. And the world's tallest building, the Burj Khalifa, was dedicated and opened in Dubai on January 4. At 2,716 feet (828m), the Burj is considerably taller than the previous tallest buildings, the Taipei 101 (1,666 ft.), the Shanghai World Financial Tower (1,614 ft.) and the Petronas towers in Kuala Lumpur (1,428 ft.). In the United States, the tallest building is now the One World Trade Center or Freedom Tower in New York City (1,776 ft.). The Burj boasts the world's highest occupied floor, the tallest service lift, and the highest observation deck (124th floor).

However, no view is greater nor perspective grander than that which Nile nobles and their ladies receive when helping and supporting Shriners Childrens' Hospitals. Paraphrasing an old Shrine slogan: No one stands so tall as when they stoop to help a child in need.

Nile's net membership at the end of 2010 fell below the 2000 mark and finished at 1996.

Chapter Twelve

THE TWENTY-TEENS –
THE RISE OF THE SOCIAL MEDIA

If the first decade of the 2000s ended in a downward cascading recession, the Twenty-Teens (2011-2019) rose in a crescendo of wars, weather disturbances, political turmoil, and digital noise. The continued rise of the Social Media Age in the Twenty-Teens transformed United States society and indeed most societies throughout the world at a faster pace than had ever been witnessed by historians since the invention of the printing press and in later years the inventions of the telephone, television and the Internet.

Entrance to Nile Shrine Center Mountlake Terrace WA

Richard M. Kovak

The widespread use of cell phones, e-tablets, and other Internet of Things (IoT) devices allowed easy access to social media platforms, the Internet, and the cloud. Social media outlets, such as Facebook, Instagram, Snapchat, Pinterest, Twitter, Reddit, YouTube, LinkedIn, and more allowed networks to form electronically among individuals, groups, and whole communities. Communication, one of the essential building blocks of civilization became almost instantaneous as popular messages and their responses went "viral" (spreading as fast as a communicable disease) across electronic space. This wash of information eventually raised concerns about privacy, censorship, and the dangers arising from over dependence, taunting, shaming and unawareness of physical surroundings.

Politically, the world turmoiled into the Twenty-Teens with the Arab Spring revolutions and the rise of the Islamic State in Iraq. The Levant extremist movement erased the borders between Syria and Iraq. Sunni, Shiites, and Kurds struggled against each other. Strongmen were overthrown in several countries. Europe bore the brunt of a migrant crisis as refugees from those areas in turmoil came to European countries en masse. Russia annexed the Crimea and Great Britain sought to extricate itself from the European Union, the so-called Brexit maneuver. And China emerged on the world stage as the next great superpower.

In the United States, recovery from the Great Recession of 2007-2010 was slow and ponderous, but the economy improved from year to year until the DOW, NASDAQ and S&P started recording new highs in 2018 and 2019. The Presidency of Barrack Hussein Obama lasted from 2009 until 2017. He was the first African-American to be elected to the presidency. His most notable accomplishment was the Patient Protection and Affordable Care Act (Obamacare). He also helped enact into law the American Recovery and Reinvestment Act, the Tax Relief Act, the Unemployment Insurance Reauthorization Act, and the Job Creation Act of 2010, all of which provided economic stimulus to a nation suffering from the Great Recession.

In 2016, an upstart billionaire businessman, Donald Trump won election to the presidency over Democratic opponent Hillary Clinton. To many people, this was a surprise result, since Trump lost the popular vote yet won the electoral vote sending many citizens to search copies of the United States Constitution to try to figure out what is the Electoral College. Nevertheless, on January 20. 2017, Donald John Trump was inaugurated as the 45th President of the United States.

Despite the rash of hurricanes, wildfires, tornados and earthquakes that plagued the world, the vagaries o f the ups and downs of the economy and the political disturbances during the Twenty-Teens, the Nobles and their ladies of Nile marched onward in orderly fashion, electing their next rounds of leaders, weathering the Nile's monetary problems and continuing to warmly support the Shriners Hospitals for Children programs. Time and space do not permit an extensive review of each Twenty-Teen potentate's year. A supplement to this book is being prepared which will detail those years. Nevertheless, below listed are the names of those Twenty-Teen potentates and their ladies.

2011 David E. "Dave" Ramich and lady Kathy
2012 Roland D. Jennings and lady Suzanne
2013 James L. Hutchins and lady Marilyn
2014 Craig A. Jacobson and lady Cynthia
2015 David M. Brady, Sr., and lady Karen
2016 Donald E. "Don" Lane and lady Denise
2017 Gale H. Kenny and lady Jayne
2018 Larry A. Bronner and lady Annie
2019 Steven L. Dazey and lady Susan

The elected 2020 Divan and their ladies are the following:

Potentate – Michael J. Riley and lady Kimberly
Chief Rabban – Larry J. Gillespie and lady Shirley
Assistant Rabban – J. Dale Newman and lady Kimberly
High Priest & Prophet – Ned Daniels and lady Linda
Oriental Guide – Brent Arnold and lady Sarah

And so, with 2020 begins the start of the Twenty-Twenties for the Nile Shrine Center.

The rest of the story of the Nile Nobles and their Ladies remains to be written. The detailed events of each Potentate's year in the Twenty-Teens and the Twenty- Twenties must await a future installment or a full-blown sequel. Nevertheless, the fun, fellowship and philanthropy continually felt by the Shriner families in their never-ending quest to make the Shriners Hospitals for Children the best children's care facilities in all the world carries on from year to year. To paraphrase an old axiom – the present is but prologue to the future.

CAVEAT –This book is being published while the world is still in the grip of the Great Coronavirus (COVID-19) pandemic of 2020. No detailed reporting of that event can be completely told at this time. Its story will be included in the supplement and sequel that recounts the years of the Twenty-Teens and Twenty-Twenties.

Chapter Thirteen

SPECIAL GROUPS AND ACTIVITIES

The SS Nile and The Ark and Anchor Masonic Club

Herein lies a tale of how Nile nobles and their ladies used to celebrate an important event and how they entertained visiting dignitaries. In those days, Nile had a Patrol unit with two platoons each containing 40 members. It had a large band with 60 members. In 1915, Nile had just hosted the Imperial Council Session in Seattle. It was in the process of making a name for itself on the national stage of Shrinedom.

In 1919, Potentate John C. Watrous of Nile Temple invited Imperial Potentate Freeland Kendrick and his lady to visit Nile during their tour of Northwest Shrine temples and that Nile would be honored to have Mrs. Kendrick christen a brand new 10,000 ton steamship that was being finished at the nearby Skinner and Eddy Shipyard. On November 15th of that year, the Imperial Potentate, his lady, and the touring Imperial entourage left El Katif Shrine Temple in Spokane and journeyed across Washington arriving in Seattle late at night. The next day, the Imperial party attended church services at First Presbyterian Church in Seattle where they were impressed by a wonderful sermon delivered by Senior Pastor, Reverend Dr. M.A. Mathews, a Nile noble. Dr. Mathews had previously addressed the Imperial Council in 1914 and was part of the group from Nile that had invited the Imperial Session to meet in Seattle in 1915. After church, the Imperial Potentate and his lady were treated to luncheon at the Washington Hotel and then were given a motor trip around the city arriving at the Seattle Golf Club where a reception for them was held by the Nile Divan, past potentates, and many important city officials.

On November 17 the morning dawned dark and cloudy with threat of rain. But after breakfast, the nobility of Nile began assembling in large numbers. The First Section of the Nile Ceremonial was performed at the hotel. Then the Nile Band and the Patrol came in their resplendent uniforms. A color guard arrived and a parade was formed for the march to the shipyards of the Skinner and Eddy Corporation where the new SS Nile sat proudly waiting to begin its career as a steamship plying Puget Sound waters and beyond. The SS Nile had started out with a tentative name of the SS Crittenden, named for a United States Secretary of the Treasury, but through artful negotiation influential Nile nobles were able to convince the United States Board of Shipping and Trade to have it renamed the SS Nile.

When the parade, headed by the Color Guard, the Band and the Patrol followed by hundreds of nobles and then the Imperial party in cars, reached the shipyard they were greeted by several thousand men and women, but most impressively by 1200 Masons who composed the Ark and Anchor Masonic Club. This club, made up almost solely of shipyard workers, were all Masons belonging to one or more lodges in the Puget Sound area. Many were Shriners and they held this in common: their work was done in the old-fashioned Masonic way with brother Mason helping brother Mason, not competing against each other for money or honors. In Masonry, the Ark and Anchor are, respectively, emblems of a well spent life and a well-grounded hope in the future of mankind. The Ark is symbolic of that Divine Ark which safely carries us over this earthly sea of tempestuous troubles and the anchor is that secure Divine Presence which will safely moor us in a peaceful harbor at the end of our voyage.

The Ark and Anchor Club had arranged a marvelous surprise at the shipyard – they had transformed the entire shipyard into a Shrine Oasis! Novel scenery had been erected all along the way depicting life size camels, large pyramids, Zem Zem springs, green palms, and white fountains. There were also draperies, banners, and regalia of the Order. A large picture of the Imperial Potentate had been set up under a long welcome banner and a trail of sawdust representing "hot sands" extended a whole mile from the entrance of the shipyard to the point where the ship stood waiting to be launched. The platform next to the ship had been decorated with the national colors as well as the emblem and colors of the Mystic Shrine. On reaching the platform, the Imperial Potentate and his lady were greeted by shipyard President D. E. Skinner who spoke eloquently of patriotism, Masonry, and the Shrine. Imperial Potentate Kendrick then spoke and dwelt principally on Americanism and the need for United States ships of trade after the end the Great War in Europe. He liberally thanked his hosts for this great honor that had been bestowed upon the Imperial Shrine and himself and his lady. During his speech, the sun broke through the clouds basking all in sunlight as though the great Architect of the Universe smiled approval of this great event.

Then the time for the great event arrived. Mrs. Kendrick stood by the prow of the ship with an arm full of roses in one hand and a beautifully decorated bottle of champagne in the other hand. At precisely 12:30 PM, the Nile Band started playing and Mrs. Kendrick delivered a well-placed blow of the bottle upon the ship's prow that started it moving down the wooden cradle that held her. Faster and faster the ship sped down the launch way until it hit the water with a surge of foam that nearly splashed back up onto the platform. As the crowd cheered, from out in the bay came a glorious response. Hundreds of ships that had lined up to watch the launch blew their horns and whistles. Factory whistles blew from all over the area. As the SS Nile hit the water, a large sign on her prow declaring "Smile with Nile" unfurled and became visible. The massed thousands roared their approval. President Skinner then presented Mrs. Kendrick with a beautiful diamond pin to mark the occasion.

That night after dinner at the Washington Hotel, the ladies were escorted by Nile Greeters to the theater while the rest of the nobles retreated to the hotel ballroom to witness the second and third sections of the Nile Ceremonial. After the two groups reunited, a series of introductions was made. The Imperial Officers, visiting Potentates and other distinguished visitors were introduced through open lines of the Nile Band and Patrol. Afterward the Patrol presented a competition between its two platoons and the Imperial Potentate had the honor of awarding a silver cup to the winning platoon. Although both platoons performed admirably and both were loudly applauded by the spectators, it was the Patrol's Second Platoon that won the silver cup in the eyes of the judges. Finally, a burlesque performance by Nile Patrol's Second Section was put on parodying the launch event. Only this time the Imperial Potentate himself was the bottle popper and surprise got the better of him when the bottle failed to break despite numerous attempts to christen the faux ship prow and merely bounced around the floor when the prow started squirting water on him, as the audience laughed their approval of this novel stunt.

After all was said and done, the Imperial party retired for the night and left for Afifi Temple the following day. As he departed, Imperial Potentate Kendrick thanked everyone at Nile for the lavish and royal treatment that he and his lady had received and stated that they would always remember their "pleasant Smile With Nile."

Historian's Note: The very next year, Imperial Potentate Kendrick would return to the Northwest and introduce the famous resolution at the 1920 Imperial Session in Portland that, when passed, created the Shriners Hospitals for Children. This resolution, championed by Potentate Forrest Adair of Atlanta's Yaarab Temple in his famous "Bubbles" speech, laid the ground for the building of the first Shriners Children's Hospital in Shreveport, Louisiana in 1922. Shortly afterward, Shriners Childrens' Hospitals were built in Portland and Spokane in 1924 as well as elsewhere throughout the 1920's.

The 1915 Imperial Session - Nile Reaches the National Scene

At the Fortieth Imperial Session held at Yard Temple in Atlanta in May, 1914, Nile's Patrol and Band were sensational. Nile had the largest delegation in Atlanta (258) which included the 35-man Patrol under the direction of Capt. George R. Drever and the 32-man Band under the direction of Harvey J. Wood. They came with Shriners from other Northwest temples in an 11-car train. The Northern Pacific made sure that the crews of this train were made up completely of Shriners who worked for NP. The polished drills of the Patrol and the sparkling music of the Band impressed everyone so much that the Atlanta Constitution newspaper got behind and supported Nile's bid to host the next Imperial Session. Said the Constitution reporter on May 12, 1914: "...the services of the Constitution have been tendered the Seattle delegates in their fight for the 1915 Convention of Shriners. We think, as we hope, that Seattle will win."

The Imperial Council recommendation committee came out 4-1 in Seattle's favor. On the following day the Imperial Session Assembly unanimously voted to locate the 1915 Imperial Session in Seattle. Paradoxically, although Atlanta knew the result 15 minutes before Seattle, Seattle knew it 2-3/4 hours before Atlanta because the telegraph report reached Seattle on Pacific time which was earlier in the day than Atlanta's East Coast time.

The Forty-First Imperial Session in Seattle was one of the greatest events in Seattle's young history. Over 50,000 visitors came from all over the country and from Canada to attend it. 15,000 Shriners marched in the Grand Parade. Over 50 temple bands and 82 Patrols participated. Business sessions were held at the Moore Theater. And Nile Temple was the heart and soul of the festivities. Said Seattle Mayor Gill: "I have not been mayor for quite a few days. Nile Temple has been mayor. My duties have been limited to providing special police protection. I am proud of Nile Temple."

Joseph A. Salwell was Nile Temple Potentate that year and Frederick R. Smith was Imperial Potentate. But it was the scores of committees and hundreds of nobles from Nile that made this convocation successful all under the direction of Noble J. E. Chilberg, Chairman of the 1915 Executive Committee. The beautiful program put out by Nile Temple for this session, is a tribute to the hard work of Nile nobles in acquiring advertisers and sponsors. The City of Seattle Chamber of Commerce worked to raise $150,000 to help defray the expenses of the session. Paid ads, sponsorships, and temple fundraising brought in a matching amount.

The ceremonial held in conjunction with the Imperial Session brought in 186 new nobles, notably Congressman William E. Humphrey and Seattle Chief of Police Louis Lang, and was attended by 2,500 sideliners. The 40-man Nile Patrol, 30-man Auxiliary Patrol, the 40-man Band and the 40-man drum and bugle corps all participated in a parade at the Ceremonial.

The Liberty Bell was brought in from Philadelphia for a one-day stop on Seattle on July 15, 1915. Many were able to see this major American artifact for the first time in person. Patrol and band competitions were held at Woodland Park and many thousands were in attendance to witness the colorful displays of costumes and maneuvers.

It was just prior to the advent of this Imperial Session that the famous "Smile with Nile" slogan was created. Although sometimes credited to John B. McLean, P.P., the real story involves Executive Committee Chair J. E.

Chilberg calling for suggestions for a convention slogan that would capture the heart and spirit of Nile for the upcoming event. After much spirited debate the suggestion by Noble Herbert A. Schoenfeld, "Smile with Nile," was eventually adopted. And although most ad hoc slogans are quickly forgotten after the end of the event for which it was coined, this slogan came to be recognized throughout Shrinedom as one of the most enduring and recognizable in Shrine history. After the slogan was adopted, Band Director Harvey J. Wood decided to write a song for the convention. Unlike the Smile with Nile song put to the tune of The Caissons Go Rolling Along which is sometimes sung today, Wood's Smile with Nile is an original work. It is an uplifting melodic piece that has catchy lyrics by John R. ("Doc") Hager.

Upon leaving Seattle after the convention, new Imperial Potentate J. Putnam Stevens said: "I have attended 13 Imperial Sessions and Seattle has set the pace for all of them."

The 1936 Imperial Council Session in Seattle and the Imperial Potentate From Nile Who Never Served

The 1936 Imperial Council Session held in Seattle Washington on July 13-16 remains one of greatest achievements of Nile nobility and their ladies. This convention, which occurred during the height of the Great Depression, during the greatest heat wave in North American weather history (see below), and while Hitler was taking the Sudetenland from Czechoslovakia, has been documented in a previous Smile with Nile article and part of it will be reprinted below.

But the strangest aspect of the Imperial Convention of 1936 was the mysterious declination of the Imperial Potentate's position by Nile's Hugh M. Caldwell. Hugh was an attorney by profession and had been elected Mayor of Seattle in 1920. Already at that time a member of Nile's Divan, he was elected Potentate of Nile in 1922 and served as such with distinction. In 1927, he ran for and was elected Imperial Outer Guard. He labored nine long years in that 10-man line, all the while keeping up his legal and business interests, and in 1936 was due to be elected Imperial Potentate. As a Nile noble, he naturally chose Seattle as the home venue for the 1936 Imperial Session Convention. The business of the convention was fairly short that year and the Imperial elections were one of the main concerns of the council. Hugh was duly nominated and was unanimously elected as Imperial Potentate. But as soon as he rose to give an acceptance speech, many nobles noted an aura of sadness in his demeanor. He thanked the nobles for their vote, but stated that for health, business, and personal reasons he must decline to serve. A major hubbub then occurred among the assembled nobles, so much so that a recess was declared. Several Nile nobles rushed the stage and wept with Hugh as he himself shed bitter tears. After the recess, Hugh resumed the podium and nominated Deputy Imperial Potentate Clyde I. Webster to take over the office of Imperial Potentate. Webster was unanimously elected and Caldwell sat down. Webster accepted even though this honor had come to him a year earlier than expected. He has assumed that he would be elected Imperial Potentate at the 1937 Imperial Session in Detroit Michigan, the site of Moslem, his home temple. Hugh was then elected an ad vitam (for life) member of the Imperial Council, but could never call himself a Past Imperial Potentate because he had never served his term as such.

The question as to exactly why he declined the honor has been debated for years. Most likely some of his contemporary members of Nile know the real reason, but that reason has never been made public. Hugh had been in the Imperial line for almost 10 years and had never once given an indication that his business and legal interests were suffering because of his Shrine duties. In fact, his business interests were said to have profited from his position with the Shrine of North America. His travels never seemed to have affected his health, although they may have affected his home life. He was not known to have had any serious health problems prior to this time, although fatigue and stress could have been working havoc on his body. And why did he wait until after he was elected Imperial Potentate to announce his declination to serve when he knew very well that he was not going to follow through with that high office? He could just as well have told the Imperial Council of his intentions ahead of time and notified Webster that Webster would be nominated instead of himself.

One reason posited for this sudden declination is Hugh was reputed to be a very gregarious person prone to be attracted to ladies other than his wife. It may well be that Mrs. Caldwell had caught him in some previous romantic indiscretions and had refused to serve as his First lady if he took the Imperial Potentate's position. Vain man as he was,

Richard M. Kovak

Hugh still wanted to taste the title even though he knew he could never serve his term due his wife's determined stance. Anyone who has more definitive information on this matter is welcome to contact this writer at his email address below. No other Nile noble has ever come close to being elected an Imperial Potentate. The only other two Imperial Sessions held in Seattle, in 1915 and 1969, celebrated the ascension to the Imperial throne of Noble J. Putnam Stephens and Afifi Past Potentate Ellis M. Garretson respectively.

55,000 Shriners Attend 1936 Imperial Session in Seattle and 300,000 People Turn Out for Shrine Parade

Over 55,000 Shriners attended this event despite the economic effects of the Depression. From Islam Temple in San Francisco came close to a thousand Shriners together with their 100-foot-long Dragon. Zuhrah Temple in Minneapolis sent several hundred Shriners with their "Largest Drum in Shrinedom," a 6-foot diameter bass drum mounted on carriage wheels. Abu Bekr Temple from Sioux City, Iowa sent its famous 24 horse White Horse Patrol. And Syria Temple from Pittsburgh, Pennsylvania sent its Wheels of Steel motorcycle unit. In addition, the United States Navy Fleet Week coincided with the Imperial Convention and 412 Navy ships brought over 12,000 sailors and officers to celebrate with the Shriners in Seattle at the same time. The Old Times Building (former home of the Seattle Times) in downtown Seattle was transformed into Shrine Headquarters. The fifth floor was made into an Egyptian temple for meetings and social events. The fourth floor was the domain of the Chanters who featured a picturesque Klondike Dance Hall. The third floor held offices, a pressroom, a switchboard, and a completely equipped first aid hospital. The second floor was Band headquarters and the first floor housed executive offices, registration desks and other administrative activities. On most of the floors were spacious lounges for female guests.

WHERE THIS WEEK THE SHRINERS OF THE NATION WILL "SMILE WITH NILE"

● The Old Times Building in Times Square, resplendent in its decorations as headquarters for the Sixty-Second Imperial Council Session of the national Shrine organization in Seattle this week. About it will revolve the elaborate program of entertainment arranged for thousands of visiting Shriners by Nile Temple of Seattle, convention host.

PART FIVE

SEATTLE WELCOMES The Shriners And the Fleet

Nile Headquarters 1936 Imperial Session

A beautiful program book was published. The book extolled the virtues and advantages of not only Seattle, but also Tacoma and the rest of the Northwest.

Hotels were booked to capacity and even private homes could not accommodate all the visiting Shriners. So, a Fez City was created, consisting of hundreds of Pullman cars parked near the King Street and Union Pacific Railway stations just south of the business district. Fez City would eventually hold 10,000 Shrine visitors. Street lights were installed in the lanes between the tracks. And the railway companies put in sanitary facilities, power lines, phone connections, running water and shower baths, and porter service. All the cars were air-conditioned. It was only a short walk from Fez City to Pioneer Square and the Seattle downtown area, but what a relief for Shrine and city planners to have housing of this magnitude so close to heart of the city.

The Grand Parade held on Tuesday July 14, 1936 presented 126 units with over 5000 marching Shriners. The parade lasted almost three hours. 50,000 other Shriners were among the 300,000 people who watched the parade from the sidelines. It was the greatest number of people ever assembled for a single event in the history of the Northwest said Chief William Cole of the Washington State Patrol whose officers were called on to assist Seattle Police to manage the huge throng. An anecdote of note is in order here. A bit of Shrine courtesy by the Al Malaikah band from Los Angeles drove the crowds into a frenzy. They repeatedly played "Bow Down To Washington" as they marched. And, even though they would occasionally play other schools' fight songs, whenever they returned to "Bow Down," which they did frequently, the crowds went wild.

Many events were held on the University of Washington campus including the massed bands concert witnessed by 30,000 spectators in the great horseshoe grandstand at Husky Stadium. This band, composed of 2500 band members from 40 different temples consisted of 300 trombones, 166 sousaphones, 800 clarinets, 400 trumpets, 100 saxophones, 500 horns, 30 bassoons, 50 piccolos and many other instruments. They played a rousing concert program ending with the Smile with Nile March composed and directed by Noble William G. Marshall, Director of the Nile Band.

Hollywood movie stars of the day arrived to participate in some of the entertainment shows: Allan Jones, Sally O'Neil, William Farnum, Patsy Ruth Miller, and Monty Blue. Ironically, silent film star Monte Blue served as a very talkative Master of Ceremonies for several events. Great fun was had when Ms. Miller and Ms. O' Neil were met at the airport by Nile P.P. Van S. McKenney, accompanied by a detachment from the Nile Patrol and Potentate the camel. Upon being introduced to the two starlets, Potentate immediately stretched out his neck, chomped down and ate the bouquet of roses and ferns that Ms. Miller was carrying and then beckoned Ms. O'Neil to jump on for a ride which she promptly did in her white culotte pants. Policemen assigned to control the crowds obtained the autographs of the stars on blank traffic tickets. Clark Gable was to have been there, but had to cancel because of studio business down in Los Angeles. However, the two female stars so captivated the crowds that Clark was not missed.

The other major event that occurred in 1936 was the formation of Nile's Legion of Honor unit. Talked about for years, this unit came into being largely through the efforts of Noble Col. Robert M. Watkins. The spur to formation was the coincidence at the 1936 Imperial Session of the National Association of Legion's of Honor annual meeting. Aware of Nile's intentions, National Commander Henry H. Green (Yaarab Temple, Atlanta, Ga.) brought three LOH Drill Teams to Seattle, which performed with the utmost military precision. Sensing the opportunity, Watkins approached Nile Potentate Tom Holman for permission to form a Nile LOH unit that year. Potentate Holman gave his permission to Watkins and his committee to investigate the feasibility of such a unit. The committee's report was presented at the December 10, 1936 stated meeting, officially accepted, and the new unit was sanctioned to come into being. On the following day, the first Nile LOH meeting occurred with Col. Chester Chastek elected as Commander, Watkins as Senior Vice Commander and Kenneth Hodges as Junior Vice Commander. 41 members were signed up including members of the Nile Drum and Bugle Corps. Petition was immediately made to NALOH for a charter and on December 21, 1936 the NALOH elected Nile LOH as its 10th member unit. Col. Watkins became Commander for 1937. The LOH served Nile long and gloriously and much more will be said about its activities in future articles, including hosting the NALOH Conventions in 1954 and 1985.

Other events did happen at Nile during 1936 including the potentate's Ceremonial on April 25 (71 new nobles), the Imperial Ceremonial on June27 (129 new nobles), the coast to coast broadcast of the Nile Band and Chanters on CBS on April 18, the Sixth Pilgrimage to the Orient (Manila, Hong Kong, Shanghai and Yokohama), a Thanksgiving Ceremonial on November 28 (11 new nobles) and the Sixth Ice Carnival on December

11-12. Most remarkable of these was the trip to the Orient. For on that trip in Manila at the Ceremonial conducted at the Bamboo Oasis Shrine Club, a young military officer by the name of Douglas MacArthur was made a Nile Shriner. In January of 1936 the Grandmaster of the Philippines made MacArthur a Mason on sight. Because many United States military officers were members of Bamboo Oasis, word of Nile's impeding pilgrimage from July 18 to August 16 came to MacArthur and he petitioned for membership. Since that date he became one of Nile's most famous and storied members.

Heat Wave Kills Over 5000 in the United States

The summer of 1936 also saw the most severe heat wave ever to affect the United States in recorded weather history. It followed one of the coldest winters on record. From late June through August, temperatures soared to record highs in most states, in particular the Midwest states. The heat wave brought severe drought conditions to states with already dry and exposed soil. Crops failed and harvests that year were particularly poor. As a result, corn and wheat prices rose steeply. It is said that in several of the Dust Bowl states soil temperatures reached the 200-degree mark at the 4 inch or 10-centimeter level of depth. That super-heated soil effect on the farming environment was devastating. Such torrid soil temperatures killed the nitrogen fixing bacteria and other microbes essential for crop growth and propagation. July was the hottest month. Ohio and Iowa experienced several days of temperatures at the 110-degree level. Steele, North Dakota reached 121 degrees which remains the North Dakota record to this day. In September, the heat wave and drought had lessened in intensity even though many states were still drier and warmer than normal. Normal seasonal temperatures resumed in the fall.

The 1969 Imperial Session in Seattle

1969 is memorable to Nile nobles for two great events: the Imperial Council Session held at the Seattle Center Exhibition Hall June 29-July 4, and the first manned landing on the moon by United States astronauts on July 20. Vernon Bell presided as Potentate that year and what a year it was! The first public installation ever held of Nile officers and the ensuing program was presented on January 11 at the Opera House. The pageant "Look To the West" was performed and narrated by Nile Noble Judge John Cochran. Imperial Potentate Chet Hogan was the Installing Officer. The big event of the year of course was the Imperial Convention (95th Imperial Council Session). Over 100,000 Shriners and their ladies and families attended the various events that comprised the Convention. Beginning with the Chester A. Hogan Ceremonial held June 28, through the Grand Parade with over 200 Shrine Units participating on July 1, and ending with a closing session and a night parade on July 3, the 95th Imperial Session was a great success in large part due to the organizational and management skills of Nile Noble Aurie Thompson, P.P. 1963.

Noted Seattle Times columnist Don Duncan described Aurie as the husky, gray haired owner and President of Piston Service, Inc. in Seattle. But for the time of the convention and for many months prior to that he was the Director General of the biggest convention Seattle had seen since the 1936 Shriners' Convention, also held in Seattle. After it was all over, Thompson would be, according to Duncan, "just another fez in the crowd."

But wait! Charles "Chick" Hogan was a Past Worshipful Master of Corinthian Lodge #38 of Tacoma and a Past Potentate of Afifi Temple, Nile's mother temple in Tacoma. Why Seattle? Well, Chick had run for the Imperial line shortly after his term of office as potentate of Afifi Temple and won. When it came time for him to head the 95nd Imperial Session as Imperial Potentate, it was apparent to him that Tacoma could not accommodate the growing number of Shriners and their ladies attending these sessions. So, an arrangement was made by which the City of Destiny deferred to the Queen City (as it was then known) to host the Imperial Session. The main events would be held in Seattle at Nile facilities (recall that Nile offices were located adjacent to the Seattle Center in 1969), and elsewhere in the Seattle area and co-hosted by Afifi, Nile and El Katif Temple of Spokane. The expenses would be shared. Since Nile took on the laboring oar of securing facilities and accommodations, a Past Potentate of Nile, Aurie Tompson (Past Potentate 1963) was chosen as Director General.

And what an Imperial Session it was. Past Imperial Potentate (1949-1950) Harold E. Lloyd (Al Malaikah Temple) attended and was honored as Shriner of the Year. Governor Daniel J. Evans gave a stirring keynote address at the banquet held at the Civic Opera House on July 2. Besides the Imperial Shrine Divan, included in this audience were Frank E. Ulin,

Grand Master of the Most Worshipful Grand Lodge of Free and Accepted Masons of Washington, Floyd Miller, Honorable Mayor of the City of Seattle, United States Senator and Nile Noble, Henry F. (Scoop) Jackson, the heads of all Scottish Rite and York Rite bodies as well as many other dignitaries.

Governor Evans implored all citizens to rise up to face and help resolve the challenges to our society raised by the newly emerged civil rights, human rights, and minority rights movements, concluding with these words:

> "Let those who must, dissent, but let the rest of us remember that by our positive action and by that alone will come the resolution of the American dilemma. A great nation cannot remain great if its people stand silent in criticism; it cannot remain great if its people succumb to fear and labor a false patriotism. It can only remain great if its people become involved and restore to nationhood a clear sense of individual commitment and purpose. This is our challenge. This is your challenge. To set aside the agony of adversity and take up the challenge of hope and to rekindle in every American the faith that from his works a nation can survive.

In 1936, Shriners came mostly by railroad car and a Shrine city of Pullman cars was created at the King St. Station railroad yard to house them. In 1969 most came by plane and Seattle-Tacoma Airport set a record that year for most air passenger traffic in its history. Hotel accommodations for the 1969 Shriners stretched across 90 miles up and down the I-5 corridor. 900 Shriners and their ladies came down from Gizeh Temple in British Columbia. Gizeh budgeted $200,000 for their trip and of course much more was spent on their shopping sprees in the State.

Two parades were held. There was a day parade on Tuesday, July 1, and a night parade on Thursday July 3. Both followed the same route, starting at Fourth Avenue and Madison and winding up at the Seattle Center Coliseum. Over 300 Shrine units from 42 Temples participated in each parade, including a dozen pipe bands, 20 brass bands, 18 chorus units (including Nile's own Chanters), 30 Arab patrols, 19 clown groups, 20 motorcycle patrols, 15 Oriental bands, a dozen drum and bugle corps and hundreds of convertibles, mini car and other assorted vehicles.

Other activities included competitions for drill teams, horse patrols, and motorcycle patrols, Oriental Band, concert band and Chanter competitions, clown competitions and drum and bugle corps competitions. Band concerts, both scheduled and impromptu, occurred periodically throughout the city and often took place in hotels, bars, and restaurants or wherever Shriners gathered.

Two anecdotes connected with the convention that were reported in the Seattle Times are worth sharing. One was that a Seattle citizen, indignant that Shriner motorcycle riders were wearing fezzes and not the legally mandated helmets, filed suit in King County Superior Court to force them to wear helmets in accordance with the State of Washington motorcycle helmet law. However, Presiding Superior Court Judge Story Birdseye threw out the suit saying that it was a convention and a parade convenience to wear the fezzes. It turns out that the plaintiff, one Jack Zektzer, had been arrested many times for driving a motorcycle without a helmet and had been convicted on most of the charges. He wanted the same law applied to Shriners as it was to him.

The other anecdote comes from Seattle Times columnist Val Varney who wanted to test the theory that Shriners are fun-loving wolves who love their wine, women and song and would jump at the chance to make a pass at or at least wolf whistle a pretty woman while they were on convention. Val is a very attractive woman and, attired in a red, white, and blue mini skirt, long stockings, and high heels, went over to the Headquarters Olympic Hotel to test the theory. To her wonderment she found the Olympic Hotel lobby filled with both men and women – the Shriners had brought their wives! She sat down on a sofa in the main lobby, crossed her legs, put on a fetching smile, and waited – nothing! Finally, she got on an elevator filled with Shriners and no women. But the elevator trip was silent. The only thing she sensed was the smell of bourbon. Back downstairs, she made a few more strolls around the lobby but received only two more long Shriner stares and a few winks. She concluded her report to the Times: "Maybe Shriners still like their wine and song, but now they bring their wives to conventions. Sorry, girls, they're not the wolf pack I'd always heard about."

In the end, the convention elected J. Worth Baker, an Indianapolis businessman (Murat Temple) as the incoming Imperial Potentate. And, after the convention, Chick Hogan presumably went back to Puyallup to resume his business of developing shopping plazas.

However, one more note of interest is worth reporting. During the Thursday night parade, the Seattle skies opened up and it started raining. However, most of the parade onlookers stayed to see Bertha the high strutting elephant from Kerak Temple in Reno Nevada. She wore a huge fez and led the Kerak Oriental Band which also boasted a bare-chested, dripping with rain, kettle drummer. Then the well dampened Medinah Temple Chanters, seated on an open backed semi-truck came along singing: "The bluest skies you've ever seen are in Seattle." So ended Nile's last hosting of an Imperial Session in Seattle. The only sad note about the convention came from the State of Washington Liquor Control Board which reported that the Shriners drank less liquor than anticipated and the State was left holding the bag on 80,000 cases of liquor that it had overbought for the convention. Said Richard King, the State liquor store purchasing agent: "(Inventory) might have been high, but we felt that, if a Shriner went into a store to get a certain brand, we'd better have it for him. We couldn't have him go away and say 'That bureaucratic State of Washington didn't have the booze I wanted'."

Later that month came one of great events of all time, not only for Nile and America, but for the world. Throughout history humankind had speculated about the moon, the closest celestial body to Earth. From poetic notions to pretty shrewd guesses about its composition, man has longed to journey to its nearest celestial neighbor. The Soviets were thought to be well in the lead in achieving this goal through their Luna series which photographed the never-before seen back side of the moon and actually landed (probably crash landed) a human made object on the moon's surface for the first time. But the United States, under spurring from President Kennedy in the early 1960's, rushed to catch up. Americans watched in awe as first the Mercury, then the Gemini and finally the Apollo series of launches brought the United States closer and closer to that age-old goal. The climax came on July 20, when after the Apollo 11 space capsule landed on the moon, the commander of the Apollo 11 mission, civilian Neil Armstrong, stepped out of the lander and walked on the moon. He was ably backed up by command module pilot Mike Collins and lunar lander pilot Buzz Aldrin, a noble of Arabia Temple in Houston. However, Armstrong's first words: "That's one small step for a man, and one giant leap for mankind" came out as "That's one small step for man..." because of radio difficulties. Nevertheless, the 500 million people watching this historic event rejoiced that the impossible had been accomplished. Most social commentators acknowledge that this lunar landing and walk is one the defining moments in human history.

General Macarthur Visits Nile Temple

When President Dwight David Eisenhower was asked by a press reporter as to whether he knew General MacArthur, he replied: "Know him, why I studied dramatics under him for seven years."

Later, when MacArthur was asked what he thought of President Eisenhower, Mac replied: "He was the best... clerk I ever had."

In April, 1951, President Truman recalled General MacArthur from Korea and relieved him of his command. MacArthur had just recently executed one of the most brilliant tactical maneuvers in military history. In November, 1951 Noble MacArthur visited Nile Temple, his home temple, for one of the most memorable stated meetings ever held at Nile.

But how did MacArthur come to be a Nile noble and when?

Well, it happened during Nile's Sixth Pilgrimage to the Orient (Manila, Hong Kong, Shanghai, and Yokohama) in 1936. For on that trip, while Potentate Tom Holman and the Nile Divan were in Manila performing a Shrine Ceremonial at the Bamboo Oasis Shrine Club located there, a young military officer by the name of Douglas MacArthur was made a Nile Shriner. Prior to that event, in January of 1936, the Grand Master of the Philippines made MacArthur a Mason on sight. Because many United States military officers were members of the Bamboo Oasis Shrine Club, word of Nile's impeding pilgrimage to the Orient from July 18 to August 16 came to MacArthur and he petitioned for membership. Since that date he became one of Nile's most famous and storied members

Douglas MacArthur was born January 26, 1880 at the Arsenal Barracks in Little Rock, Arkansas where his father, Arthur MacArthur was stationed at the time. His mother, Mary Pinckney Hardy was from Norfolk, Virginia. He was raised on a succession of army posts and as he said in his memoir, Reminiscences, "I learned to ride and shoot even before I could read and write – indeed almost before I could walk and talk."

He attended the West Texas Military Academy and graduated at the top of his class. After obtaining an appointment to West Point from Congressman

Theobald Otjen, he again graduated at the top of his class. Upon graduation he was commissioned into the United States Army as a Second Lieutenant in the Corps of Engineers. He served as an engineer until October 1905 when he was selected by his father, now a major general and Commander of the Department of the Pacific, to be his aide de camp. His military career skyrocketed after that. He achieved the rank of major in 1915. Following the entry of the United States into the Great War in 1917, he was instrumental in the formation of the 42ndRainbow Division, made up of soldiers from several states' National Guard units, and became its chief of staff with the rank of colonel. The 42nd fought well in France, so much so that MacArthur was awarded the Croix de Guerre from France and the Silver Star and Distinguished Service Cross from the army. He was promoted to brigadier general on June 26, 1918 making him, at the time, the youngest general in the American Expeditionary Force. The 42nd continued to fight with distinction through the Great War earning great accolades for itself and its leaders. By the end of the Great War, MacArthur had earned six more Silver Stars, another Distinguished Service Cross and the Distinguished Service Medal.

Between the two World Wars, he became the Superintendent of the United States Military Academy, where he made many reforms including the temporary elimination of hazing of the plebes. In 1922 he left West Point to assume command of the Military District of the Philippines, and then command of the 23rd Infantry Brigade. In 1925, he became the army's youngest major general. Thereafter, he received several appointments of command in both the United States and the Philippines, including a short stint as president of the United States Olympic Committee in 1927. In 1930, he was sworn in as United States Chief of Staff with the rank of full general.

After finishing his stint as Army Chief of Staff in 1935 he was awarded another Distinguished Service Medal. When the Philippines received semi-independence in 1935, President Manuel Quezon of the Philippines asked MacArthur to supervise the creation of a Philippine Army. He would be paid a salary in addition to his United States military pay and given the rank of Field Marshal. With President Roosevelt's approval MacArthur took the post and arrived in Manila in October, 1935. He brought with him several assistants, including Captain Thomas J. Davis, Major Dwight D. Eisenhower, and Major James B. Ord. An interesting side note is that while aboard the SS President Hoover bringing him to Manila, he met a 37-year-old divorcee socialite, Jean Marie Faircloth, whom he would later marry.

It was in Manila that the Grand Master of the Philippines heard of his coming and invited him to a local lodge in January 1936 where he made MacArthur a Master Mason on sight. MacArthur later visited the Bamboo Oasis Shrine Club which was a favorite hangout of many top-ranking United States soldiers in Manila. There he learned of the upcoming visit by the Nile Temple Divan and participated in the Manila Shrine Ceremonial in August 1936. Later that month he officially received his title of Field Marshal from President Quezonin of the Philippines in a ceremony at Malacañang Palace. The Philippine Army was formed from universal conscription, but had a difficult time getting organized due to lack of equipment and arms. President Quezonin felt that MacArthur was the man who could transform this army into a respectable fighting machine.

On April 30 1937, MacArthur married Jean Faircloth in Manila and in February 1938 had a son by her, Arthur MacArthur IV. On December 31, 1937, he officially retired from the army, but stayed in Manila as a civilian advisor to President Quezon.

His activities in World War II are so well known and so extensive that there is not sufficient room to delineate them in this article. Suffice it to say that he was recalled to active duty as a major general in 1941 when President Roosevelt federalized the Philippine Army. He was named Commander of United States Army Forces in the Far East and by December 20 had the rank of full general once again. His forces had to retreat to Bataan where they held out until May 1942. MacArthur escaped to Australia where he was named Supreme Commander of the Southwest Pacific Area. During this retreat he uttered his famous line: "I shall return." For his defense of the Philippines he was later awarded the Medal of Honor, joining his father, Major General Arthur MacArthur who had received the Medal of Honor in 1890 for conspicuous heroism during the American Civil War. They were the first father and son winners of the Medal of Honor.

After two more years of fighting he made a triumphant return to the Philippines in October 1944 fulfilling his famous promise to the Philippine people: "I shall return." He was promoted to the rank of General of the Army, a five-star general, in December 1944. It is said that his first set of five stars was crafted by a Philippine jeweler who made them from melted down coins from the United States, Philippines, United Kingdom, Australia and the Netherlands, the countries whose troops he commanded. He accepted Japan's surrender on September 2, 1945 aboard the USS Missouri. After that he oversaw the occupation of Japan from 1945 to 1951, making many reforms and overhauling the government of post-war Japan.

MacArthur's Involvement in the Korean Conflict

After Japan's surrender in 1945 the Soviet Union and the United States agreed to divide the Korean peninsula into two occupation zones with the 38th North latitude as the dividing line. Unfortunately, this situation resulted in the formation of two separate competing governments, the Republic of South Korea under Dr. Syngman Rhee and the Democratic People's Republic of Korea under Kim Il Sung. At Dr. Rhee's inauguration as President of ROK, MacArthur promised Rhee that if North Korea ever attacked South Korea, he would "defend it as I would California."

After the Soviet and United States forces withdrew from their occupation zones in 1948 and 1949 respectively, the expected happened. On June 25, 1950, North Korea invaded South Korea. The UN responded with a resolution to create a UN peacekeeping force to protect South Korea, Ordinarily, such a resolution would have been vetoed by the Soviet Union, a permanent member of the UN Security Council, but the Soviets were out boycotting the Security Council that day due to a previous perceived grievance. The Joint Chiefs of Staff recommended MacArthur to serve as Commander of the UN Force and he was immediately selected. Dr. Rhee then placed all of his army under MacArthur's command. However, by this time, the North Koreans had already pushed the South Korean forces down to the Pusan perimeter.

In order to stem the advance of the North Korean Army in South Korea, MacArthur conceived and launched a daring amphibious assault on the city of Inchon deep in North Korea. Violent tides at this location and a strong enemy presence made this a dangerous operation, which was opposed by the Pentagon. However, on September 15, 1950, MacArthur launched the attack anyway, and proved to be decisively successful. The North Koreans were caught off guard. The North Korean Army advance in South Korea was cut off from its supply lines and began a fast retreat into North Korea. The U. N. troops pursued the invaders back into North Korea across the North Korean border and right to the border of Red China. In Washington, D.C., this was judged to be a violation of the U. N. peacekeeping charge which was simply to defend the South Korean border and keep the peace. MacArthur, however, argued for extending the conflict not only through North Korea but across the Yalu River into China where there were Chinese bases supplying the North Koreans with munitions and other supplies. He also strongly advocated using nuclear force on China if necessary. China appealed to the Soviet Union for help, which responded with supplies and air power, but with little manpower. Truman, alarmed that this conflict could turn into a Third World War, and perhaps a nuclear one, ordered no further advance. In the meanwhile, the Chinese Volunteer People's Army (composed of mostly Red Chinese Army regulars) stormed across the Yalu River to aid the North Koreans and caused the UN forces to retreat across the border. MacArthur wrote to the Republican House majority leader, Rep. Walker, expressing his concerns and displeasure about President Truman's decisions concerning the course of the war and, in effect, asking Congress to take appropriate action directly. Truman blew up over this perceived attempt to set the Legislative Branch against the Executive Branch over this issue and promptly recalled MacArthur in April 1951. The order recalling MacArthur went out April 10 over General Omar Bradley's reluctant signature.

Fighting would continue in Korea until July 27, 1953 when a cease fire was declared, by this time the positions of the armies involved were back at the 38th parallel and a Demilitarized Zone (DMZ) was established around this dividing line. An armistice was signed by the North Koreans and the United States but not by the South Koreans.

Nile Temple, of course, strongly supported its outspoken Noble General. As a result, an outstanding event of 1951 occurred in connection with the Nile November stated meeting to which Potentate H. Dan Bracken Jr. had invited Nile Noble MacArthur. Over 4000 Nile nobles attended that meeting! After General MacArthur finished speaking in which he strongly defended his actions and his rationale for the use of nuclear weapons against the Chinese if necessary, to end the war, Nile Noble Judge William J. Wilkins gave a heartfelt response which said in part:

> "Moreover, history will record that you demonstrated your true greatness as an American when, upon your return to these shores-unselfishly and without rancor-you gave freely of your time, as you did last night, in bringing forcibly to the American people the true conditions, both at home and abroad, as they confront us today and you have revived our spirits and our will to fight. But, General MacArthur, we are proud of you because you typify and represent, better than anyone else, the high ideals of Masonry and Shrinedom. You possess to a high degree

great moral courage, sterling honesty, a sincere belief in fair play and in your fellow man and, in the words of our Shrine Ritual, you have given us an example of a clean, honorable, wholesome and manly life.

Noble MacArthur Attends Nile Stated Meeting Nov. 1951

Later, MacArthur would address a Joint Session of Congress ending his remarks with these words:

I am closing my 52 years of military service. When I joined the army, even before the turn of the century, it was the fulfillment of my boyish hopes and dreams. The world has turned over many times since I took my oath on the plain at West Point, and the hopes and dreams have long since vanished, but I still remember the refrain of one of the most popular barracks ballads of that day which proclaimed most proudly "old soldiers never die, they just fade away." And like the old soldier of that ballad, I now close my military career and just fade away, an old soldier who tried to do his duty as God gave him the light to see that duty. Good Bye.

Historian's note: MacArthur was never able to return to Nile. He lived out the remainder of the last years of his life with wife, Jean, at a suite in the Waldorf-Astoria Hotel in New York and died in 1964.

SPECIAL UNITS

The First Units

In anticipation of a series of articles to be written about the presently surviving units and clubs of Nile Temple, this article is offered as a reminder of Nile's early history and the First Units of Nile.

In the first part of this History of Nile Temple we documented the granting of dispensation to Nile Temple at the Thirty-Fourth Imperial Session held at St. Paul, Minnesota on July 14-15, 1908 based upon a petition of 466 nobles from other temples, mostly Afifi. Ernest B. Hussey, P.P. of mother temple Afifi, was elected as Nile's first potentate at that Imperial Session. Stated meetings were held at Elks Hall in the Alaska Building in Seattle until better quarters could be obtained. With a divan in place and a meeting place secured, Nile got down to the task of organizing itself and recruiting new members.

(Note: Imperial also required a head count of how many Commanderies existed in Nile's jurisdiction (5); how many Consisteries (1); how many present Nile members were members of those Commanderies and Consisteries (625); the distances from other temples (37 m. from Afifi and 337 m. from El Katif), and the proposed dues ($3)).

Could Imperial refuse such a gifted group of nobles? For they were, at the time, the largest group of nobles ever to petition for dispensation and were now, in their first year of existence, making the longest pilgrimage

(5,600 round trip miles) to date for a temple to initiate new nobles in Nome, Alaska. Of course not. At the next Imperial Session held at Louisville, Kentucky on June 9, 1909 Nile was awarded its charter as were Hillah and Rizpah temples.

The Nile Arab Patrol

The first unit formed at Nile Temple was the Nile Arab Patrol. Although the exact date of its inception cannot be pinpointed, Patrol Historian Charles A. Manning wrote in 1915:

> With no available authentic records to determine the exact date of the inception of the Patrol...the only source of information are the memories of the Nobles who at that time were interested in the work of the early days. From such facts as your historian has been able to glean, it is probably safe to set the first getting together of the squad as sometime in September or October of 1908.

Referring to the First Roll Call document, historian Manning goes on to write (Fn. 2):

> There is some doubt as to whether this was really a list of the original members or whether it was simply a list of a Commandery drill team from which the early members of the Patrol were drawn for at that time the two drill teams were so closely intermingled that it was difficult to differentiate one from the other...However, it is safer to assume as the first actual Patrol those who participated in the First Drill given at the First Ceremonial of Nile Temple held in the Moore Theater Dec. 2, 1908. Of this we have undisputed proof for a group photograph was taken on this occasion. In this picture I have been able to secure identification of all but two members. The picture contains 26 men instead of 27 but this is accounted for by one, Noble Klemptner, had scruples against having

his picture taken, and stepped out of ranks before it was
secured.

First Nile Arab Patrol, Dec. 1908

With the exceptions noted the Original Patrol as appearing in this
picture are as follows:

Captain Donald B. Olson, Lieutenants W. D. Freeman,
L. S. Winnans, 1. (Name Unknown), 2. Morris, D. W.,
3. DeVries, L. Y., 4. Drew, F. G., Adjutant, 5. Chestnut,
R. E., 6. Hamill, A. F., 7. Loer,, Dr. T. R., 8. Wood, E.
W., 9. Campbell, J., 10. Hitchcock, R. C., 11. Peter, H., 12.
Dunn, F. C., 13. Ghent, Dr. J. A., 14. Sanders, W. H., 15.
Clementson, G. H., 16. (Name Unknown), 17. Wilcox, G.
W., 18. Brown, J. E., 19. Knight, F. E. A., 20. Plants, D. D.,
21. Cooper, R. B., 22. Tillotson, H. H., 23. Donnelly, D. H.,
24. Klemptner (Not in picture).

The First Ceremonial was a rousing success. Other historians, notably
Freddie Hayden and Frank Lazier have stated that 121 new nobles were

taken in that day in 1908 at the Moore Egyptian Theater in Seattle. Even more amazing was that almost a thousand nobles (many from Afifi) were in attendance to witness this first attempt by the new temple to grow its membership. A picture of the First Ceremonial Divan is pictured below. Unfortunately, we do not have a list of those participating, but it can be reasonably assumed that several of the temple divan's took active part. The Patrol did the Second Section in those days, but we have not been able to discover any documentation of the number and type of stunts used.

First Ceremonial Divan, Dec. 1908

Nile's Second Ceremonial and the Patrol's Second Public Drill took place at the Alaska-Yukon-Pacific Exposition grounds (what is now the University of Washington campus) on August 25, 1909. However, shortly before that event, Nile had become a fully chartered temple. On May 25, 1909, Recorder E.C. Beede wrote to the Imperial Council requesting a charter. He documented how Nile at its First Ceremonial took in 121 Novices and afterward took in several affiliates making the membership total 629 as of the date of his letter. In addition, Nile now had 48 novices elected, six more awaiting action and five more affiliates pending. There would be a Ceremonial held in Nome,

Alaska in July of that year for which 39 petitions had been received to date. He describes the stated meeting and the Ceremonial locations in Seattle and concludes his letter to Imperial as follows:

> "We enclose a copy of our bylaws for your approval and also a draft for $50 as is required by your new bylaws. We have expended in Paraphernalia, including handsome costumes for the officers and the Arab Patrol, about $2000. We feel that we are well equipped and competent to conduct and manage a first-class Shrine and we respectfully pray for a Charter of Constitution that we may continue the good work already begun. Courteously and Fraternally Yours, E.C. Beede.

The Second Drill of the Nile Arab Patrol (its name was changed to Nile Patrol in 1912) was held in the Auditorium of the AYP Exhibition Grounds. In January of 1912, the Patrol obtained the use of the old armory in Seattle for their drills and meetings. That same year the Patrol attended their first Imperial Session in Los Angeles and participated in their first competition. According to the P.I. news report of May 10, 1912, the Nile Patrol won enthusiastic applause from the 20 thousand spectators. Fifty patrols participated and all were given loving cups by Imperial Potentate W. J. Cunningham. The Patrol later attended Imperial Sessions in Atlanta, Georgia (1914) with great success and many more thereafter eventually winning numerous awards for its sterling drill performances.

Sadly, the Nile Patrol last performed in 1994 and was disbanded shortly thereafter.

The Nile Temple Band

Out of small acorns large oak trees grow. The Nile Ceremonial of 1911 held at the old Armory Building in Seattle might not be much remembered except for the new nobles brought into Nile and the Oriental oboe music provided by Walter Searle and Harry H. Thomas. That musical serenade at the 1911 ceremonial prompted several other Nile Nobles who were musicians, several of them members of the Seattle Musician's Union, to consider forming a band to play for Masonic events. This group, consisting of Nobles Harvey Woods, Harry H. Thomas and C. J. Young, (Clarinet); Walter Searle, (Oboe); R. W. Billings, C. D. Wilson, and William H. Westedt, (Cornet); William Murray (Bassoon); S. B. Limerick, (Trombone); and L. P. Schaffer (Bass), together with two Blue Lodge Masons, Henry W. Deutcher (Clarinet) and L. D. Reed (Clarinet) at first thought of making this group a Knight Templar Commandery Band.

They soon dropped this idea and approached Potentate Dan B. Trefethen in 1912 with a petition to form a Nile Temple Band. Dan took no action on this petition, but a year later, one of their supporters, who happened to be Potentate John L. McLean was quite enthusiastic about the concept of a Nile Band. The group held a meeting with the Potentate at the Sherman and Clay Music store in downtown Seattle on June 16, 1913 and hammered out the details of a Band Uniformed unit. Potentate McLean promptly chartered the new unit and thus came into being the second of Nile's Uniformed Units, the Nile Temple Band.

Potentate McLean put Noble Emil Enna of Al Kader Temple in charge of the band to shape it into a "Shrine military band." Noble Enna was impressed with the splendid material of the band and directed the band for 11 rehearsals to get it started. Potentate McLean was elected president of the Band and Harvey Woods was elected Business Manager. When Enna left to back to Al Kader he was succeeded by Noble Harvey Woods as Band Director.

Shortly afterward, several other Nobles joined the Band: Fred Carcer, W.H. Marnes, Burton Stare, W.W. McGuire, and W.D. Allen. In September, Joseph Barton, Isadore Singerman, Ned Yeaton and Joe Cohen joined. Now boasting over 20 members, many of whom were professional musicians, the Nile Temple Band sponsored a Nile Shrine dance in November, 1913 which proved to be an immediate success. All local Master Masons were invited and they and the Shrine nobles crowded the Shrine Auditorium with their ladies to dance the night away to the tuneful sound of a Big Band.

The Band's membership continued to grow and in late June, 1914 the Band was off to its first appearance at a Shrine Imperial Session, that year being held in Atlanta, Georgia. Thirty Band members participated.

The Great War took its toll on the Band and for a couple of years the Band's numbers shrank in size as many of Nile's nobles were called to duty overseas. But after the Armistice in 1919, the Band's membership again grew. The Band accompanied the Nile divan, Patrol, and newly formed Chanters to Portland in 1920 for the Imperial Session held there.

This was the historic Session in which Potentate Forrest Adair of Yaarab Temple in Atlanta gave the famous "Bubbles" speech which so aroused the membership that they voted to create the Shriners Children's Hospitals system at that session, And who is to say that it may not have been a Nile baritone horn player playing "I'm Forever Blowing Bubbles" over and over at 4:00 AM outside the Portland hotel where Forrest Adair had his room the night before that historic session day which was the inspiration for his famous speech? After all, the particular baritone horn player was never identified, although several temples claimed afterward that it was one of their band nobles.

The 1920's brought a revival of both Nile's membership and the Band's numbers. Because many of the Band's members were professional musicians and dependent upon paying gigs for their living, friction would occasionally arise with the Nile Temple Divan in conjunction with Nile's musician hiring practices. On February 9, 1928, the Band filed a complaint with the Divan that the Band musicians were being overlooked as performers for Nile functions. They were concerned that Nile was hiring non-union musicians for temple activities to save money. Needless to say, Nile responded by toeing the line with union musicians. After all, it was the Roaring 20's and money was no object. The Great Depression changed all that. And, in a later year, the Band would not be so successful in its dealings with Nile Potentates.

The early Directors of the Band were Harvey Woods 1913-1932; William Marshall, 1933-1937; Emil Podhora, 1938; Clyde Morris, 1939-1950, Charles Decker, 1950-1988. More recent directors were Jack Parks 1989-90, Ed Krenz 1991-2002, and Winston Vitous 2003-2010.

Band Presidents have numbered several past potentates and/or potentates-to-be including: John McLean (1913), Joseph Swalwell (1915), Glenn Carpenter (1952), Fred Sethman (1955), Walter Woodburn (1960), Bob Kercheval (1971) and Warren Ploeger.

Of course, in all the other years, talented Nobles filled the office of Band President, one of the oldest survivors being Ted Bendel (1970).

The Band survived the 30's playing all over Northwest and attending PNSA Conventions and Imperial Sessions whenever there was enough money to be had to pay for a trip. The Band was a key element of the 1936 Imperial Session held in Seattle performing regularly and leading the 2500-member massed band which was a highlight of the convention. The Band sponsored and occupied a full floor in the Old Times Building in downtown Seattle which was headquarters for Nile Temple that year. However, the 1940's brought some serious changes to the Band.

In 1941, for reasons unknown to many but will be divulged below, Potentate Louis J. Dowell ordered the Band dissolved and kicked off the Nile premises. This was quite a blow to the Band since the Temple subsidized the Band's trips to PNSA and Imperial. This author's investigation has revealed that by the 1940's many Band members were making a decent living again performing at union assignments. At Nile they performed for free. There was just too much economic sacrifice and inconvenience to many of the members to turn down paying jobs to comply with requests to play for free. Apparently, on several occasions during this time period, the Band, through their controversial Band Manager, F.D. Mande, refused to heed certain Pote's Calls for the Band to perform. Again, the reason was that many of the best players were occupied doing paying gigs. However, Potentate Dowell felt that the Band "was getting too big for its breeches" in ignoring his calls and June 23, 1941 wrote a letter to the Band demanding the expulsion from the Band of Mande. The Band voted to retain Mande and wrote a letter back to the Potentate telling him that they refused to expel Mande. Four days later, Potentate Dowell notified each band member that the Band had been dissolved. He relieved each of the officers of their duties and ordered that all of the equipment be turned in. Of course, each musician who personally owned an instrument would keep his own piece. Nevertheless, there was a substantial amount of band material that had been purchased by the Band with Band finds, which in turn were Nile funds, and thus Nile property.

Order was restored in September, 1941, when Potentate Dowell wrote to various former bandsmen of a reorganization of the Nile Shrine Temple Band. A reorganization meeting took place on October 13, 1941 at which time Howard Eash was elected President and Clyde Morris Director. Charter members of the reorganized Band included 21 full and 16 associate members, most of whom were not union musicians. There is no record which this author could find as to whether or not a Band Manager position was reinstated at this time.

Although several musicians were drafted and or volunteered to fight in WWII, by 1943 Band membership stood at 59, the year that Jerry Sampson was President. At the end of 1946, Band membership had swelled to 80 members. In 1949, new articles and bylaws were adopted, and that same year, Potentate Ken Howe had the temple buy new fezzes for all the uniformed units, including the Band. The special uniformed unit fezzes were to be worn only when in uniform and were to remain the property of the temple under the care of the quartermasters of each unit.

In the post-war years the Band continued to grow. They played at the 1950 Harold Lloyd Ceremonial held at Nile and were a major participant in the "On The Road To Mecca" operetta which premiered that year. In ensuing performances of that famed operetta, the Band usually played the Overture, the music for actors' entrances and exits, during the intermission and at the close.

That same year they were a celebrated unit at the 76th Imperial Session in Los Angeles presided over by Imperial Potentate Harold Lloyd. After those highpoints, the Band continued to distinguish itself at PNSA Conventions and Imperial Sessions over the next four decades winning numerous trophies and awards in competitions with the best temple bands from across North America. They played at the 1982 and 1983 Imperial Sessions in Orlando and Denver respectively and came away with second place trophies each time outdoing all other bands in North America except the Charleston, W. Virginia band in 1982 and another band in 1983. Most impressive of all was their consecutive first-place wins at PNSA conventions from approximately 1967-1978. The Band members were actually relieved when another band won the year their string was broken so embarrassing had their streak become for other temples' bands.

One special anecdote is worth retelling. In 1978, Ted Bendel, through his wholly owned travel agency, booked a Greek ship for three temples (Nile, Al Aska and Al Kader) to take a joint Pote's trip consisting of a cruise around the Caribbean Sea ending at San Juan, Puerto Rico. Musicians from all three temples' bands signed up for the cruise and they wound up becoming the musical hit of the voyage. In the afternoons, the bands' members would assemble on the fantail of the ship and provide a concert for the ship's passengers and crew. So entrancing were these concerts that a scheduled stop in Haiti was missed and no one complained.

The Band played at the Kids' Christmas Parties, at the Nile Family Picnics, at ceremonials, dances, and special events. They went on the road to play at other temples or for Scottish Rite and Masonic Service Bureau events and dances. The Pote's Band, a spinoff from the Big Band during Potentate Aurie Thompson's year (1963), consisting of several virtuoso performers From The Band made listeners want to hear more from the Big Band. Scotty Kelley (trumpet and President of the Seattle Musician's

Union) led these indomitable performers wherever the Potentate went for many years. In Shrine parades the Pote's Band would ride on an old fire truck provided by Potentate Bob Wright and stunned the bystanders with their jazz and Dixieland music improvisations. The Pote's Band was so good that Imperial Divan members made it a point to gather and listen to them at Imperial Sessions. Overall, the Nile Temple Band players were for almost a century, quite simply, one of the finest ensemble bands in the country.

In the last decade, the Band has suffered a serious decline in membership due to falling numbers of new nobles, deaths and demits. There are a few veteran members yet around but the Band no longer functions as a performing uniformed unit. The instruments are eerily stacked down in the Nile basement as if awaiting a resurrection of those magnificent horn players and drum beaters of the past. Drums are in cases and horns rest in velvet linings in their satchels as if all were patiently awaiting the return of the magical touch of their musicians' hands and lips. The thousands of music scores are sitting in cardboard boxes and in old metal file cabinets while the ravages of time spur them to eventual disintegration. The music stands lie idle and the whole Band room has the musty smell of impending final darkness.

But there those rare occasions, sometimes at a Nile Family Picnic or at a get together of some of the Band veterans when the old sparks of musical excellence and ensemble camaraderie, which are the hallmarks of the Band, still flare into an uplifting, sonorous performance reminiscent of the old days when this Band was the best in the land.

The Chanters Unit

After the formation of Nile Patrol (1908) and the Nile Band (1913), the next unit to be formed at Nile was the Chanters unit. Early in January, 1920, Potentate Archie F. Hamill attended a rehearsal of the Seattle Scottish Rite Choir at the downtown Scottish Rite Center. After hearing their presentation and being duly impressed by their musicality, he decided to form a choir at Nile. He immediately recruited 22 of the Scottish Rite singers since they were also Shriners. In keeping with the Arabic theme of Nile he promptly named the new choir, The Chanters.

We can now name these original 22 Chanters: F. A. Bates, C. B. Ogle,

L. J. Mackay, Per Olsson, Accompanist, L. Nash, A. A. Nelson, C. C. Emmons, W. J. Reseburg, A. E. Boardman, David F. Davies, Director, Roy G. Rossman, President, A. W. Pollock, Walter Eckart, Maurice Friedman, Librarian, John Lang, Jr., A. K. Marriott, J. W. Thatcher, A. Wrenall, Magnus N. Peterson, H. J. Cone, J. E. Atkinson, and W. R. McClintock, Secretary-Treasurer.

Now 1920 opened with a shocker. On January 1, Babe Ruth was traded by the Boston Red Sox to the New York Yankees for $125,000, the highest price ever paid to obtain a ball player up to that time. Potentate Hamill opened the Nile 1920 Shrine year with a Ceremonial on January 29, the very day that the 18th Amendment (Prohibition) took effect. The Ceremonial netted 150 new nobles. The Imperial Council Session to be held in Portland that year was the prime goal of Nile's units and nobles. Al Kader would be hosting Imperial Council and they expected a large delegation from their growing sister temple at Seattle. The Band and the Patrol were busy practicing and drilling for Portland. And the newly chartered Chanters were preparing their songs under the able leadership of Noble David F. Davies. However, Potentate Hamill wanted another Ceremonial on June 11 to further boost Nile's ranks before the Portland Imperial Session, which would be attended by General John J. Pershing, a noble at Sesostros Temple in Lincoln, Nebraska. The June Ceremonial boosted Nile by another 618 new members.

Because Seattle was a gateway to the Northwest over 10,000 Shriners eventually passed through Seattle in June of that year on their way to Portland and Nile gathered almost 1000 automobiles to squire them around Seattle and show them the Puget Sound area. On June 21, the 60-member Band, 43-member Patrol, 22 member Chanters and 1400 regular members left Seattle in two special trains of the Great Northern Railroad for Portland. Several hundred other nobles headed down by automobile or on other trains so that Nile's total representation at Portland was closer to 2000 nobles.

After much rehearsal and a scramble to find uniforms, the Chanters borrowed white overalls from the Nile Arab Patrol for their day performances and each Chanter brought his tuxedo for evening performances. The Chanters would eventually adopt uniforms modeled after the Patrol's uniforms with colorful vest jackets, pantaloons and sweeping sashes. Later, they would adopt a maroon sport coat, white pants, white shoes, and white shirt with a striped crimson and gray ("Cougar") tie. Today, the Chanters wear dark pants and dark shoes with their maroon sport coats, but they still sport the striped Cougar tie, much to the dismay of some Husky alumni.

Under the directorship of Noble David F. Davies the new Chanters unit acquitted itself very well in Portland, even to the point of joining with several of the more established Chanters units from around the country to serenade the assembled nobility and their ladies in a mass choir performance of several hit tunes of the time. And, of course, as would become the custom for many years to come, the Chanters marched in the Grand Imperial Parade singing a series of swell songs for the parade onlookers. Until recent times, the Chanters attended all Imperial Sessions, except for the 1934 session in which no Nile units participated due to economic hard times, and all PNSA summer events.

As the Chanters unit grew, and they would eventually reach 45 to 50 singers at any one-time, other directors came on board. From 1920 to 1923, the Director was David F. Davies. From 1923 to 1926, it was Adam Jardine. In 1927 Orin "Jack" O'Dale took over. During the Depression years and into the war years (1932-1944) the Director was Arville Belstad. One of the most colorful directors was August Werner who directed the Chanters from 1944 to 1965. He was a Professor at the UW School of Music, sang with Seattle Opera, composed musical pieces, and performed regularly as a soloist at community events. Fred Sethman took over from 1966 to 1974 and from 1975 to 1980 the Director was Ed Ottum. Since then, a variety of great directors have worked with the Chanters, including, Neil Laurence, P. P. Bob Wright, Jim Hart, Alvin "Bubba" Hendricks, P.P. Fred Oliver, Al Dillan and currently serving as Director is Ed Grimes.

Like the Patrol and the Band, the Chanters early on began participating in Imperial Session and PNSA competitions. They won many awards, too numerous to mention here. They were frequently invited to "sing for their suppers" at other Masonic organizations such as the Scottish Rite, the Masonic Service Bureau, Eastern Star, Daughters of the Nile, and the Ladies Oriental Shrine. They performed for various community groups and participated in town parades all over the Northwest with their singing and staged antics.

In 1936, when the Imperial Session was held in Seattle to honor Nile P.P. Hugh Caldwell who was to be elected Imperial Potentate, the Chanters used the fourth floor of the Old Times Building to build a replica of a Klondike Gold Rush Saloon at which they dispensed both suds and songs in such a delightful manner that the Saloon became a hit of the downtown festivities.

But in 1950 something special happened. Noble George T. McGillivray had composed an Arabian operetta, later titled "On the road To Mecca," which was to debut at Nile's Harold Lloyd Ceremonial on Saturday May 20, 1950 held at the Civic Auditorium in downtown Seattle. The Patrol, the Band and the Chanters would all participate. The operetta consisted of two acts and four scenes. In Act I, Scene I, a caravan of novices, played by the Chanters, assembled in the City of Berbera for a pilgrimage to the Sacred City of Mecca to entertain the potentate and his divan and to receive their rewards. The Chanters sang "The Open Road," "Allah Have Mercy On Us" and the Arab Marching Song. Soprano soloist Jean Gray sang the role of the Water Girl, "Wanting You" by Sigmund Romberg. In Scene II, the caravan camps on the banks of the Nile River, entertaining themselves with song followed by the Evening Prayer. Chanter soloist Dr. Edwin Palmason, in the role of Abu Bekr, sang "Softly As In A Morning Sunrise." He joined Jean Gray for the beautiful duet "One Alone" and Chanter soloist L. Edwin Mackay sang "To The Faithful for Prayer" as Muezzin-Azan. The Chanters then sang "Song of the Seraphim."

In Scene III, the pilgrims encounter a fierce desert storm with special lightning, wind and thunder effects provided by the First and Second Sections. One of the unlucky pilgrims, Usama, sings "Till The Sands of the Desert Grow Cold," beautifully performed by Chanter soloist, George Peckham. In Act II, Scene I, the pilgrims make it to Mecca and the Ceremonial Cast takes over in the usual manner seen in today's ceremonials. However, the singers were not done. To entertain the Potentate at Mecca, the Chanters sang several songs, Dr. Palmason sang the "Kashmiri Song" by Finden; Jean Gray sang the beautiful "Only A Rose"; George Peckham sang "On the Road To Mandalay"; and Ed Mackay sang the "Prayer Song" with a background chorus of Chanters.

This operetta would continue to be performed for almost four decades after this event with different songs and different singers. The spectacular backdrops for these four scenes are still boxed in the First Section shack at Nile. In 2008 the palace scene backdrop was brought out by Noble Dave Ramich for the first time in almost 20 years, was set up in the ballroom and used that year at ceremonials honoring Past Potentate Don Cameron and Nile's 100th formation Anniversary. At this latter Ceremonial, visiting Imperial Potentate Doug Maxwell had several pictures taken of himself and his lady, Patricia, in front of this wonderful backdrop, two of which were printed in the Imperial Session guidebook for the 2009 Imperial Session in San Antonio.

The Chanters also started the annual Children's Christmas Party in 1929 and were the sponsoring unit on this special event for several decades. A special story line was created each year with Chanters and other nobles acting and singing the parts of the storyline characters. The event, now known as the Kid's Christmas Party, is presently sponsored by the Nile Clown unit with the Chanters always participating and leading the children and adults in a variety of seasonal songs, ending with "Rudolph, The Red Nosed Reindeer" as Rudolph and Santa appeared.

The Chanters would practice every week under motivated directors to hone their skills. As time wore on, and membership in Nile dropped, so did membership in the Chanters unit. It became harder and harder to find men who wanted to be a "singing Shriner." Yet today the Chanters unit continues to practice and perform the national anthems of the United States and Canada at stated meetings and PNSA. Occasionally, they perform at other events such as a February Nile Sweethearts Dinner or a March St. Patrick's Day luncheon.

This article will close with the words of Past Director and Past President, Fred H. Oliver, P.P.:

> "It truly is a success story with these Nobles rehearsing once a week under inspiring directors who stimulated the unit to turn their talents into wonderful performances. Our thanks to these musical directors, Nobles who spent countless hours and days to lead the Chanters to successful musical presentations and the achievement of many awards and honors through the years. A special thanks also goes out to those men and women who were the accompanists during these years, people who added greatly to the quality of the Chanters' performances."

This history would not be complete without also mentioning those Nobles who served as Presidents of this honored unit of Nile, from the first President, Noble Roy G. Rossman to the current President, Noble Robert Starowski. These Nobles dedicated their years to successfully managing the

Chanters and their ideas and creativity have made the Chanter experience so worthwhile with peace and harmony prevailing.

Finally, we offer thanks to the many Nobles from other Units and from the Divan who assisted the Chanters in their National Anthem presentations at stated meetings when their current ranks were thinned through age, sickness or other unavailability."

If you are interested in becoming a Nile Chanter, please contact President Robert Starowski at rmstarowski@yahoo.com or Director Ed Grimes at ejgrimes@yahoo.com. No sight reading is required. As long as you can carry a tune or are willing to learn to carry a tune (rehearsal practice CDs are available in all voices), you are welcome to join the Chanters as they prepare to invigorate their programs with new material and to plan for future event performances.

The Legion of Honor and Legion of Honor Drill Team

When speaking about a group of valiant men who come together to share their common experiences and service to country such as these men of the Legion of Honor, it is important to understand what this organizational unit is about and why it exists. A Legion of Honor is a Shrine unit composed of nobles who have served in the military service of their country, whether active or veteran, honorably discharged or retiree, volunteer or draftee, officer or enlisted. They are all proud to be doing or having done whatever their country required of them to keep their country and its citizens safe from all real and perceived threats to security and wellbeing. This includes service in the United States Army, United States Navy, United States Air Force, United States Coast Guard, Marines, Merchant Marines, or any reserve component thereof.

The stated objectives of a Legion of Honor are to foster a spirit of patriotism and love of country and flag; to perpetuate the memory of fallen comrades who gave their lives for their country while members of the armed forces; to unite more closely former comrades in arms in the continuing service of God and country, and Masonry and Shrinedom; to maintain a Color Guard and a Uniformed unit for representation of country and Temple in ceremonials, parades and other social functions; and, as both individuals and Legion of Honor Units, to develop an increase in friendship and cooperation among Legion of Honor Units and among other units of Shriners International.

Talked about for years, the Legion of Honor (LOH) unit at Nile came into being largely through the efforts of Noble Col. Robert M. Watkins. The spur to formation was the coincidence at the 1936 Imperial Session, held at Seattle and hosted by Nile Temple, of the National Association of Legions of Honor (NALOH) annual meeting. Aware of Nile's intentions, National Commander Henry H. Green (Yaarab Temple, Atlanta, Ga.) brought three LOH Drill Teams to Seattle, which performed with the utmost military precision. Sensing the opportunity, Watkins approached Nile Potentate Tom Holman for permission to form a Nile LOH unit that year. On Armistice Day of that year (November 11) Potentate Holman gave his permission to Watkins and his committee, consisting of Watkins, Chester Chastek and Colonel Walter Pollitz to investigate the feasibility of such a unit. The committee's report was presented at the December 10, 1936 Nile Temple stated meeting, officially accepted, and the new unit was sanctioned to come into being. On the following day, the first Nile LOH meeting occurred with Col. Watkins was elected as Commander; Chastek as Senior Vice Commander; and Kenneth Hodges as Junior Vice Commander. Other charter members were Hugh Shaw, Finance Officer; Dr. Barton E. Peden, Surgeon; Irvin F. Heise, Chaplain; Manuel Laskey, Quartermaster; Harry Stengel, Adjutant; and Jack Wait, Provost Marshal. In addition, a Constitution was drafted and it as well as bylaws were adopted.

Petition was immediately made to the NALOH for a charter and, on December 21, 1936, NALOH elected Nile LOH as its 10th member unit.

Chastek was elected Commander of Nile LOH for 1937. And in that year, a Legion of Honor Drill Team was assembled, having received permission from Potentate Carl Croson in March of that year to do so – 32 men in line and four officers. The four LOHDT officers were: Robert Scheible, Captain; Arthur Swanson, First Lieutenant; Elmer E. Watkins, First Lieutenant; and Cecil O. Temple, Second Lieutenant.

Captain Scheible, as Drill Master of the team, apparently showed little mercy to his charges. He drilled them relentlessly twice a week until he made a crack drill unit out of those rookies. Regular drills were held at a waterfront location near the old Albers Milling Company in good weather and, in bad weather, the drills were conducted at the old Washington National Guard Armory.

1937 was a very good year for Nile's LOH. That year, Henry Fisher and Past Commander Watkins attended the NALOH Convention held in Atlanta, GA where Colonel Watkins was elected as National Sixth Lieutenant Commander of the national organization. As it turned out, Colonel Watkins served the National up until he reached the office of National Second Lieutenant Commander when he had to resign in 1941 for health reasons.

But in late 1937, the drill unit was almost ready to perform. Nile Temple purchased special uniforms for members of the drill team and their debut that year was a rousing success. The following year, Potentate Harrison J. Hart, extended an invitation to this new unit to join the other Nile uniformed units (Patrol, Band, Chanters) on a pilgrimage to the 1938 Imperial Session in Los Angeles. Captain Schieble's hard drilling paid off as a fully formed marching Nile LOH Drill Team showed up in Los Angeles to stun the crowds of assembled nobles by taking a podium award for LOH Drill Teams.

During the period of the drill team's existence several prominent nobles have served as Drill Team Captains, including Robert Scheible, Cecil O. Temple, Jack Wait, Charles Kessler, John Cerjence and Ted Fonis. More recently, John Lien, Walt Lain, Bob Colton, Manny Ventoza, and Travis Dean have served as Drill Team Captains.

Many prominent nobles have served as Nile's LOH Commanders, including Chester Chastek, Robert Watkins, Jack Wait, Past Potentates John G. Jones, John G. Lien and Edgar R. Davidson. The present Commander is Noble Jim Erickson.

However, despite Nile LOH's prestige and national presence, its luck in producing National Commanders from its ranks has been problematical. As you saw above, Col. Robert Watkins had to resign for health reasons after reaching the rank of National Second Lieutenant Commander. In 1945, Noble Bert Snyder died in office after reaching the rank of National Third Lieutenant Commander. And, Noble Julius C. Anderson, who had been elected to take Noble Snyder's position, died in 1947 after reaching the rank of National Third Lieutenant Commander. It was not until Noble Jack Wait, who also had been elected to the position of National Fourth Lieutenant Commander following Noble Anderson's death, that Nile had an LOH member who made it to the top as National Commander. (It should be noted that the line to the top takes eight years in various National Lieutenant Commander divisional positions before assuming command as National Commander).

The 1953 National Association of Legions of Honor (NALOH) Convention in Seattle

As the elected National Commander in 1952, Noble Wait now had the privilege of holding the LOH National Convention in his home temple. And from May 20-23, 1953, the Nile Legion of Honor hosted its first NALOH Conference. Nile Noble John H. (Jack) Wait, Nile LOH Commander in 1940, reigned as National Commander. The Benjamin Franklin Hotel in Seattle was the convention headquarters. A Memorial Service at the Public Safety Building honored all war dead and especially the late Tom Holman, Nile Potentate 1936, under whose administration the Nile LOH was chartered. After the business of NALOH was concluded on Friday May 22, a huge Banquet and Ball took place at the Nile Country Club ballroom. On Saturday May 23, the visiting LOH members were treated to a tour around Lake Washington and a midnight supper. The convention was a great success and Nile's LOH took great pride in this singular accomplishment. As noted above, Nile LOH would have had a National Commander emanate from its ranks years earlier but for the untimely ill health and deaths of three other LOH nobles who had been in the NALOH line. After Noble Wait, it would be another 32 years before Nile could boast of another National Commander from its ranks.

The 1985 NALOH Convention in Seattle

In 1985, Roland J. Hoefer's year as Potentate was marked by several interesting events. Besides the move of Nile Temple headquarters to its new facility on the Country Club grounds, on March 26-29, 1985, Nile's Legion of Honor hosted the 54th Annual Meeting of the NALOH. Nile LOH Past Commander (1978) Fred E. Clyne made it through the eight-year line of the National LOH leadership to become National Commander. The NALOH Convention was held at the Red Lion Motor Inn in Sea-Tac. Almost 1500 Legion nobles and their ladies from all over North America attended the convention. The Directors General for the Convention were Nobles Don Pells (Nile LOH Commander 1985) and Walt Odom (P.P. 1979) with Nobles John Lien (Nile LOH Commander in 1978), Bob Stephens (P.P. 1984) and Gene Murray as Deputy Directors. Special guests at this gala event were Governor Booth Gardner, Seattle Mayor Charles

Royer, Imperial Potentate Gene Bracewell, Admiral Herb Bridge, and Seattle historian and author Bill Speidel. Earlier that month Noble Mel Blanc appeared at a Nile Supper Show, but could not stay around for the NALOH Convention due to other commitments. Once again, the Nile LOH proved itself a most worthy player among the 100 or so LOH Units in North America at the time.

Imperial Nixes Separate NALOH Conventions

But before this significant event in Nile's history could take place, a gray cloud from Imperial had to be removed from the skies of Nile. It seems that in November, 1982, Imperial Council met in special session and decided to instruct NALOH to change its bylaws with respect to its annual meeting date. Instead of NALOH's bylaw allowing National Commanders to host the annual NALOH Conventions in their home temples, Imperial demanded that the Annual NALOH Convention be held in conjunction with Imperial Session during and at Imperial's time and location. Imperial would allow NALOH to have a mid-year meeting not less than 90 days before or 90 days after Imperial, but the annual convention had to coincide with Imperial Session. The ostensible reason given by Imperial was to deter "fragmentation of the Order" should Shrine unit National organizations continue to meet at times and places other than at Imperial Sessions. Imperial sent a strongly worded letter to NALOH regarding this order but at the same time gave NALOH two years to comply. Thus, the NALOH Conventions for 1983 and 1984 could be held respectively at Gatlinburg, Tennessee and Oklahoma City, Oklahoma as planned, but the 1985 Convention would have to take place at Atlanta, Georgia where Imperial Session would be held that year.

One can imagine the consternation among LOH Units and individual members, especially at Nile, that developed over this edict. Numerous letters and phone calls poured into Imperial protesting the order and testifying to the value and service of LOH Units to their country and to their temples. Fred Clyne wrote an impassioned letter to Imperial Second Ceremonial Master George Powell, whom he personally knew, asking him to intervene on behalf of Nile for 1985. Past Potentate Loren McFarland of Tehran Temple wrote most eloquently to all Imperial Divan members that forcing NALOH to meet during Imperial, rather than at National

Commanders' home temples, would cause undue time constraints and expense on NALOH activities and attendees and may In the end "ring down the curtain" on NALOH. The compromise reached, through the efforts of then National Commander Bud Farmer, Fred Clyne and Imperial Sirs Dr. Bowers and Gene Bracewell, was that NALOH could conduct all of its annual business and elections at a National Spring Meeting yet still sponsor its "annual meeting" at Imperial Session for those who wished to attend. The Spring Meeting could be held anywhere at the call of the National Commander. Thus, the day was saved for Nile's NALOH Convention in 1985.

NALOH has since become the International Association of Legions of Honor (IALOH) in keeping with Imperial's name change of Shriners of North America to Shrine International. IALOH now consists of over 9,000 nobles in 150 Legion of Honor Units throughout the world. The association continues to provide overall coordination of and guidance for its member units.

State Of Washington Plaque at Tomb Of Unknown Soldier

Another anecdote about Noble Clyne involved his effort to have a plaque in honor of the veterans of Washington State placed at the Tomb of the Unknown Soldier. It seems that Noble Clyne, during one of his visits to the annual Wreath Laying Ceremony at the Tomb in Arlington, Virginia, noticed that in the adjacent rotunda awards room there was no plaque honoring Washington State veterans as there were for almost every other state. In February, 1982, at a meeting of the Ballard Shrine Club at which Senator Henry Jackson was presented with a Nile fez bearing the title "Senator," Fred spoke with Senator Jackson about this anomaly. Senator Jackson promptly wrote letters to the Department of the Army and to Governor John Spellman and had the situation corrected. On October 20, 1983, Fred and several members of Nile's Legion of Honor had the privilege of seeing Governor Spellman present the Washington State plaque to the Superintendent of the Tomb for installation in the rotunda. The heads of every Washington State veteran's organization were present for this ceremony.

But the Nile LOH is much more than NALOH or IALOH. It has been a vital part of Nile Shrine Center activities for over 75 years supporting the potentates, attending Nile, PNSA and Imperial Shrine activities, and hosting events such as the LOH Drill Team's Annual Spaghetti Dinners and the LOH Mother's Day Breakfasts held in the Spring of each year. The Nile LOH has a Color Guard unit which carries the flags of all countries of Shrine International in parades, recently adding the Philippine flag after Mabuhay Shrine Center in Manila was chartered in 2010. The Color Guard also carries and posts the colors at Nile stated meetings and at other Nile events. The Ladies of LOH members are among the most dedicated of all Nobles' spouses helping out and, in many cases, taking over command of the preparation of the social functions of the LOH and the Drill Team. Without their love, assistance, and support, many of the LOH events would have languished in the trenches and in the scuppers of male procrastination.

The Nile LOH has served Nile long and gloriously and much more can be said about the stalwart men who comprised in the past and to this day continue this illustrious unit. The Nile LOH presently meets on the first Friday of the month at 6 PM in its meeting room on the first floor of Nile except for the months of January, June, July, and August. Nevertheless, you can see the drill team and other LOH members in parades with their "Desert Storm" Jeep, flags flying and arms waving. The LOH Color Guard will always be out in front of all the Shrine units in any parade showing the colors and in smart 100 steps per minute march time arousing the patriotism and gratitude of bystanders and onlookers.

Today, any Shriner in good standing who is a veteran of the United States Military or of the armed forces of United States Allies is eligible to become a member of the Nile Legion of Honor. Call the Nile office at 425-774-9611 at x 213 for information and referral to an LOH member.

OTHER GROUPS

The Nile Oriental Band

Although relatively recent as a unit compared to the Patrol, the Concert Band and the Chanters, the Nile Oriental Band has more than proved its worth to Nile as a fund raising, award winning and marvelously entertaining working unit. But what do we know of its origins, and of the origins of Oriental bands in general? And what about the name "Oriental"? Surely these Arabic looking entertainers could not possibly have derived their costuming and grooming from the Far East.

Indeed the term Oriental, as used by Western historians prior to the mid-20th century, referred to the lands of the Eastern Roman Empire, in particular, the lands of the Eastern Mediterranean, including Turkey, ancient Palestine, Syria, Persia (now Iran/Iraq), Egypt and other parts of northern Africa and some of the Balkan states. As European scholarship followed explorers farther eastward, the term shifted to be more associated with the Far Eastern countries. Nevertheless, when Billy Florence and Dr. Walter Fleming astounded the world in 1872 with the Ancient Arabic Order of Nobles of the Mystic Shrine, Oriental meant the Near East, i.e., the Arabic and Hebrew/Aramaic speaking countries of the Eastern Mediterranean Sea. Technically, the term Oriental is derived from the Latin root "oriens," which means rising. Thus, Oriental referred to the areas where the sun rises in the East and to Western Europeans that looked like the Near East.

It should be noted that the use of the term Oriental has been prohibited by Washington State law from being used in the state's official public documents. (Engrossed Senate Bill 5954 2002) (use "Asian" instead). The reason given was that in recent years the term Oriental was being used pejoratively when referring to persons of Asian descent.

Shrine Oriental Bands

It might surprise some readers to learn that Shrine Oriental Bands have been around since the turn of the 20th Century. The inspiration for such bands came in 1893 when, during the Chicago World's Fair, several Turkish exhibits and shows displayed the work and talents of their country. A great sensation at the fair was a show starring "Little Egypt," a justly famed belly dancer. To call attention to the show, the barker had two musicians near him, one playing a musette, or reed horn, and the other a tom-tom. Nobles of Medina Temple of Chicago visiting the fair were so impressed by these musicians that they decided to organize a band composed of these instruments plus a few other percussion instruments. So, in 1899, Potentate Frank Roundy of Medinah Temple commissioned the temple organist, George Kurzenknabe, to form such a band. But no such instruments were to be found in Chicago. A German instrument maker was retained to produce a musette like the Turkish one. When done, the price turned out to be $20 and it did not sound right. But after further diligent inquiry, the organist found a similar horn made by the Sing Fat Co. of San Francisco, and it did sound right and only cost $1. Once the horns were procured and a Chinese gong and a triangle were added to the tom toms, the Medinah Oriental Band was off and running or at least playing a strange form of music.

However, they had only one tune to play called "The Midway." After numerous renditions of it at the temple, nobles were threatening to use ripe tomatoes, seltzer bottles and other like items to quiet this raucous band. Understandably, George Kurzenknabe quickly found the time to compose several more pieces for the strange combination of musette and drum. The Medinah Oriental Band went public at the 1901 Imperial Session in Kansas City, and within two years had refined its playing so much that it began to assume the swagger that Oriental bands demonstrate to this day over ordinary brass bands. Other Temples soon clamored to have their own Oriental bands and the stampede was on its way throughout Shrinedom. All adopted Arabic costuming, beards, and the jewelry that we still see today.

The West Seattle Shrine Club Oriental Band

The story of the Nile Oriental Band began in West Seattle. In 1957, a group of nobles from that club began to meet in the basement of Noble Ray Schick's home. Inspired by the Oriental bands which some of them had seen play in other parts of the country, they decided to form their own enterprise. The first musettes were made in the machine shop where Noble Hugh Benedict worked. The group decided that their musettes were to be double-reeded to be more authentic, unlike the single reed musettes used by other Temples' bands. Although the double reed is harder to play, it produces a lovelier and stronger sound than the single reed. Today, most Oriental bands order their musette reeds from Zenobia Temple Oriental Band which has sold a very good plastic reed since 1961.

The West Seattle Shrine Club Oriental Band (WSSSCOB) was then organized with Ray Schick as its first President, and George Jory as Director. Other charter members were Hugh Benedict, Frank Richardson, Mel Harris, Earl Knight, Al Mills, Francis Reeder, John Shukis, and Ike Eskenazi. They were soon joined by other nobles such as Angus McMillan, Ken Northrup, Harry Greenblatt, and Ken Kinsey, Sr. Although membership was at first limited to West Seattle Shrine Club members, that requirement was soon dropped to allow other nobles from Nile to join in the fun.

They held their practices on Monday evenings in the West Seattle

High School auditorium and their marching practices on the athletic field. Regular business meetings were held at the West Seattle Golf Course Clubhouse. They performed at the 1958 Issaquah Salmon Days as well as playing and marching in the West Seattle Seafair Hi Yu parade. They soon received invitations from all sorts of community parade organizers and very quickly, the Potentates of Nile Temple recognized the impact that this band had on the public. In 1958, the band was visited by Potentate Jimmy Cain at one of their West Seattle rehearsals and, at his request, performed at several Nile functions that year. In 1959, Potentate Lloyd X. Coder asked the band to represent Nile Temple at PNSA in Calgary, Alberta. According to legend, none of the Nile units could attend, and unless some unit representing Nile attended, the Potentate himself could not march in the PNSA parade. The WSSCOB went to that convention paying all of its own expenses and the Pote marched in the parade.

Yet despite its performance on behalf of Nile in 1959, the WSSCOB was not invited to become a working unit of Nile Temple. Perhaps, the members themselves resisted amalgamation into Nile fearing that they might lose some of their artistic freedom. Rumor has it that a petition was made in 1959, but for some reason it was not acted upon. So, the WSSCOB continued on its own, marching in numerous parades, gaining parade awards and accolades wherever they appeared. Then a strange thing happened. The September 1962 issue of the Smile with Nile carried an ad seeking nobles to form an Oriental Band at Nile Temple as a working unit. Guess who answered the call?

Nile Oriental Band Chartered

Since most nobles who were interested in Oriental Band participation were already members of the WSSCOB, very few nobles at Nile answered the call. Then, a hat in hand call to the officers of the WSSCOB by the Nile Divan resulted in a wholesale transfer of the WSSCOB into Nile as a working unit. An organizational meeting was held in December, 1962 and the new Nile Oriental Band was chartered. Bylaws were approved in January, 1963. Elected as officers of the new Nile Oriental Band were George Jory as President, Clifford Glass, First VP, Ike Eskenazi, Second VP, Charles Ferris, Secretary, and John Shukis, Treasurer. Later, the officers' names were changed to be more in keeping with the OB's Arabic theme. President became Sultan, the

VP's became Pashas I and II, the Secretary became Keeper of the Scrolls, and the Treasurer became Keeper of the Purse.

Potentate Aurie J. Thompson kept the new Nile Oriental Band busy that year. In addition to representing Nile at PNSA in Billings, Montana, the Nile OB performed at the two ceremonials and the Nile Picnic, participated in the Waterland Festival in Des Moines, marched in the West Seattle Hi Yu parade and gave a concert to the residents at the Masonic Home.

Once the Nile Oriental Band came into existence, its meeting and practice place changed to the old Nile Shrine Temple building in downtown Seattle where they remained for several years. When construction began on the new Nile headquarters building at the Country Club premises and the old Temple building had to be vacated, the OB moved their meeting and practice place to the Ballard Eagles facility. In February 1983, the band moved to one of the shacks on at the new Temple site. And in September 1983 Potentate John G. Jones III gave the band room in one of the new unit rooms in the Temple. The band now regularly meets and practices in the basement of the present Temple building. Meeting and practice nights have been changed to Tuesday nights.

Since its inception, the Nile Oriental Band has won numerous awards in PNSA competitions. Its stature as one of the top Oriental bands in the country was confirmed in 1974 when it won the World Championship Trophy at Reno, Nevada sponsored by the Western Association of Oriental Bands. An interesting anecdote from that marvelous event is that during the Shrine Parade, after the Nile OB had won the Fantasy Competition for large bands, a multi-million-dollar robbery took place at a casino along the parade route. The spectators were so entranced by the Oriental bands marching by that they took no notice of the cops and robbers confrontation taking place right there on the sidewalk of the parade route.

The Nile Oriental Band has had only a few directors during its existence and many of them were band members. Following George Jory were Ed Jones, Jack Schwartz, and Bernie Press. Press was an outsider, a professional musician brought in during the 1960's to upgrade the Oriental Band to national caliber. At the time, he was neither a Mason nor a Shriner, but the Oriental Band paid his initiation fees and dues into a local blue lodge, then into Scottish Rite and finally into the Shrine. (In those days Shriners had to be a member of either the Scottish Rite or the York Rite to become a Shriner. That requirement was dropped by Imperial Shrine in 2000). Bernie was paid a salary as Director. However, he also served as Sultan in 1970.

When his health began to fail in 1992, Howard Beck, Keeper of the Purse, took over as Director. But in 1993, at the PNSA in Casper, Wyoming, the Nile Chanters Director, Jim Hart, Jr. (MBA from USC 1954), was talked into becoming the Musical Director. Jim took that post, even though he had his hands full as Nile Recorder, and has not looked back. He remains its current Director. And it was Director Hart who led the Nile Oriental Band to its next biggest triumph, the Imperial World Championship at the 2002 Imperial Session in Vancouver, B.C. Competing against the best Oriental Bands from the East and the West, Nile won the large band Fantasy Competition in style and took overall honors as well.

Over the years, the Nile Oriental Band has won numerous awards and trophies, the two biggest being the 1974 WASOB World Championship and the 2002 Imperial World Championship, and continues to this day to provide entertainment at Nile functions, ceremonials, and other events. Several of its members have served as the president of the PNSOBA. These include Bob Jones, 1964-65, Ike Eskenazi, 1975-76, Bert Carlson, 1981—82, Norm Wold, 1992-3 and 1994-5, George Wohlleben, 1997-98, Bruce Garner, 2001-2, Ben Neff, 2004-5, Bo Lindgren, 2007-8 and another Nile OB member, Dave Barney, is coming up through the PNSOBA line.

Several Nile Potentates have served as Sultan, most notably Wayne Sheirbon (Pote 1981, Sultan 1990) and Harry Grove (Pote 1993, Sultan 1996) and George Wohlleben (Pote 2005, Sultan 1994). The OB has taken steps to assure its continued existence by actively recruiting Divan members to join the band. The current (2020) Sultan is Mark Goldberg.

Since 1971, the Nile Oriental Band has conducted a very successful Crab Feed as its major fund raiser. The OB members obtain fresh crab, corn and salad fixings and turn the Nile auditorium into a gigantic feeding frenzy while the band both serves as waiters and entertainers during the event. Today, over 40 years later, the OB Crab Feed still serves 400-500 guests at its Annual Crab Feed in the Nile Ballroom. Funds raised go to support Nile OB members travel and other expenses of the band as well as providing monies to contribute to the Ladder of Smiles.

ASOB and the Ladder of Smiles

No article on the Nile Oriental Band can conclude without mention of the Association of Shrine Oriental Bands or ASOB. It is the national/

international organization for Shrine Oriental Bands. Founded in 1928 at the Imperial Session in Chicago, Illinois, it provides an umbrella organization for the dissemination of news and communication among Shrine Oriental Bands everywhere. It produces the only professionally formatted publication in Shrinedom, Na Khabar, which in Arabic means "the news" or "the message." Yearly dues go to support this magazine, but with the advent of only one hard publication per year, only 50% of dues paid to ASOB now go toward this publication.

The ASOB is also renowned for its Ladder of Smiles. This fund, founded in 1961, contributes the monies raised by participating Temple Oriental Bands directly to the Shriners Hospitals for Children, making ASOB one of only two national organizations with working Shrine units to do so. The other is the Clowns Red Sneaker Fund. The Ladder of Smiles as the fund-raising arm of the ASOB has contributed well over 2-1/2 million dollars to the Shriners Hospitals for Children since 1961. Often right at the top of the list of Oriental Band contributors is the Nile Oriental Band. It annually ranks in the top three among all Oriental bands in funds raised for the Ladder of Smiles and very often takes its usual place at the top of the list by year's end. One secret to Nile's success is the Bad Word Jar at Nile Oriental Band business meetings. Rumor has it that band member Norm Wold has almost singlehandedly kept this fund in the black. And speaking of Norm Wold, allegedly the World's Greatest Cymbal Player, he is the only Nile Oriental Band member to achieve the great success of being elected to the National ASOB line and becoming president of the ASOB in 2006. His term was marked by many improvements in the functioning of ASOB and for an upsurge in contributions to the Ladder of Smiles. Norm is also and has been for several years now the Nile OB Keeper of the Purse.

Today, the Nile Oriental Band is still searching for nobles to learn to play the musette or to beat a drum with the band. There are also tambourines and other percussion devices to play. Members now ride in a large band wagon, obtained from Afifi Temple in 2009, and need not fear marching the streets. Call the Nile office at 425-774-9611 to sign up to play "the sweetest music this side of Mecca."

THE DAUGHTERS OF THE NILE

Formation and Early History

Much has been written about Nile Temple's founding nobles were originally members of Afifi Temple in Tacoma and members of an Afifi Shrine Club in Seattle for several years before petitioning Imperial Session and being granted a dispensation to form Nile Temple in 1908. But did you know that a similar genesis preceded the formation of another great social and philanthropic organization, the Daughters of the Nile, and Hatasu Temple No. 1 in particular?

It turns out that many of the wives, daughters, mothers, widows, and sisters of our early founders also participated in Afifi Temple activities through an Imperial approved organization known as the Daughters of Isis. Seattle women belonging to the Isis Court in Tacoma also had a club in Seattle known as the Daughters of Isis Club which regularly met at the homes of several of its members in the Seattle area. When Nile was granted its dispensation in July, 1908 and then its charter in June 1909, Seattle Isis women could no longer participate in the Tacoma Isis Court. However, they kept alive their Seattle Club hoping that an Isis Court would be chartered at Nile. For jurisdictional reasons hard to fathom today, Imperial denied the chartering of an Isis Court in Seattle. So, in December, 1912, the Seattle Isis Club disbanded. Nevertheless, hope sprang eternal in the hearts of several of these women and at that last Isis Club meeting in December, 1912, Mabel R. Crows invited several of the Isis Court members to her home to meet on February 20, 1913. At this meeting, she led discussion about an organization that she had heard about from her mother, that in Minneapolis, Minnesota, Zuhrah Temple had a lady's club, independent of the temple, known as Zuhrah Ladies. She spoke enthusiastically of forming a similar independent club in Seattle to be known as The Ladies of Nile Club whose members would be women whose husbands were members of Nile Temple. The new club was promptly organized with Mabel Krows as President, Minnie Jefferey as Vice President, Gertrude Lazier Hodgson as Treasurer and Elizabeth Davies as Secretary. At a meeting on March 20, 1913, the club members voted to offer membership opportunity in the club to all wives, daughters, mothers, widows, and sisters of any noble from any temple, thus paving the way for universal expansion of the organization.

Later that year, several club members expressed the desire to take their club to a higher level and to reorganize as an Order, totally independent of a Shrine Temple with its own mission and purpose.

One may marvel at the chutzpah of these women, but it should be noted that women in Washington State at this time were just starting to get a feel for their influence and power in a so-called man's world. Washington State had just recently voted on November 8, 1910 to give women the right to vote in all elections. This action broke a 14-year deadlock in the national women's suffrage rights movement making Washington State only the fifth state to grant women the right to vote. This momentous event opened the floodgates for several other Western states (California, Utah, Wyoming) to enfranchise women, whereas women in most Eastern and Southern states had to wait until Congress passed, and the states ratified, the Nineteenth Amendment to the United States Constitution which events did not occur until June 4, 1919 and August 26, 1920 respectively.

Now an Order, in the fraternal sense, is defined as a group of people living or meeting together under a uniform set of rules with the group having a common purpose. Behavior in the group is regulated by these rules and enforced by a set of regulations, proscriptions, and penalties. Generally meeting in closed lodges or chapters, new members would undergo an initiation rite and meetings may be conducted according to a set ritual. An Order might also adopt or require a particular style of dress for its members to be worn at stated meetings and/or the wearing of distinctive badges, pins, clothing, or the like. Finally, secret passwords, grips, signs, or tokens may be adopted by the Order to permit easy recognition of fellow members.

The women present voted to develop such an Order with the stated purposes as follows: To assist in charitable work, to aid in the advancement and elevation of the standard of womanhood and to provide for the social and friendly association of its members. But before proceeding further, they needed a ritual to establish the ethical, moral, and fraternal framework for the new organization. To this end it was suggested by Gertrude Lazier Hodgson that Nile Noble Charles Faustus Whaley be contacted to draft a ritual to be approved by a Ritual Committee consisting of Hodgson, Cleo Kline, and Edith Gattis. Information tells us that Edith Gattis eventually prevailed upon Noble Whaley to write the ritual. Whaley was a noted author of the time and was experienced in writing ritualistic prose. After laboring throughout the summer of 1913 and conferring with the Ritual Committee, he came up with a ritual based upon some impressive ceremonies found in Egyptian history. The name for the new organization was suggested as Daughters of the Nile. Although this name evoked memories of the Daughters of Isis and the Ladies of the Nile Club, it was actually based on the name of the Nile River in Egypt and was a reflection of the importance of the Nile River to Egypt's people. Like the Nile River, whose overflowing brought agricultural prosperity to the ancients, so too would this new Nile organization bring joy, peace and prosperity to its members and their families.

Noble Whaley created a panoply of new officer names as well. In keeping with the Egyptian motif, the presiding officer would now be the Queen. Her associate officers would be in order: Princess Royal, Princess Tirzah, Princess Badoura, Princess Recorder, Princess Banker, and additional Princesses of the Court with the names Nydia, Zulieka, Zenobia, Zora and Zuliema. In addition, there was to be a Princess Chaplain, a Princess Marshal, a Princess Musician, two Attendants, a Lady of the Keys, and a Lady of the Gates.

Impressed by this beautiful ritual and the new array of personages, the ladies promptly voted into existence the new organization and the ritual was adopted. The first ceremony of initiation occurred on September 18, 1913 with Mabel Krows, the President of the Ladies of the Nile Club giving the obligation to the charter class of members. The group would henceforth be known as the Daughters of the Nile. On October 16, 1913, the first temple was organized and officers for the new group were elected. Minnie Jeffery was elected Queen, Edith Gattis as Princess Royal, Gertrude Lazier Hodgson as Princess Tirzah, Levelia West as Princess Badoura, Mabel Krows as Princess Recorder, and Andrewette Patton as Princess Banker.

The name Hatasu for the new temple was suggested by Queen Minnie Jeffery. Hatasu has been described as a noted Queen of Egypt whose rank and influence indicated the high esteem with which women were held in ancient Egypt. But the true story of Queen Hatasu is much more involved.

Hatasu, also known as Hasheps or Hatshepsut, meaning Foremost of Noble Ladies, actually became the fifth Pharaoh of the Eighteenth Dynasty of Ancient Egypt. She was born 1508 BCE and, after the deaths of her mother and three older siblings, ruled as Queen with her father Thutmose I. After her father died, her younger brother assumed the throne as Thutmose II, but he was a shallow ruler with not much stomach for royal politics. In fact, to legitimize his reign as Pharaoh he had to marry his sister because it was through her and her mother's ancestors that the true royal bloodline flowed. On the other hand, Hatasu had learned the art of ruling a country from their father and was a strong willed, clever, and bright administrator. When Thutmose II died in 1479 BCE, Queen Hatasu assumed the title of Queen Regent for her nephew, Thutmose III who was next in line in the pharaonic order. However, he was a mere child and after a few years she declared herself Pharaoh in 1473 BCE and was accepted as such by the people.

Her reign of almost 22 years was marked by a peaceful respite from the wars that previous rulers had fought and she embarked upon one of the most productive and successful building periods in the history of Egypt. For example, she completely renovated the old temple of Ammon at Karnak. She built a very elaborate temple at Medinet Abou near Thebes which advanced the level of architecture in Egypt from the simple unicell temple of the reign of Usurtisan I to a complex multicell design built on a cruciform floor plan with numerous pillars, columns, porches, and offices for the priests. She had a fleet of merchant trading ships built and personally conducted a famous trading mission to the Land of Punt, variously identified as southern Arabia or the lower Somali coast, to bring back spices and incense. She built obelisks and other monuments to her ancestors and to herself. And she did not neglect her people. She made sure that the granaries were full and available for public dispersal during lean years. She built sanctuaries for women who were widowed or infirm or aged. She forged peace treaties with neighboring states that would ensure peace for her time. Unfortunately, her ambition probably overwhelmed her young nephew, Thutmose III, for after her death circa 1458 BCE, he tried to have her name erased from all the monuments that were built during her reign. Nevertheless, her skill in administering one of the most advanced countries of its time, her building projects, the reopening of long dormant trade routes and her popularity with the people have caused the admiration of Egyptologists, anthropologists and historians so much so that she is widely regarded as one of greatest Pharaohs of any dynasty of ancient Egypt.

That the women of Hatasu No. 1 chose such an auspicious name for their temple confirms their belief that they are indeed the Mother Temple of the Daughters of the Nile and worthy successors to an ancient line of wise female rulers and giving philanthropists.

In Part 2, we will discuss the formation of the Supreme Temple, the spread of temples across the North American continent, the establishment of the Daughters of the Nile Foundation and the Canadian Trust, and the history of giving to the Shriners Childrens Hospitals. Special thanks is hereby acknowledged to Hatasu No. 1 for allowing this author the use of the booklet, History of the Founding of the Daughters of the Nile as a reference source for this article.

Just as the Shriners found the need to form a supreme governing body for their fledgling organization in 1876, the Daughters of the Nile had the foresight to create a Supreme Temple of Daughters of the Nile in 1913. At the time, the organization consisted only of the initial Hatasu Temple of Seattle and there were only 22 members. But at a meeting held at the home of Edith Gattis on October 30, 1913, a Supreme Temple was organized with Levelia K. West elected as the first Supreme Queen. Later, on November 21, 1913 at the home of Elizabeth S. Davies, the rest of the Supreme Temple officers were elected and appointed. Needless to say, there was substantial overlap between the officers of Hatasu Temple and Supreme Temple.

Now that there existed a Supreme governing body, Hatasu could be chartered as a temple under the Supreme Temple. And so, it was that Hatasu Temple No. 1 petitioned for and soon received its charter from Supreme Queen Levelia West on March 23, 1914. Ceremonials, using the ritual written by Charles Faustus Whaley, quickly followed bringing more members into the organization. The first annual session of Supreme Temple was held on June 25, 1915 at the home of Supreme Queen Levelia West at which meeting the Constitution and Bylaws of the Supreme Temple were adopted. Minnie Jeffery was elected Supreme Queen and one of her notable accomplishments was organizing Miriam Temple No. 2, Victoria, B.C. on May 2, 1916. She also organized Tirzah Temple No. 3 in Butte, Montana on June 3, 1917.

Other temple organizations were quick to follow. Supreme Queen Edith Gattis organized Nydia temple No. 4, Portland, OR on April 23, 1919 and Zora Temple No. 5, Tacoma, WA May 8, 1919. But the real kickstart toward making Daughters of the Nile a national and later an international organization was the astounding recruiting trip made by Edith Gattis across the country in 1921. Crisscrossing the country she was able to help organize Lotus Temple No. 7, Duluth, MI, on April 24, 1921; Zenobia Temple No. 8, Chicago IL on April 26, 1921; Zuleika Temple No. 9, Binghamton, NY May 31, 1921; Pyramid Temple No. 10, Davenport, IA, May 6, 1921; Netaker Temple, No. 11, Des Moines, IA, May 6, 1921; and Mokattam Temple No. 12, Los Angeles, CA, May 21, 1921, thus providing Daughters of the Nile with an Atlantic to the Pacific presence.

That same year, through an introduction provided by local State of Washington Congressman Miller, she was able to meet with Mrs. Warren Harding, the President's wife and convince her to accept membership into Daughters of the Nile. Mrs. Harding graciously accepted and was soon made a member of the closest temple to Washington, D.C., Zuleika Temple in Binghamton, NY. After giving Mrs. Harding her obligation, Supreme Queen Gattis presented Mrs. Harding with a platinum diamond set pin, which had been donated by jeweler Joseph Mayer of Seattle for the occasion.

By now, the famous Imperial Session of 1920 had been held in Portland, Oregon at which session the attendees voted to create the Crippled Childrens Hospitals of the Shrine. The first hospital opened its doors for this purpose in September, 1922 in Shreveport, Louisiana. In 1923, Past Supreme Queen Edith Gattis offered Imperial Shrine the support of the Daughters of the Nile for this great endeavor. Imperial Potentate Conrad Dykemann wrote back to Mrs. Gattis in pertinent part "it would be unthinkable to refuse so gracious an offer for so worthy a cause." And so, began a generations long affiliation between Daughters of the Nile and the Shriners Childrens Hospitals. In 1924, $2,503.50 was raised for the Orthopedic fund of the hospital system. Imperial Potentate James Chandler gratefully accepted the donation and his acknowledgement of it is recorded in the minutes of the 21st Annual Session of Imperial Shrine for 1925.

Hatasu Temple No. 1, as the Mother Temple, pioneered the way organizationally for the growth of the group as a whole. Nine different women from Hatasu have served as Supreme Queens, the most recent being Murial V. Knapp (2008-9). And Hatasu Temple itself has had a succession of strong leaders, including the mother daughter tandem of Alice Kennedy and Kathy Ramich (1988 and 2008 respectively). The present Supreme Queen (2020-21) is Heather Krastins Lambert of Mat-Sha Temple No. 62 in Miinnesota, and the present Queen of Hatasu Temple (2020-21) is Joan Breda.

The Convalescent Relief Fund and the Endowment Fund

The support that Daughters of the Nile temples have given to the Shriners Childrens Hospitals of North America has been unflagging and constant. In 1931, a Convalescent Relief Fund was organized to provide monetary support for the hospitals. It was primarily supported by voluntary contributions. In 1949, a Convalescent Relief Endowment Fund was created to provide a perpetual source of funds to contribute to the hospitals. All interest from the endowment fund investments would be added to interest from government bonds held by the fund and to donations subscribed to this fund and would be added periodically to the Convalescent Relief Fund from which the contributions to the hospitals were being made.

The Canadian Trust

By 1997 there were 12 Daughters of the Nile temples in Canada. All money raised by these Canadian temples for the Convalescent Relief Fund and the Endowment Fund were funneled for processing through the United States bank accounts of Supreme. However, the variation in the value of the Canadian dollar vs. the United States dollar at the time was great, giving the Canadian dollar an unfair discounted value in the United States Also, because Canadian donations were being sent outside of Canada for charitable purposes, Canadians were being deprived from claiming such donations as charitable deductions on their personal income tax returns. It was decided by Supreme to register the Canadian accounts for the Convalescent Relief Fund and the Endowment Fund as a Canadian charity to be called the Canadian Trust. This was accomplished on April 1, 1997 and, on that date, the Charities Division of Revenue Canada formally recognized and registered the Canadian Trust as a bona fide Canadian charity. Although the Canadian donations in Canada would have to be used solely to support the Montreal Shriners Hospital, the way was now clear for Canadian citizens to claim their charitable donations to the Shriners Hospitals as charitable deductions on their personal income tax returns.

Daughters of the Nile Gold Plaques in the Hospitals

It is now a matter of legend that Daughters of the Nile have contributed $1 million to each of the 22 Shriners Hospitals for Children as represented by a gold plaque in the lobby of each hospital honoring this significant achievement. As of 2011, 11 of these hospitals have received a second million dollars in donations as represented by a second gold plaque acknowledging that level of giving, and rest are not far behind. But what is most surprising is that the Canadian Trust has generated an accelerated level of giving by both the Canadian and United States Daughters of the Nile Temples to the Montreal Hospital. The first million-dollar plaque at Montreal went up in 1995. The second gold plaque was presented in 2002. And on July 18, 2009, a third gold plaque was installed, making the Montreal Hospital the first of the 22 Shriners Hospitals for Children to be the recipients of more than $3 million in donations from Daughters of the Nile.

The Daughters of the Nile Foundation

In 2007 the Daughters of the Nile as a 501(c) (10) private foundation was expanded to become a 501(c)(3) public charity to be known as the Daughters of the Nile Foundation. On February 16, 2007 the Foundation was formally incorporated as such in the State of Washington. Assets from the Convalescent Endowment Fund were transferred to the Foundation and assets from the Convalescent Relief Trust Account were transferred to the Foundation's Convalescent Relief Investment Management Account that same year.

Clothing for Kids

But aside from donations of money, the Daughters of the Nile temples have gained fame through their sewing efforts. Although some temples had been sewing clothes for the Shriners Hospital children for years, at the Supreme Session in 1929 in Los Angeles, Supreme Queen Victoria Crouse encouraged all temples to have a sewing day at least once a month to make clothes for the children being treated at the hospitals. And over the years this challenge has more than been met. Hundreds of thousands of garments have been sewn or bought for the children of the hospitals. This work has expanded to include toys and gifts for these children on their birthdays or at Christmas time if they happen to be in the hospitals at these times.

The War Bond Effort

One other anecdote about the generosity and resourcefulness of the Daughters of the Nile bears mentioning. During World War II, all citizens were urged to buy war bonds to support the war effort. Daughters of the Nile Temples were leaders in raising money for the war effort through the sale of these bonds. In 1944 Hatasu Temple No. 1 of Daughters of the Nile embarked on a project to raise money to buy a B-29 Super Fortress Bomber for the war effort by selling Series E War Bonds during the Sixth War Bond Drive.

For those readers not familiar with the War Bond Drives of World War II, be assured that this was not some quixotic quest designed to quiet unrest at home. Liberty War Bonds were sold during World War I to help finance that war effort. During the interim between the two great wars, small denomination "baby bonds" were sold to keep the economy rolling along. In 1940, after the fall of several European countries to the Nazis, it became evident to the Roosevelt administration that money would have to be raised to defend the United States against encroaching aggression. British economist, John Henry Keynes, had suggested that the money should be raised through taxes and enforced savings programs, but Secretary of the Treasury Henry Morganthau saw the value of restructuring the "baby bond" sale program as "defense bonds" which would be sold to individuals as Series E bonds. However, the Japanese attack on Pearl Harbor soon caused the administration to rename the Series E bonds as war bonds. The War Finance Committee took charge of the sale of the bonds and massive publicity campaigns using celebrities, cartoon characters, contemporary art, musicians and fraternal organizations created a buying mania in the United States Hugh rallies were held throughout the country to draw customers for the bonds and to celebrate the patriotism and loyalty of United States citizens to the war effort. In particular, Nile Temple staged a rally in Victory Square on June 3, 1944 in downtown Seattle to celebrate they had sold over $5 million of war bonds during the Fifth War Bond Drive, the second largest amount by any organization in the country.

Now, in late 1944, a Sixth War Bond effort was needed and into this patriotic milieu strode the proud members of the Daughters of the Nile, Hatasu Temple No. 1. Audaciously, they announced to then Potentate Ray L Eckmann that they were going to sell enough war bonds, $600,000 worth, specifically to buy a B-29 Super Fortress for the war effort. They asked for the help of the Nile Shriners in this effort. Queen Kathleen Barnett wrote to Potentate Eckmann in pertinent part as follows:

We have pledged the sale of sufficient funds to purchase a B-29 Super Fortress priced at $600,000. Will you, Nobles of Nile, in the name of General Douglas MacArthur, help us to keep our pledge by buying your bonds through our organization. Pay Roll Bonds may be assigned to this project.

This turned out to be a particularly popular project since the B-29s were built by the local Boeing Company. Special applications to purchase the bonds were created denoting that this bond money would be earmarked to buy B-29s.

Hatasu Temple installed a sales booth at the Nordstrom store located at 5th and Pike in downtown Seattle and sold bonds to customers there. They persistently hawked their sales pitches at friends, acquaintances, and other temples. By December 16, 1944 they had sold enough war bonds to purchase TWO Super Fortresses ($1,200,000)!

Today, there are 143 Daughters of the Nile temples throughout the United States and Canada. They have developed a support group called The Gentlemen of the Creeks which consists primarily of nobles related to members of DON members by marriage or family. The Daughters of the Nile celebrated their 100th Anniversary in 2013. Formed initially for the character development of their members, the organization has become a centerpiece in American and Canadian societies for social bonding and philanthropic endeavor. Through their donations of volunteer time, games, books, clothing, quilts, pre-op dolls, and other items to the children being treated by Shriners Hospitals for Children, the Queens, Princesses and Ladies of the Household have set a standard of giving for all to follow.

LADIES ORIENTAL SHRINE
OF NORTH AMERICA

Founded in Wheeling, West Virginia in 1903, the Ladies Oriental Shrine of North America (LOSNA) is another group which today supports the Shriners Hospitals for Children system while being a fun social and mutually supportive union of ladies. According to their history, ladies of Nobles of Osirus Temple were attending the Osirus Spring Initiation

Ceremony at the McClure Hotel in Wheeling West Virginia. Once the men departed for their men only initiation ceremony, many of the ladies "were having so much fun, they didn't want to stop." A secure conference room at the hotel was found and behind closed doors the ladies organized a ladies-only group to be called Isis Court No. 1, the first court of a larger body to be called the LOSNA. This group would be separate and distinct from what was then known as the Ancient and Accepted Order of Nobles of the Mystic Shrine (AAONMS), but it would support the Nobles and their activities while conducting their own affairs. Members of Isis No. 1 would be called Ladies and their executive head is called the High Priestess. They would wear as headgear a distinctive fez, white with a red tassel. Although membership in Isis Court No. 1 was limited to ladies of families of Osirus Shriners, ladies in other Shrine temples in the near geographic area soon learned of this new organization and demanded to be part of the fun of this new group. Soon, Courts in Pittsburgh Pennsylvania (Allah Court No. 2) and Parkersburg West Virginia (Hathor Court No. 3) were instituted as Courts 2 and 3. These courts no longer exist, but LOSNA went on to prosper when in 1914, the three existing courts recognized the need for a grand governing body to be called the Grand Council. On July 24, 1914, representatives from these three courts met to form the Grand Council of LOSNA. The overall Executive head was denominated the Grand High Priestess. From that point on, LOSNA really started to take off with new courts being instituted in Tulsa, Oklahoma (Aaba Court No. 4 October 14, 1914), Columbus Ohio (Thea Court No. 5 August 23, 1917) and Cleveland Ohio (Kheedawee Court No. 6 April 19, 1919). In 1920 six new Courts were instituted and seven more came into being during the rest of the decade of the Roaring 20's. Growth slowed with the Depression and World War II with only two more Courts being added, but post-war prosperity and enthusiasm in the late 40's brought in nine more Courts, including Ahmes Court No. 41 in Seattle Washington (April 14, 1948). Eight new Courts were instituted in the 1950's, four in the 1960's, and a whopping 14 new Courts in the 1970's. Several more Courts were added throughout the 1980's, 1990's and 2000's with the most recent addition being Aziza Court No. 108, Savannah Georgia on February 28, 2014.

Today there are 62 Courts in the United States and one in Canada (Bokhara Court No. 22 in Toronto, Ontario).

With the founding of the Shriners Hospitals for Children system in 1920, the activities of the Ladies of LOSNA took on an even more focused perspective. They adopted the Shriners Hospitals as their recognized charity and philanthropy and started raising funds to support these institutions. Millions of dollars have been raised and donated to the Hospitals by the Ladies of the various Courts in addition to the blankets, quilts, stuffed animals, and other items which have been donated to the children served by the hospitals. Every year at the Imperial Sessions of what is now Shriners International, LOSNA makes a sizable monetary donation to the Shriners Hospital fund.

Membership in the Ladies Oriental Shrine is open to women aged 18 and over who are related by birth, marriage, or adoption to a member of the Free and Accepted Masons or to a woman who is recommended by two current members who are in good standing in LOSNA. Its original purposes of fun, fellowship and the betterment of its members have been augmented since the 1920's by its support for the Shriners Hospitals for Children. Ladies take an active role in the events of their Nobles' respective Shrine Centers, participate in parades, mini clinics, Shrine circuses and other fund-raising ventures. Each Court has sub-groups within it which can be Oriental bands, Patrols, Clowns, Dance, or other such units.

Ahmes Court No. 41, instituted April 14, 1948, is one of the more active Courts in LOSNA. The Ladies of Ahmes Court primarily support the Shriners Hospitals in Spokane Washington and Portland Oregon. In addition to monetary donations, items produced by the Sewing Club, and many more items specifically purchased for the children of these hospitals, have been donated. Over the last 10 years, the value of the donations by Ahmes Court to these two hospitals has been well over $100,000. Ahmes Court regularly holds an auction event at Nile Temple in Mountlake Terrace Washington to raise funds for the hospital giving program. The Clown unit always attends the Nile Shrine Annual Picnic and delights the children with balloon animals and the adults with a baked goods tent. Other units of Ahmes Court perform at the Nile Initiation ceremonies, in particular, the Patrol and Dance units.

Afterword by Author

This project or multiple projects started out as a series of newspaper articles originally published in the *Smile with Nile* in house newsletter edited by my good friend Donald C. Moore. It was to be a compilation of the Nile's potentates' years from the inception of Nile as a member of the Imperial Shrine organization known as the Ancient Arabic Order of Nobles of the Mystic Shrine (AAONMS), now known as Shriners International to supplement and complement the various piece-meal histories of Nile written by other authors. It grew to include key moments in history captured for the information of readers who may have long forgotten the incredible events of past years or may have never lived through them to even be aware of them. These events put into perspective and sociocultural context the doings and lives of a group of people living in a small corner of the country. I truly believe that this type of history and herstory, if you will, can be compiled of any social organization in the country and for that matter the world. The story of Nile is not unique. It is representative of what human beings do and can do wherever they are located and united in the pursuit of fun, fellowship and philanthropy and who believe in a Divine Creator, be that Entity known as God, the Almighty, the Supreme Being, Allah, or the Pure Light of the Universe, but it is One in whose name we labor to do what we have been commanded to do – to serve others and, by doing so, become better human beings for our group and the world.

Brief History of Your Smile With Nile Newspaper

No history of the Smile with Nile newspaper can be written without first remembering from where that marvelous name and slogan was derived. In 1915, as Nile was preparing for its first great event, the Forty-first Imperial Shrine Session, to be held in Seattle in July 1915, a contest was begun by Nile to come up with a catchy slogan which would capture the spirit and enthusiasm of the event. Of the hundreds of nominee slogans which were submitted two stood out: Celebrating in Seattle and Smile with Nile. The story goes like this:

It was just prior to the advent of this Imperial Session that the famous "Smile with Nile" slogan was created. Although sometimes credited to John B. McLean, P.P., the real story involves Executive Committee Chair J. E. Chilberg calling for suggestions for a convention slogan that would capture the heart and spirit of Nile for the upcoming event. After much spirited debate the suggestion by Noble Herbert A. Schoenfeld, "Smile with Nile", was eventually adopted. And although most ad hoc slogans are quickly forgotten after the end of the event for which it was coined, this slogan came to be recognized throughout Shrinedom as one of the most enduring and recognizable in Shrine history. After the slogan was adopted, Band Director Harvey J. Wood decided to write a song for the convention. Unlike the Smile with Nile song put to the tune of The Caissons Go Rolling Along which is sometimes sung today, Wood's Smile with Nile is an original work. It is an uplifting melodic piece that has catchy lyrics by John R. ("Doc") Hager.

After 1915, the slogan Smile with Nile became one which adorned many bulletins, meeting notices and Potentate's Messages which were issued from time to time by the Nile office. For a short time starting in February 1919, a news bulletin entitled "The Nile News" was produced by the Nile Recorder's office. But there was no regularly published Smile with Nile newspaper until February 1934 when Potentate John A. Bennett and Recorder Frank B. Lazier issued Vol. 1 No. 1 of what would become a regularly occurring newsletter. As Potentate Bennett explained on the front page of this issue:

"Here is the first issue of "SMILE with NILE" stepping out to make its bow to the nobility of Nile. It is published and sent to you each month under the auspices of Nile Temple, A.A.O.N.M.S. for the purpose of keeping the nobility informed regarding the affairs of the Temple, and thereby making a closer contact among the members, wheresoever they may be dispersed. You will be given the news and happenings of the Temple as its history is made from month to month. This news concerns you personally, and therefore the success of this publication will greatly depend upon your efforts."

First Issue of Smile with Nile Feb. 1934

Thereafter, Smile with Nile was published every year, eleven issues per year since the July/August issues were usually combined into one. Even during the war years of 1941-1945 Smile with Nile was published without missing an issue. And who were the stalwart editors who compiled, researched, spellchecked and even wrote articles for this highly popular medium?

It started with Recorder Frank P. Lazier (P.P. 1911) who edited and produced that historic first issue. He continued as Editor (and Recorder) until November 1949. In 1949, Frank's health began to fail and the task of editing Smile with Nile was turned over to an appointed Editorial Committee whose members included Nobles Garl Watkins, Chair, W.J. Abrams, F. Clyde Dunn, Lang M. Goodwin, Cliff Harrison, Joseph Huddleston, L. Max Kelly and Stuart Whitehouse. The work on Smile with Nile performed by Frank P. Lazier and his assistants for the prior 15 years can only be imagined since they had to be replaced by a committee of eight Nobles! For a several years thereafter Garl Watkins was listed as the Editor-in-Chief, then starting with the February 1951 issue, Frank T. Rosenquist assumed the Chief Editor's position as the membership of the Editorial Committee changed over time. After a few years the Editorial Committee devolved into one Editor who had complete charge and control over input and publication. The flip side of that job was that the Editor did most of the work in soliciting articles and shaping them into publishable form. From time to time, an Advertising Manager whose job it was to solicit paying sponsors, is listed on the masthead.

Horace W. Port was Editor-in-Chief for a couple of years beginning with the February 1953 issue. Frank T. Ostrander was the Editor for the March 1954 issue. After the format change in 1954 (see below) and through the 1960's, it was difficult to tell who the editors were because their names no longer appeared in the masthead. It was just about at this time that Nile Headquarters were moved from the address at 1005 American Building in Seattle to the new headquarters at 229 3rd Ave. N. Seattle (located at 3rd Ave. N. and Thomas Streets diagonally across from the old State Armory building). Then in the 1970's with the change to an even larger format Harry M. Lehrbach took over and edited Smile with Nile for more than a decade until September 1984 when Mary F. Hamilton took over. Yes, folks, a Lady! And quite a Lady she was. She almost singlehandedly put together and published the Smile with Nile issues until the early 90's. George Minnick took over as Editor for a few years in the 1990's. Brief stints as Editor were performed by Karen J. Palmer and Kathi Naff in the 90's. In 1998, Linda St. John took over the editorial reins and brought Smile with Nile to publication through the calendar year of 2000. In 2001 Noble John Lien (Past Potentate 1994) assumed the Editor's job and he successfully produced Smile with Nile until September 2003 when current editor, Noble Don Moore, took over. Don brought the SWN to new heights of prominence when issues produced by him won Imperial's Dromedary Award for Best Newspaper in a Large Temple for two years in a row 2008-2009. Don's tenure at the editor's helm ceased in 2016 when budget considerations caused Nile to convert the newsletter to a much shorter and briefer format.

The shape and format of the Smile with Nile newspaper has changed considerably over the years. When it started out it was published as a small booklet 6" by 9". That format lasted for two decades. Beginning in 1954 it became a larger issue of 8" by 11-1/2" which could be folded in half for mailing distribution. In the 1970's it evolved into the familiar 11-1/2" by 17" format we know today. The paper on which it was printed also changed over time to save costs and shipping weight until it now resembles the newsprint paper on which most newspapers are printed. This article cannot go into the technological changes in printing SWN which have occurred over time. Suffice it to say that now editing, compiling and printing is all done digitally.

Thus, for over 80 years Smile with Nile has been regularly published as the main communication arm of Nile Temple/Nile Shrine Center. It has provided the nobles and their ladies, and indeed all who have had the great pleasure of reading its content, with not only the news and information of Nile, its divans, its units and its shrine clubs, but also memorials, biographies, national and international events which affected us, tributes, jokes, announcements, and advertisements of interest to Shriners. Whatever the future may bring in terms of format, location and publication mode, we all look forward to continuing to read our Smile with Nile.

Printed in the United States
By Bookmasters